President Kennedy and Britain

PRESIDENT KENNEDY AND BRITAIN

David Nunnerley

ST. MARTIN'S PRESS
NEW YORK

AFFILIATED PUBLISHERS: Macmillan & Company, Limited,
London – also at Bombay, Calcutta, Madras and Melbourne
– The Macmillan Company of Canada, Limited, Toronto

Contents

To my parents

Author's Foreword

The chief source of this book has been the systematic interrogation of as many as possible of the principals involved with this critical period in the history of the Anglo-American relationship. This process of close verbal questioning was made essential by the absence of most of the official papers. Those documents which were available were, of course, consulted but proved to be of only limited value. It was therefore necessary to seek out the men who had personally helped to shape events or who, in some cases, had written the relevant papers, currently closed to examination, or who simply had gained valuable insights into the processes of decision-taking. It is well known, moreover, that some of the steps in the making of government decisions are never, nor could ever be, fully documented. Public records all too often tend to disclose reasons rather than motivations. And we are all entitled to try to understand the human mind in all its complexity. This is not of course to underestimate the extreme difficulties and dangers involved in reliance on interviewing techniques. Memories of what should have happened tend in time to be confused with recollections of what actually happened. The author merely hopes that he has made due allowance for the natural propensity of men, and none more than politicians, to speak mainly in terms of self-justification.

Unfortunately the reader is not made privy to the complexity and delicacy of this balance between fact and fancy because, to many of my informants, I promised anonymity. Some were willing to permit direct quotation, but I concluded that it would be too cumbersome to define what they said and at the same time observe the anonymity of others. To have so done, moreover, may have been, by sheer elimination of possibilities, to have identified specific personal sources wanting to remain anonymous.

I have therefore merely listed below those who so generously gave of their time. Even then I cannot name all those who were interviewed, or distinguish those who preferred to respond by letter or telephone, and, on many occasions, correspondence amplified personal interviews. But, to all my informants, I express my sincere gratitude. Without their help and encouragement, this book would not have been possible.

I want particularly to record my gratitude to Lord Harlech. He was always a most willing and tireless source of information and encouragement and his many comments have, I am sure, greatly improved the balance and the accuracy of this text. Nor would any acknowledgements be complete without my thanking the many friends and colleagues who so generously gave of their time to examine my manuscript critically. Among those who offered invaluable comments, I want especially to thank Dr Colin Seymour-Ure, lecturer in Politics at the University of Kent, and Mr Neville Bailey, a long-time family friend with an almost unequalled command of English grammar. I am similarly grateful for the many improvements suggested by Mr Guido Waldman of The Bodley Head. His patient and penetrating examination of this volume undoubtedly made my responsibilities in this respect less onerous. I am further heavily indebted to both the Politics Department at the University of Kent and the Social Science Research Council, the former for inviting me to undertake the research work which forms the basis of this book, the latter for generously providing me with the means to do so. My greatest debt, however, is owing to my family. Had it not been for their encouragement and loyalty, I would assuredly have never completed this book. Of course, the responsibility for any errors in the text is mine alone.

David Nunnerley
Sevenoaks 1972

List of Persons Interviewed
and Office Held (where pertinent)

Dean Acheson: Former Secretary of State; adviser to President Kennedy on Berlin.

Joseph Alsop: Columnist, *The Washington Post.*

Julian Amery: British Minister of Aviation 1962-64.

Willis Armstrong: State Department official.

George Ball: U.S. Under Secretary of State 1961-66.

Charles Bohlen: Assistant to Rusk on Soviet Affairs; U.S Ambassador to France, 1962-68.

Robert Bowie: State Department adviser.

Henry Brandon: American correspondent, *The Sunday Times.*

David Bruce: U.S. Ambassador to Britain, 1961-69.

Alastair Buchan: Director, the Institute of Strategic Studies.

MacGeorge Bundy: Special assistant to the President for National Security, 1961-66.

William Bundy: U.S. Deputy Assistant Secretary of Defence for International Security, 1961-63.

Lord Caccia: U.K. Ambassador to U.S., 1956-61; Permanent Under Secretary, F.O., 1961-65.

Lord Caradon: U.K. Mission to the U.N.

General Lucius Clay: President Kennedy's Representative, Berlin, 1961-62.

Don Cook: European correspondent, *The New York Herald Tribune*, 1960-65.

Arthur Dean: U.S. Disarmament expert.

Sir Patrick Dean: Permanent U.K. Representative at the U.N., 1961-64; U.K. Ambassador to the U.S., 1965-69.

Major-General Sir Rohan Delacombe: G.O.C. Berlin (British Sector), 1959-62.

Douglas Dillon: U.S. Under Secretary of State, 1957-61, Secretary of the Treasury, 1961-65.

James Douglas Jr.: U.S. Deputy Secretary of Defence, 1959-61.

Sir Alec Douglas-Home: Foreign Secretary, 1960-63; Prime Minister, 1963-64.

Earl of Dundee: Minister of State, F.O., 1961-64.

Sir Harold Evans: Public Relations Adviser to the Prime Minister, 1957-64.

Thomas Finletter: U.S. Ambassador to NATO, 1961-65.

William Foster: Director, U.S. Arms Control and Disarmament Agency, 1961-69.

Hugh Fraser: British Secretary of State for Air, 1962-64.

John Freeman: U.K. Ambassador to the U.S., 1969-71.

Senator William Fulbright: Chairman, Senate Foreign Relations Committee.

Thomas Gates: U.S. Secretary of Defence, 1959-61.

Roswell Gilpatric: U.S. Deputy Secretary of Defence, 1961-64.

Joseph Godber: Minister of State, F.O., 1961-63.

Lord Paul Gore-Booth: Permanent Under Secretary, F.O., 1965-69.

Sir Dennis Greenhill: Minister, British Embassy, Washington. 1962-64; Permanent Under Secretary, F.O., since 1969.

Lord Harlech: U.K. Ambassador to the U.S., 1961-65.

Averell Harriman: U.S. Ambassador-at-large, 1961; Assistant Secretary of State, Far Eastern Affairs, 1961-63.

Louis Heren: American Editor, *The Times*.

Roger Hilsman: Director, Bureau of Intelligence and Research, State Department, 1961-63.

Arthur Hockaday: Private Secretary to British Ministers of Defence, 1962-65.

Field Marshal Sir Richard Hull: Chief of the General Staff, 1964-65.

Lord Inchyra: Permanent Under Secretary, F.O., 1957-61.

Admiral of the Fleet Sir Caspar John: First Sea Lord and Chief of the Naval Staff, 1960-63.

Senator Edward Kennedy: Brother of President Kennedy.

Foy Kohler: U.S. Ambassador to the U.S.S.R., 1962-66.

General Lyman Lemnitzer: Chairman, U.S. Joint Chiefs of Staff, 1960-62.

Selwyn Lloyd: Foreign Secretary, 1955-60; Chancellor of the Exchequer, 1960-62.

John McCloy: U.S. Disarmament expert.

Geoffrey McDermott: H.M. Minister, Berlin, 1961-62.

Malcolm MacDonald: Leader, British Delegation to Laos Conference, 1962.

Robert McNamara: U.S. Secretary of Defence, 1961-68.

Livingston Merchant: Head, U.S. M.L.F. Mission, 1963.

Drew Middleton: London correspondent, *The New York Times*, 1953-63.

Richard Neustadt: Adviser to President Kennedy.

Paul Nitze: U.S. Assistant Secretary of Defence for International Security, 1961-63.

General Lauris Norstad: Supreme Allied Commander, Europe, 1956-62.

Henry Owen: State Department official.

Marshal of the Royal Air Force Sir Thomas Pike: Chief of the Air Staff, 1960-63.

Paul Rankine: Official, British Embassy, Washington.

Lord Redmayne: Government Chief Whip, 1959-64.

Sir Patrick Reilly: U.S. Ambassador to the U.S.S.R., 1957-60; Deputy Under Secretary F.O., 1960-64.

James Reston: Washington correspondent, *The New York Times*, 1953-64.

Sir Frank Roberts: U.K. Ambassador to the U.S.S.R., 1960-62; Permanent U.K. Representative on the North Atlantic Council, 1960-62.

Henry Rowen: U.S. Deputy Assistant Secretary of Defence, Planning, 1961-65.

Dean Rusk: U.S. Secretary of State, 1961-69.

Arthur Schlesinger Jr.: Special Assistant to the President, 1961-64.

Sir Robert Scott: Permanent Secretary, Ministry of Defence, 1961-63.

Lord Sherfield: U.K. Ambassador to the U.S., 1953-56; Chairman, U.K. Atomic Energy Authority 1960-64.

Ronald Spiers: State Department official.

Sir Christopher Steel: U.K. Ambassador to West Germany, 1957-63.

Robert Stephens: Foreign Editor, *The Observer*.

Sir Hugh Stephenson: Deputy Under Secretary, F.O., 1960-63.

General Maxwell Taylor: Chairman, U.S. Joint Chiefs of Staff, 1962-64.

Llewelyn Thompson: U.S. Ambassador to the U.S.S.R., 1957-62.

Lord Thorneycroft: British Minister of Defence, 1962-64.

Lord Trevelyan: U.K. Ambassador to the U.S.S.R., 1962-65.

William Tyler: U.S. Assistant Secretary of State, European Affairs, 1962-65.

Viscount Watkinson: British Minister of Defence, 1959-62.

Dr Jerome Wiesner: Special Assistant to the President for Science and Technology, 1961-64.

G. Mennen Williams: U.S. Assistant Secretary of State, African Affairs, 1961-66.

Peregrine Worsthorne: Deputy Editor, *The Sunday Telegraph*.

Sir Michael Wright: British Disarmament expert.

Adam Yarmolinsky: Special assistant to U.S. Secretary of Defence, 1961-64.

Eugene Zuckert: U.S. Secretary of the Air Force, 1961-63.

I
Kennedy and the
Special Relationship

Ten years ago on a cold December day, Dean Acheson, the former Secretary of State, made an important speech on the prospects for European union. Halfway through his address at West Point military academy, Acheson told his student audience, 'Great Britain has lost an empire and has not yet found a role. The attempt to play a separate power role—that is, a role apart from Europe, a role based on a "special relationship" with the United States, a role based on being the head of a "commonwealth" which has no political structure, or unity, or strength and enjoys a fragile and precarious economic relationship by means of the sterling area and preferences in the British market—this role is about played out.' Flashed across the Atlantic on the press-agency wires, this small part of Acheson's address, even though taken out of context, provoked a huge public outcry in Britain. There were cries of outrage and wounded pride. *The Daily Express* bewailed what it regarded as an American 'stab in the back' of her British ally. Analysing the former Secretary of State's inexcusable tactlessness, *The Sunday Times* concluded that America's recent triumph in the Cuban missile crisis must have 'gone to his head'. *The Daily Telegraph* meanwhile contented itself with the observation that Acheson, always more immaculate in dress than in judgement, was 'extremely unlikely ever again' to hold high office. Fully sympathetic to the unenviable political dilemma in which the British Prime Minister had been put, President Kennedy personally telephoned his friend, Macmillan, urging him to grin and bear the outburst of a disillusioned man rather than be drawn into a public debate. Instead, his decision determined by the force of British indignation, Macmillan felt compelled to rebuke Acheson publicly for falling 'into an error which has been made by quite a lot of people in the course of the last four hundred years, including Philip of Spain, Louis XIV, Napoleon, the Kaiser and Hitler'. Whatever the precise relationship between such diverse characters, it was certainly to take many weeks and much effort on the part of both President Kennedy and Mr Macmillan before the atmosphere in relations between Washington and London returned to anything resembling normality.

Probably no single phrase has been more used and a greater source of heated debate than that most presumptive of terms, much beloved by British politicians, of a 'special relationship' between Britain and the United States. It has evoked both adoration and cynicism. It has been almost the holy grail of successive Prime Ministers. To take a stab at the 'special relationship' has in the past been for many to take a stab at the very heart of Britain. Yet in 1972 the whole thing seems so much less sentimental, so out of date, so unimportant. Few of the trappings of a masquerade are any longer maintained. America, it would seem, has become bored with Britain. Impatient of Britain's illusions of continuing grandeur, tired of bailing governments out of their recurrent economic crises and furious with the apparent politicking with Vietnam peace initiatives, the United States quite simply no longer sees much point in continuing to observe the time-honoured conventions of the Anglo-American relationship. But a few years ago, Britain and America would eagerly dispatch their most able—and, of no coincidence, their most attractive—diplomats to be each others' ambassadors. These men would take their places in the very corridors of power. Nowadays, in contrast, a British Ambassador, in terms of his right to private Presidential audience, might just as well come from Tibet. The great love affair, it would thus seem, has finally come to an end. Britain's stock of sentimental credit with America has finally been exhausted. Yet even for Britain, having at last determined that her future now lies within Europe, the sentiments surrounding the Anglo-American relationship are much less emotionally charged than they once were. No longer do remarks, like

Acheson's 'played-out' speech, invoke the indignation they did but a decade ago. In fact much starker appraisals than Acheson's have subsequently been made—Britain is now regarded by many as a 'mini-state', a 'third-rate' power of the stature of Sweden or Holland—without producing xenophobic reactions. It would thus seem, therefore, that Anglo-American relations have become much less emotional precisely because Britain in 1972 has accepted in her assessment of herself much of what Acheson said in 1962!

Far from being merely the aberration of a disgruntled man, Acheson's general view of Britain's dilemma was one shared by many people in both Britain and America. Indeed, had it not been so obviously inappropriate, President Kennedy himself might have been inclined to agree with much of what Acheson said. For the 'special relationship', based on an equality of status, had long since become a thing of the past. The joint effort during the Second World War had reflected a successful partnership between two allies, unprecedented in their history. But then it had also somewhat superficially sustained Britain's importance. Britain may certainly be forgiven for concluding that victory brought not rewards but only problems. For, if the configuration of international relations was to necessitate major changes in American foreign policy, its implications for Britain were to be no less momentous, and in probability much more painful. Near-bankruptcy compelled Britain drastically to reduce her world commitments. The Empire was no longer the exclusive Anglo-Saxon club, the great dream of Rhodes and Salisbury. Instead, with the emergence of the new nationalism, the collective political meaning of the Commonwealth withered to little more than a congeries of bilateral trade arrangements between the mother country and the ex-colonies. Still, the possible roles for Britain in the post-War world remained numerous—possibly too numerous—and it would perhaps have been more beneficial for Britain had the façade as well as the furniture of great-power status been destroyed by war. As it was, not only did Britain see herself as leader of a loosely-federated Commonwealth, but also as a kind of independent 'great' power, a European partner, an honest broker in the Cold War, and, above all, a special partner of the United States. Unfortunately she tried, at various times,

3

to play all these roles, even though some of them were so obviously in mutual contradiction. Thus, for example, did the cultivation of a 'special relationship' with the United States make impossible for Britain an unreserved entry into Europe. Its consequences, projected on a long-term basis, have indeed been unfortunate. For, as De Gaulle was to argue so forcefully against Britain's Common Market application, how could Britain expect to enter an economic, political and military union with Europe in 1963 but leave her nuclear deterrent (the very core of Britain's defence retained at Nassau) outside until 1980 at the earliest? At the same time the very recognition in Britain that the continued effectiveness of the Anglo-American alliance is dependent upon the excercise of American power has inevitably put great strains on its cohesion. For Britain's assumption in the post-War world of the role of America's most reliable lieutenant in the business of resisting Soviet expansionism was in large part self-imposed. Rightly or wrongly—how easy it is to be wise after the event!—successive British governments made a deliberate and calculated choice to emphasise Britain's value as an ally of the United States, thereby assuring continuing American interest in the relationship with Britain, which from 1945 seemed all the more uncertain, all the less secure. Quite simply, Britain, in return for loyalty and support, insisted on a 'special relationship'. And only then did it become emotionally charged, for the United States could never attach the same importance as Britain to the relationship. It was thus that as British power declined, there developed a tendency in Britain to carp and criticise: to carp at American actions, at American methods, at American timing, at American thinking. It was basically jealousy, infantile resentment on the part of the attitude of an 'older brother', who finds he has been displaced as the centre of attention, (if not affection), by a 'younger brother'. Traditionally, the older brother is wiser and more experienced, the younger brother more impetuous: certainly Englishmen think of themselves as wiser than Americans. For many Americans, however, Britain is not an older brother but of a different generation. Britain is so much older, so much less obviously energetic, apparently so tired. Yet there is a wealth of experience and cunning: Americans will credit Britain with any amount of deviousness and of Machiavellian skill in manipulating others to her own ends. 'It is a matter of sacred tradition,' wrote Robert Sherwood, 'that when an American statesman and a British statesman meet, the former will be plain, blunt, down to earth, ingenuous to a fault, while the latter will be sly, subtle, devious and eventually triumphant.'[1]

For many Americans, Britain is infuriatingly know-all, even wicked, yet practically never rash or foolish. For many Britons, America is frequently rash and often foolish. And this is cause for apprehension when the feeling in Europe now is that Americans, rather than doing too little in the world, are in fact doing too much. America's allies, declared Selwyn Lloyd in 1963, 'are getting increasingly tired of the feeling that they are being pushed about.' The consequences for Britain, with her self-elected dependence on the United States, have been much greater as was clearly, and tragically, demonstrated in the Suez Affair of 1956, certainly the gravest crisis for the two allies since the War.

Suez really challenged all the presumptions about both the 'special relationship' and also Britain's role in the world. At stake, at least for right-wing Tories, was nothing less than Britain's survival as a world power. Unless Nasser were brought to his knees, they argued, Britain would become another Netherlands. It had been intolerable for them that Britain was party to an alliance so dominated by the United States, especially since it was widely believed that the Americans were determined to get Britain out of the Middle East. Suez was thus for them not an example of typical American naïvety in foreign affairs—as incredibly it seems to have been for Eden; it was rather the culmination of a deliberate American policy. And to their surprise, as the crisis developed, this case against the Americans, expounded for some years, became both plausible and popular. It was in effect a convenient way to explain the ensuing events as a conspiracy against British interests.

For Eden—and in this he was not alone—the policy of the Eisenhower Administration, and in particular Foster Dulles, was much to blame for the failure of the Anglo-French venture. 'If the United States Government had approached this issue in the spirit of an ally,' Eden wrote in his memoirs, *Full Circle*, 'they would have done everything in their power, short of the use of force, to support the nations whose economic security depended upon the freedom of passage through the Suez Canal. They would have closely planned their policies with their allies and held stoutly to the decisions arrived at . . . It is now clear that this was never the attitude of the United States Government. Rather did they try to gain time, coast along over difficulties as they arose and improvise policies, each following on the failure of its immediate predecessor. None of these was geared to the long-term purpose of serving a joint cause.'[2]

Dulles' role in the whole affair was inexcusable. At no time did he tell his so-called allies candidly, precisely and comprehensively whether American policy in all circumstances absolutely excluded the use of force. Excruciatingly moralistic, in so far as Dulles understood compromise, he completely despised it. Trained as a lawyer, his whole instinct was to try to outsmart his rivals, whom he never really distinguished between friend and foe. As in a legal battle, where his client was first and last the United States, which must somehow win in the end, it was not sufficient for Dulles merely to defeat his rivals: he had to pulverise them, to humiliate them. He failed completely to acknowledge the essential truth that a nation has allies not because it is doing them a favour but because it either wants or needs them. He refused to pay anything for his allies: he even refused momentarily to forego his moralising. The consequent vibrations on America's alliances are even today being felt and the full price of Dulles is still to be completely paid. Suez highlighted the great dangers of Britain's dependence upon American power. For, despite Macmillan's efforts to continue as if nothing had ever happened, the Anglo-American relationship has never been quite the same since Suez: Britain has henceforth not undertaken any major foreign policy initiative without first securing American political, military or financial support.

President Kennedy himself fully recognised the latent emotions which surrounded any debate on the value of the Anglo-American alliance. He was similarly aware of the indispensable role the alliance had played both in the War and even after, in the establishment of NATO. As a former Supreme Allied Commander in Europe remarked, far from being harmful, the 'special relationship' had been 'probably essential to provide a working base on which we could establish the relationship with the other thirteen countries in NATO.' By 1961, however, President Kennedy was much more interested in the realities of power than in Anglo-American conversations for conversation's sake. Thus was he to view the Anglo-American relationship as an element in the central power-balance—not the decisive element but a useful element. He knew that he could never attach the same degree of importance to relations with Britain as successive British governments attached to relations with America.

For Britain, the 'special relationship' in the post-War world became a convenient means—perhaps the only means—whereby she could continue her great-power pretensions, while at the same time enabling her to withdraw gracefully from contests with the United States. Whatever the consequences, and its costs must always be set against the gains, Britain since 1945 had won enough arguments with the United States to make the cultivation of influence through a 'special relationship' seem worthwhile. If there has been, as George Ball so persuasively argued, 'a tendency on each side to exploit the "special relationship" for short-term advantages at the expense of long-term objectives',[3] it is equally true that some of the benefits so derived by both sides have been substantial. Militarily, Britain clearly benefited most. Indeed, it is almost as if a theory of historical compensation applied for where, in its early years of development, the United States prospered behind the power of the British Navy, Europe since 1945 has progressed behind the shield afforded by American missiles. Politically, the benefits derived by Britain from the alliance, in terms of influence, have been all but self-evident. Less obvious have been the advantages of the Anglo-American relationship to the United States. Yet, the central theme of this present book is to suggest that, at least during the Kennedy years, the United States gained much from its close relationship with Britain. As the pages unfold so it will be seen that, at least since Suez, Britain has not always been a liability to the United States. On the contrary, America, as Kennedy was to recognise, had much to learn from British experience. Indeed it may seem ironic that Britain has ceased to be important in American eyes at precisely the time when she has most to offer the United States, especially in terms of the need for flexibility in foreign policy,

7

in her willingness to recognise the occasional wisdom in a policy of expediency and in her success in the establishment of a non-conscript, but nevertheless professional, army. For President Kennedy it was of great importance to have as an ally a country which was reliable, trustworthy and responsive; which felt, thought and reacted in a similar manner; which was capable of projecting issues on a wide political and historical canvas; whose interests were more often complementary than conflicting; and, above all, whose actions and initiatives were, in a period of unsurpassed dramatics in the Cold War, by and large to reinforce and support American inclinations, actions and initiatives. The 'special relationship', at least during the Kennedy presidency, was not a theoretical relationship based upon historical, racial and cultural affinities. It did not derive much from the existence of a common language, common prejudices, common systems, common patterns of thought, however much these factors made for a peculiarly distinctive relationship between the British and American peoples. Rather did the nature of the Anglo-American relationship in the early sixties depend very much on the fact that the two allies were working together on important matters. 'Events', recalled a member of Kennedy's inner circle, 'threw us into the role of partners, and close partners.' Thus was the 'special relationship' made real.

Objectively, there is every reason for a 'special relationship' between Britain and the United States, since to an exceptional degree both countries look at the world through similar lenses. The distinctive nature—some would say comfort—of their relationship is that each government knows a great deal about the other's problems and that, more often than not, each will take them into account when approaching its own problems. With American foreign policy resting on a certain view of the world, and of the nation as part of that world, the United States inevitably takes a somewhat different perspective on international issues from most of its NATO allies: but it is a perspective which is to an exceptional extent shared by Britain. And this is in itself particularly gratifying for the United States when, with its global policy continually under attack, it finds itself frustrated and isolated. 'In conducting important affairs,' as a former Assistant Secretary of Defence put it, 'it is almost essential to be able to discuss the matter honestly, and with all its detail, with somebody from another country which looks at the world as a whole.' And, with France under De Gaulle refusing to co-ordinate its policy within the Atlantic Community, Britain was the only ally of the United States with both a global outlook and global commitments. In the era of American primacy, Britain's special place has been maintained by her multiplicity of attach-ments. Without her overseas interests in Africa, Asia, Austral-asia, the Caribbean and the Middle East; without her naval and air bases in the Far East, the Indian Ocean, the Persian Gulf and the Mediterranean; and without her undoubted spheres of influence throughout the world, Britain would have seemed —would have been—a small power.

By indulging British weakness, the United States has perhaps all too often encouraged the United Kingdom to act in a manner that was neither in her own larger interest nor in the West's. Too often perhaps, the United States has demanded that, in support of American policies, Britain take actions she could clearly ill-afford. One such case was American support for a continuing British military presence East of Suez. Moreover, in showing a willingness to bail out sterling, the United States only encouraged British governments to temporise with Britain's economic and financial problems. The confident assurance that America would continue to support the pound made seemingly less necessary, certainly less desirable, any British decision about putting her own house in order preparatory to entering Europe. Similarly, the perpetuation of the discriminatory relations between the two countries in the nuclear field, apart from being incompatible with Britain's European policy, served only further to sustain Britain's illusions of great-power status. Yet, whatever its disadvantages, it was precisely this outlook of Britain as a world power which was to be of most value to the United States. The deployment of British conventional forces may have drained resources from the European theatre and as such invoked criticism from America. But it was because, rather than in spite of, this deployment that Britain was in a unique position to support and complement American defence policy. And, as a former Defence Minister confirmed, the British Government saw its role in the sixties 'as to support the United States world-wide. They wanted to have some British presence with them in the world; and *the whole of our defence policy was really geared to this American requirement.*' (Author's italics).

As George Ball argued, the special relationship did indeed infuriate among others the French. On almost every possible opportunity, De Gaulle launched his assault on Les Anglo-Saxons. But, ironically, even he failed fully to realise its distinctive qualities. Had President Kennedy at Nassau offered France not merely Polaris but all the nuclear privileges which Britain enjoyed, this still would not have ended the 'special relationship' between Britain and the United States. For that relationship rested and flourished to a large degree upon the extension by Britain to the United States of a determined assumption of common interest that had—and still has—no equivalent in the Franco-American relationship. The cohesion of the alliance was similarly enhanced by a degree of confidence, openness and reciprocity rarely equalled in international relations.

It was not the distinctive and positive nature of the Anglo-American relationship which was harmful and offensive. Rather were the attempts to 'sloganise' that relationship into something more than it actually was, especially through the use of the phrase 'special relationship', both silly and unproductive. Use of the phrase, especially by certain elements of the British and American press which cling nostalgically and unrealistically to it, has been harmful for Britain's future. By characterising the relationship as 'the one that means most', the press has contributed much to Britain's own self-deception. For it has cultivated a false view of Britain's role in the world by exaggerating the importance of Britain's relationship with the United States. Such an exaggeration, moreover, has made Presidential visits to Britain and Prime Ministerial visits to Washington occasions not for realistic appraisals but for childish displays of vanity. And it was this to which Acheson took exception in December 1962. He had sought to impress upon both the British and American public that, however successful an instrument for the cultivation of British influence, the 'special relationship' had never given Britain a real base of power: that a reappraisal of Anglo-American relations need not necessarily be agonising merely because it is realistic. Britain's entry into the European Economic Community,

Acheson argued, did not mean that America would value any less its relationship with Britain. On the contrary America would continue to admire British experience, statesmanship and steadfastness. The challenge for Britain was to bring those qualities to bear in terms of policy in a world of super-powers and supranational associations, wielding influence not merely by asking for it but through the merits of her policies.

The phrase 'special relationship' has been similarly offensive to both the United States and its allies. Dealing with Britain on a different basis, as at Nassau, meant that a personal meeting with, or letter from, the President would tend to place in sharp relief the fact of American favouritism, even more than any intended benefit. It thus served only to emphasise that very element of discrimination which other allies, in particular France, found so obnoxious. Conscious of the resentment which other allies felt at American favouritism towards Britain, President Kennedy hoped that he would not have to 'play any favourites' or recognise any 'special relationships' within NATO. He hoped, though in this he did not succeed, to be able to deal with all his allies on an equal basis. But that he sought to play down the Anglo-American relationship so as to placate other allies did not mean that he wanted to downgrade in importance that relationship. Rather did he hope that he could establish with his other allies a relationship which involved the same kind of frankness and confidence that existed in his relationship with Britain. The Kennedy Administration, as one of its most senior members remarked, 'looked upon the "special relationship" not as something which necessarily sets England apart from Europe. We hoped that if England went into Europe, it would take a sense of "special relationship" with it, and that we would then have a "special relationship" with Europe.'

If the 'special relationship' has never been quite the same since Suez, it reflected, at least during the Kennedy years, a positive process in international relations. It was a relationship which was strong enough to permit differences between the two governments without putting their general relations at risk. 'If it is clear', Macmillan remarked at the time, 'that there are different approaches, quite legitimately held, to a great problem, then we know each other well enough, and have enough confidence in each other to speak frankly.' Neither government had to pretend to agree upon everything, and, indeed, each was to have its own preoccupations and each expressed them in its own way. Macmillan's position suffered in American eyes from what was felt to be an exaggerated belief in the possibilities of negotiation with the Soviet Union, a reluctance to take a firmer position against communist encroachments in South-East Asia and in Berlin, an unwillingness to maintain British conventional forces at full strength, an unrealistic complacency towards the problem of security leakages, a gratuitous insistence upon the desirability of bringing communist China into the United Nations —today, one might be forgiven for suggesting that only those who brave its dangers comprehend its mystery!—and an inability to assert the primacy of political objectives over economic considerations, as seen in his policy over the Congo crisis, on British trade with the communist bloc and even in his approach to the Common Market application. In its turn, the Kennedy Administration suffered in British eyes from its seeming inability to restrain the alarmist elements spoiling for a confrontation with the Soviet Union, its undermining of the nuclear resolve, its failure to do more to meet the sensitivities of its allies, its unnecessary interference in the British negotiations to join the Common Market, its superior attitude on decolonisation, and its excessive preoccupation with Cuba, with the dangers of a surprise Soviet attack and with rigid requirements for a test-ban treaty. Such differences of policy and approach all too often tended to receive more attention and publicity. But they were surpassed in importance by the issues on which Britain and the United States worked closely together in this period. 'The "special relationship",' as a former Cabinet Minister put it, 'consisted of the feeling that you could talk to each other frankly about mutual problems and expect help. We did help them [the Americans]. Laos was a case where we changed American policy. They were inclined to get involved. We advised against.' Weighing in very strongly against any military intervention, the British Government impressed upon President Kennedy that the only hope for a non-communist dominated Laos lay in supporting the neutralist alternative of Souvanna Phouma, who had been anathema to Dulles, the C.I.A. and even much of the State Department. Yet he was, as a former British Ambassador cryptically observed, 'the answer to the maiden's prayer: not the ideal answer but the only answer.' As in Laos, so over the Berlin and Cuban crises and over the issue of an American resumption of atmospheric tests, the British Government, in urging restraint, strengthened Kennedy's hand in overcoming the wilder ideas of some members of his Administration.

The 'special relationship' did not mean that there were channels of communication of a different order to those open to all governments in diplomatic negotiations. It simply represented, (testimony to this was the Anglo-American collaboration in the test ban talks), a willingness to use the channels available more frequently, more thoroughly and often at a higher level than is usual in diplomacy.

Of most importance, the 'special relationship' was not a one-sided relationship. During the period under consideration, the relationship will be seen to have been one not of mutual convenience but of mutual benefit. The ensuing chapters will reveal that Britain was indeed a close ally whose advice and actions were generally to be much valued by President Kennedy.

1. Robert Sherwood, *Roosevelt and Hopkins: An Intimate History* (Harper & Row, 1950), p. 364.
2. Lord Avon, *Full Circle* (Cassell, 1960), pp. 458-9.
3. George Ball, *The Discipline of Power* (Bodley Head, 1968), p. 93.

2
The Court of St James and Why England Slept

If ethnic loyalty and upbringing were always decisive influences on the attitude and outlook of individuals, President Kennedy would never have been an Anglophile: for his family was not only immensely rich and devoutly Catholic, but Irish and proud of it. And Irish-Americans, particularly those who live in the Boston area, are almost to a man staunchly anti-British. For an almost pathological antipathy towards anything British has been a persistent and recurrent theme in Irish history, and Kennedy's forefathers had brought with them to Boston a strong belief in Irish tradition. The future President was at an early age made conscious of the discrimination which Irishmen suffered at the hands of the British. He never forgot the lively, if at times exaggerated, tales recalled by his grandfathers, both of whom were also a great source of training for politics. Both were fiercely proud of their ancestry, both displayed great adroitness, both were in fact Irish politicians—flamboyant and extravagant. They represented, however, the end of the era of flamboyant politics. Kennedy himself was to symbolise the new breed of Irish politician, and ironically this new style and manner was much influenced by his experiences in Britain.

Jack Kennedy first visited Britain in 1935 when he was sent to study at the London School of Economics under the socialist academic, Harold Laski. Joe Kennedy Sr, by this time a man of considerable wealth and political influence but—to his eternal regret—with little social standing, believed that his sons would greatly benefit from exposure to the radicalism of London in the

1930s. Though a confirmed conservative himself, Joe Kennedy hoped that his sons would learn about socialism, with its ideas for the betterment of the poorer classes, and would thus know by experience the economic and political causes to support and the mistakes to avoid. This intellectual ferment was certainly an experience which for the eighteen-year old Kennedy contrasted strikingly with his highly traditionalist, staunchly Republican, education; and, even though his time at L.S.E. was prematurely curtailed by jaundice, it was during this period that his later interest in civil rights and his ideas about social justice originated and were nurtured.

Following his father's appointment in 1937 as American Ambassador to the Court of St James, Kennedy took six months off college to act as a courier, and it was then that he really came to know and love London. Thereafter he spent any time he could in London, like Johnson stimulated by what the great capital had to offer. His experiences in Britain influenced and moulded his character and accelerated his intellectual awakening. He saw the consequences of the depression at first-hand, and he was struck by the manner in which British politics sought to combat them. He held a life-long fascination for British political society, with its seemingly casual combination of deeply-held concern, steadfast commitment, dry and sardonic wit and above all sheer knowledge. Englishmen of his own generation, like David Ormsby-Gore and 'Billy' Hartington, he found altogether more sophisticated and confident than his American contemporaries. They were hardly the angry young men of the 1930s: in fact politics was for them rather light-hearted, certainly no obsession, though this very idea of politics invigorating rather than dominating society much appealed to Kennedy. But the other aspects of the British way of life equally appealed to him. He immensely enjoyed his leisured week-ends in the country homes of the great aristocratic families. At first through his father's position, he found himself regularly invited for week-ends at the Chatsworths and Lismores, respectively the English and Irish ancestral homes of the Devonshires, with whom he later strengthened his ties through his sister Kathleen's marriage to the Marquis of Hartington. The presence of other house guests, many of whom were public figures, like the Edens and the Randolph

Churchills, was in a sense history come alive for him. It had, as Arthur Schlesinger put it, 'a careless elegance he had not previously encountered'.[1] The new perspective on life to which he was exposed was of special importance since it was acquired in his formative and impressionable years, during which period he might otherwise have been content to have remained a shy and somewhat introverted personality. Instead, and, as one of his intimate friends later recalled, somewhat to his own surprise, 'he found his British friends very agreeable and he got on very well with them; and gradually what I would call the anti-British elements he grew out of and by the end you couldn't have found a more British person.'

Kennedy found London's cultural milieu especially stimulating. He greatly enjoyed reading the biographies of political personages, such as David Cecil's study of William Lamb, *The Young Melbourne*. It was essentially a love for the England of the late eighteenth and early nineteenth centuries. He found the characters of Whig England more colourful and interesting than most of the characters of his own era. He may even have recognised in Cecil's description of Whig life close similarities to his own upbringing: the Kennedys shared the supreme confidence of the Whigs over the direction in which they were going: both were fiercely competitive within the family but equally intensely loyal to it; for both, great wealth, far from debarring, actually demanded public spiritedness. 'The Whig lord', Cecil wrote, 'was as often as not a minister, his eldest son an M.P., his second attached to a foreign embassy, so that their houses were alive with the effort and hurry of politics.'[2] The Kennedy house was itself much alive with the effort and hurry of politics. Like the Whigs, who hid an adroitness in managing apparently intractable problems beneath a superficial urbanity, which permitted an almost unnerving casualness in observing society's conventions, the Kennedys knew what power was all about, where it lay, what it could buy. They were never embarrassed or overawed by it. As much as the Whigs, they were at home with both the reins and the trappings of power.

But it was the manner more than the matter of Whiggism which appealed to Kennedy—the zest, the self-confidence, the almost irritating nonchalance. Essentially an activist, Kennedy found Whiggism much too impassive as a political dogma. And though he was to remain captivated by Whig style, Kennedy, had he lived in that era, would in all probability have been a Tory Democrat.

Public affairs may have taken a second place in the young Kennedy's life to the society balls in Belgravia and the weekends at Chatsworth. London nevertheless highlighted for him the complexities and implications of politics, giving him a sense of the manner and tone in which it might be approached. It also gave him, as Schlesinger was to write, 'a rather appalling look at the way democracy responded to crisis'.[3] He witnessed, and was shocked by, the complete failure of the British people to respond to the dire warnings about Hitler, given in particular by Churchill, Kennedy's greatest hero whom unfortunately he did not meet until too late. The whole question of British appeasement so intrigued Kennedy that he selected it as the subject for his undergraduate thesis, a study which, when published in 1940 under the title of *Why England Slept*, became an immediate best-seller in both Britain and the United States. The conclusions he was to reach were to be very different from the views of both his father and also his elder brother, Joe, who, upon the outbreak of war, formed a non-intervention club at Harvard Law School. Nevertheless, it was only as a result of his father's appointment that the young Kennedy was in a position to reach conclusions on the basis of first-hand observations. Indeed, Harold Laski, who refused to write a Foreword to the book, was to believe that it would never have been published had Kennedy not been the son of the Ambassador!

Left vacant by the death of Robert Worth Bingham, the ambassadorial appointment came at a particularly crucial time in the context of the imminence of the European conflict. At that time still considered the most coveted diplomatic prize, Roosevelt's selection of a political friend understandably aroused the resentment of the career diplomats in the State Department. Since it also afforded opportunities for social preferment, Kennedy's appointment provoked considerable anger among the Boston Brahmins, who had never come to terms with the Irish invasion of their city. Roosevelt himself clearly wanted to tap Kennedy's great knowledge of finance, both to help resolve the dispute over Britain's war debts and to arrange trade agreements with Britain: though, as it happened, bargaining with London on both issues was to go badly.

Whatever Roosevelt's primary motives for appointing Kennedy, relations between the two men quickly deteriorated, especially after the President suspected that Kennedy's initial popularity in Britain was such that the Ambassador was using the Court of St James as a stepping-stone to the White House. Kennedy certainly took London by storm. All American ambassadors to Britain are news, but London seemed to greet Kennedy as the most important American citizen to cross the Atlantic since Lindbergh! Hailed as 'Jolly Joe' and 'The Father of America', the Ambassador (as for the rest of his life he was to be called) hit the headlines wherever he went and whatever he did. He shocked journalists with his habit of putting his feet on his desk during press conferences; he amazed them when at his first press conference he reproached them for expecting him 'to develop into a statesman overnight'. London chuckled at the observation that the Ambassador's official residence, at 14 Prince's Gate, big as it was (with 36 rooms) was barely big enough to cater for the whole Kennedy family. Even the Ambassador's refusal to don knee breeches for royal audiences was big news, as well as delighting his fellow Irish in Boston, who at first had been undecided on whether to welcome or frown upon his appointment. To crown everything, he even managed to play a hole in one on his very first round of golf in England.

Kennedy certainly had an immediate impact upon the British people. He also became a close friend and adviser of the then Prime Minister, Neville Chamberlain. Unfortunately, the conservatism of both men blinded them to the realities of the magnitude of the political events then taking place in Europe. The Ambassador's support for Chamberlain's appeasement policy at times knew almost no bounds, as when at a Trafalgar Day dinner, but a month after Munich, he declared that the Prime Minister's 'all but superhuman efforts on behalf of peace should command the respect of us all'. A firm, if short-sighted, advocate of American isolationism, Kennedy appealed for a good-neighbours, live-and-let-live, policy towards Hitler and Mussolini. 'After all,' he told his audience, 'we have to live together in the same world, whether we like it or not.' Such remarks were hardly likely to endear the Ambassador to the opponents of Chamberlain: they were hard enough for Roosevelt to swallow, especially since at that time he was striving to cultivate a climate of opinion in the United States acceptable to American involvement, which the President regarded as ultimately inevitable.

Even when War finally broke out in September 1939, Kennedy and, to a lesser extent, Bullitt, the American Ambassador to France, were highly defeatist about Britain's chances of survival. Joe Kennedy personally told Roosevelt in the autumn of 1939 that sending aid to Britain would only be throwing it down the drain. Unfortunately for the Ambassador, his remarks hit the headlines in Britain and he found, on his return to London, that he was no longer Britain's favourite American. Having taken him in as one of their own, Britain had at least expected the American Ambassador to plead the British cause. Henceforth, Kennedy found himself isolated and frustrated.

He was incapable of establishing any close rapport with Churchill; on the contrary, there was to be much personal animosity between the two men. Later, in the first volume of his wartime memoirs, *The Gathering Storm*, Churchill was to refer to Kennedy as an 'appeaser'; and the Ambassador in turn was to condemn those memoirs as so 'replete with serious inaccuracies' that 'they should be handled with care.' That the two men did not get on was no great surprise. Kennedy had actually advised Roosevelt that Churchill could not long survive as Prime Minister. He had even warned the President that, in backing Britain to the hilt, he would be 'left holding the bag in a war in which the Allies expect to be beaten.' Dunkirk and the fall of France merely confirmed his fears about Britain's inevitable defeat. 'It seems to me', he cabled Roosevelt, 'that if we had to protect our lives, we would do better fighting in our own backyard.'

Kennedy returned to the United States in October 1940, and letting it be known that he was unlikely to return to London, he was given a surprisingly warm send-off by Britain. Seizing every opportunity to underline the force of alliance loyalties, *The Evening News* went as far as to suggest that the Ambassador had 'single-handed . . . strengthened Anglo-American friendship in London.' And Hannen Swaffer concluded his widely-read column in *The Daily Herald* with the following tribute: 'Forever, in deeds if not in written words, Britain and America are allies. Largely, that is Joseph Kennedy's work. Goodbye Joe! Heaven bless you! Your job is done.' The victorious outcome of the Second World War will always stand as the greatest single achievement of the alliance between Britain and the United States. But it owed little to the efforts of Joe Kennedy, whose diplomatic career ended, almost as it had begun, with an indiscretion. Back in the United States, in what he assumed was an off-the-record conversation with journalists, but which was widely reported, the Ambassador imprudently suggested that 'Democracy is finished in England. It isn't that she's fighting for democracy. That's the bunk. She's fighting for self-preservation, just as we will if it comes to us.' At the same time, not content with merely slamming Britain, he also took a swipe at Eleanor Roosevelt. Thus, not surprisingly, his remarks, when made public, caused a sensation. The Ambassador promptly offered his resignation, which was just as promptly accepted.

Even in 1972 there are many people in Britain who will never forgive Joe Kennedy for his defeatism, and worse his public defeatism, as American Ambassador. For them it was indefensible that he should so desert Britain in 1940. In fact the memory of what many would consider the Ambassador's 'treachery' was such that twenty years later there were some who were to express their disquiet over the extent to which the paterfamilias had influenced his son's attitude towards Britain. Fortunately, while he was always fiercely loyal to his father, Jack Kennedy rarely accepted the soundness of his father's political judgements. In fact, as the years went by, the young Kennedy was to become increasingly conscious that his father had played a hard role in Anglo-American relations during the War. Certainly, as his thesis makes clear, he was utterly opposed to the position taken by his father.

The central argument of Kennedy's thesis was that Chamberlain may well have been compelled to adopt appeasement because of Britain's reluctance to rearm. He blamed Munich on neither Chamberlain nor Baldwin but on the failings of democracy. It was for Kennedy an event in some ways both inevitable and desirable: inevitable, as a response to British public opinion and because Britain had failed to rearm; desirable, in that it bought time to rearm. He knew that it would have been better to have halted Hitler's belligerency at the outset. But one of the weaknesses of democracy is its inability to act swiftly. 'Democracy', he wrote, 'is essentially peace-loving; the people don't want to go to war. When they do go, it is with a very firm conviction, because they must believe deeply and strongly in their case before they consent.'[4] The mistakes made by Britain carried, for Kennedy, vital lessons for the United States: indeed, basically, democracy was on trial world-wide.

Perhaps the most notable feature of Kennedy's thesis, especially in the context of the xenophobia of 1940, was the aloof, almost clinical, manner in which he described events. This emotional detachment may have owed much to his reluctance—possibly out of deference to his father—to take sides in the isolationist/interventionist debate. Whatever his reasons, he had no such qualms in the post-War world, and in fact he was to hold very definite views about American foreign policy and its mistakes. He appreciated well the magnitude of the changes in the international political scene, that the European balance of power system, having irrevocably collapsed, had been replaced by a new order of world bipolarity. This, he further knew, necessitated a reassessment not only by the United States but also by its allies. Painful as he expected such adjustments to be, he was nevertheless impatient with British and French pretensions of great-power status. As a consequence, he went further than merely approving Eisenhower's refusal to support the Anglo-French intervention in the Suez Crisis of 1956. 'Since 1945', Kennedy told telephone workers in Boston: 'we have been tremendously hampered by diplomatic ties with Britain and France who wish to preserve their colonial ties. We have taken a definite moral stand against colonialism for the first time since 1945.'

Kennedy's militant call for Algerian Independence in 1957, if it was in part to explain De Gaulle's later hostile attitude, was but a further extension of his conviction of the need to clarify American purposes in foreign policy. It was not merely a failure, on the part of American foreign policy-makers, fully to appreciate the implications of nationalism in the world. A second, and perhaps even more important, weakness in American foreign policy was, as he saw it, the lack of decision and conviction in American leadership. He was highly critical of the Eisenhower Administration's tendency to seek absolutist solutions especially in South-East Asia and its failure to give proper direction. He was above all determined to reassert American leadership in the world and to give a clear articulation of policy at the pinnacle. This determination clearly augured changes in the nature of America's relations with its allies, especially Britain which had under Eisenhower enjoyed great freedom to cultivate influence within the alliance. It was thus that at the end of 1960 the British Government, and in particular Harold Macmillan, anxiously awaited possible changes in the Anglo-American relationship.

1. Arthur Schlesinger Jr., *A Thousand Days* (André Deutsch, 1965), p.75.
2. David Cecil, *The Young Melbourne* (Constable Co., 1939), p.5.
3. Arthur Schlesinger Jr., *op. cit.*, p.76.
4. John Kennedy, *Why England Slept* (Hutchinson, 1940), p.227.

3

With Macmillan

'To those old allies, whose cultural and spiritual origins we share, we pledge the loyalty of faithful friends. United, there is little we cannot do in a host of co-operative ventures. Divided, there is little we can do, for we dare not meet a powerful challenge at odds and split asunder.' These words taken from John F. Kennedy's Inaugural Address of January 1961 both represented a pledge and also summarised the new President's hopes and fears for the Atlantic alliance. And very early in his Administration, President Kennedy set out to establish close personal contacts with his major allies to help to ensure that it was his hopes rather than his fears that would be realised. But this proved to be very difficult with three of his four major allies.

Kennedy knew that it would never be easy to establish close personal relationships with his chief partners, conscious, as he was, of the generation gap between himself and Europe's statesmen. The age factor proved particularly formidable in the case of Konrad Adenauer, the Chancellor of West Germany, Kennedy sensing he was talking not merely to a different generation but a different world. Combined with a bitter resentment at the deliberate reversal of the Dulles policy of regarding West Germany as America's chief ally, this was too much of a barrier to any close relationship Kennedy might have established with Adenauer. In the case of France, a single-minded personal ambition and obdurate pride prevented any meaningful dialogue between Kennedy and De Gaulle. As for Canada, John Diefenbaker proved to be totally incompatible with Kennedy. In consequence, it was with Harold Macmillan alone that Kennedy was successful in establishing a really meaningful and intimate relationship. He saw Macmillan first, liked him best, and indeed their meetings were more frequent than Kennedy's meetings with any other partner—they met seven times altogether, four occasions in 1961 alone. Their relationship proved to be just as close, and possibly of more importance, than Macmillan's well-publicised rapport with Eisenhower. But it was never publicly recognised as such, nor indeed was it immediately apparent. In fact Macmillan himself had been extremely apprehensive of his ability to establish a relationship with the new President as close and as valuable as his friendship with Eisenhower. That rapport had been so successfully exploited to restore the Anglo-American alliance after the Suez débâcle that, in a letter of farewell at the end of 1960, Macmillan remarked 'I cannot of course hope to have anything to replace the sort of relations that we have had.'

Macmillan's apprehension was in part due to the fact that he knew precious little about the new President, which perhaps makes it the more surprising that he genuinely preferred Kennedy to Nixon, especially since Conservatives traditionally find more in common with the Republican candidate. Macmillan had been aware of Kennedy as the son of a controversial American Ambassador to Britain and as a friend of English politicians of a much younger generation, including David Ormsby-Gore, whose special position is considered later. Macmillan clearly shared the fear that the new President's attitude to Britain might be influenced by his 'anti-British' upbringing, and his father's experience. He was also 'very conscious', as one of his advisers remarked, 'of a great hurdle to overcome' with the age difference between himself, at nearly 67, and Kennedy, a young looking 43. 'How', he asked a columnist friend, 'am I ever going to get along with that cocky young Irishman?' Arthur Schlesinger Jr. put Macmillan's apprehension thus: 'The languid Edwardian, who looked back to the sun-lit years before the First World War as a lost paradise, feared that the brisk young American, nearly a quarter of a century his junior, would consider him a museum piece.'[1] Moreover, as a statesman with vast experience in foreign affairs, Macmillan was concerned at the almost complete ignorance of the new Administration in the finer art of diplomacy, in which he believed he excelled. Nothing is as new or as ignorant in politics as a new government in the United States, and, though the Kennedy team proved ultimately to be remarkably able, they were at the outset remarkably ignorant. For, within weeks of taking office, they believed they had all the answers to world problems. But, as one senior American general remarked, 'their conclusions were either terribly, terribly obvious, too obvious to mention, or terribly, terribly, wrong.' In no area was this more a matter of concern for Macmillan than the new Administration's early crusade for an acceleration in the dismantling of the Old Empire. The wind of change, Macmillan recognised, was blowing through Africa, but he did not want it to become a hurricane.

Macmillan was finally, and not unnaturally, worried about the extent to which his own role in world affairs would necessarily be transformed with the advent to power of a President determined to assert his own leadership in foreign policy. The days of White House inertia, which had characterised the Eisenhower presidency and which had given Macmillan, particularly after the death of Dulles in 1959, great scope in world affairs, were now numbered. An ambitious intellectual team had taken over, determined to reassert American prestige in the world which they deemed had been allowed to slip away under Eisenhower. They gave the impression that they were interested only in the realities of power and cared little for the sensitivities of their allies. Kennedy, it was said, no longer needed Macmillan as a go-between in his relationship with the Soviet Union. Indeed, Macmillan's absence at the Kennedy-Khrushchev confrontation at Vienna in June 1961 seemed but an indication of the new order of things.

Macmillan's apprehensions about Kennedy were nevertheless largely ill-founded. For with surprising ease, and much to their mutual relief, Kennedy and Macmillan established a close personal rapport, and a genuine fondness for each other, which went far beyond the necessities of alliance. It was a relationship which was little short of extraordinary to witness, for the two leaders were so utterly unlike in appearance, age and mannerisms. Their first conference, at Key West in March 1961, appeared like a meeting between two men of different centuries, Macmillan in many ways symbolising Victoriana, Kennedy very much a man of the modern world. And, indeed, even though the two men apparently took an instant liking to each other, their close relationship was not immediately evident. For in seeking to make an impression both leaders, according to one official present, 'showed off in their own way'. Kennedy was, moreover, to an extent upset by Macmillan's failure to react more strongly to his premonitions about the Laotian crisis, the discussion of which was the primary purpose of the hastily arranged meeting. In fact, it was not just that Macmillan was a character who did not react strongly to anything. He was also greatly disturbed about the direction and dangers of American policy in South-East Asia.

A chain of blunders and illogicalities in American policy in Laos had, in Macmillan's opinion, directly contributed to the deteriorating situation there, where by December 1960 the two super-powers had found themselves not only recognising but materially supporting the opposing factions in the civil war. Kennedy was himself sceptical of the wisdom of his predecessor's policy in Laos, but he knew that American prestige was deeply involved and that extrication in consequence would be difficult. He did not believe that Laos was 'worthy of engaging the attention of great powers', but he knew he had first to convince the Soviet Union of this. He was not prepared, he said, 'to be trapped, provoked or drawn into' Laos but, as the situation rapidly deteriorated in the early months of 1961, this looked precisely what would happen. And with France openly hostile to any proposal for joint intervention, Kennedy sought at Key West more than just 'moral support' from Macmillan. But the Prime Minister was reluctant to commit Britain to a military enterprise not least because, with his sound historical perspective, he sensed the enormous dangers of American involvement in South-East Asia, particularly if it diverted American attention away from the central theatre, as Britain saw it, of Europe and the Atlantic alliance. History may well vindicate Macmillan's apprehensions. Moreover, in the light of the British experience in the Malayan campaign in the 1950s, the Macmillan Government knew, as one Minister put it, that 'a war in Laos would be excessively unrewarding', especially since Laos was strategically more important than Malaya to the Communists without having any of the latter's natural advantages. Macmillan in consequence advised very strongly against any military action, but with Kennedy considering Laos a test not only of Soviet intentions but also of the value of the Anglo-American alliance, Macmillan did agree, though even then 'with deepest despondency', to support the President. It was not, however, unconditional support for American policy: indeed his was the typical politician's answer. As one official recalled, 'Macmillan said he had to get Cabinet approval. Kennedy obviously thought this was an excuse. It was an excuse combined with the fear of getting involved.' Later Kennedy was to realise the wisdom of Macmillan's caution, but he came away from their first meeting disappointed with Macmillan.

Moreover though their meeting in Washington a few days later was heralded as 'the beginning of a new relationship', it remained at that stage tentative. Both Macmillan and Home were upset by what they regarded as Dean Acheson's uncompromising stand on the Berlin discussions, in which, to them at least, Kennedy had appeared excessively diffident. Nevertheless, on his return to London, Macmillan reported his first optimistic impressions of the new President: 'I was very much struck by his alertness,' he said on television, 'his gaiety, his power of listening and, I thought, his full command of the position.'

Within a week, the Bay of Pigs fiasco was to demonstrate that Kennedy was anything but in full command of his Administration. Indeed Macmillan's inability to establish an early meaningful relationship with the President was due as much as anything else to the failure of the new Administration fully to grasp the limitations as well as the extent of its newly-acquired power. Many members of the new team naïvely believed, as one columnist put it to me, that 'they had the power and all they had to do was wield it.'

The British Government's criticism of the Bay of Pigs venture was surprisingly free of moral cant, being critical less of the invasion per se than of its complete ineptitude! How, Ministers enquired with astonishment, had the C.I.A. ever reached the conclusion that, if only they could establish themselves on the island, the Cuban exiles could expect large-scale popular support? British intelligence reports, that the prospects were remote for

any general uprising against Castro, were blindly ignored by the
C.I.A. sleuths. Kennedy himself was later to wonder how a
supposedly rational and responsible government could ever
have become so involved in such an ill-fated venture. But, while
the Bay of Pigs was Kennedy's greatest blunder, by exposing his
inexperience in foreign affairs it made him much more receptive
and responsive to advice particularly from outside his Administration. Macmillan in consequence assumed his rightful place as an
older and wiser counsellor, and their third meeting at Downing
Street in June 1961 thus marked the beginning of the most astonishing Prime Minister-President relationship in modern times.
There they found, to their surprise, that no differences of age and
opionion could prevent them from getting along famously. They discovered, as Arthur Schlesinger put it; 'a considerable tempera-
mental rapport. Kennedy with his own fondness for the British
political style, liked Macmillan's patrician approach to politics,
his impatience with official ritual, his insouciance about the
professionals, his pose of nonchalance, even when most deeply
committed. Macmillan, for his part, responded to Kennedy's
courage, his ability to see events unfolding against the vast
canvas of history, his contempt for cliché, his unfailing sense of
the ridiculous. They found the same things funny and the same
things serious. "It was the gay things that linked us together",
Macmillan once told me, "and made it possible for us to talk
about the terrible things." . . . It was as if they had known each
other all their lives.'[2]

That the two leaders should have discovered such a tempera-
mental rapport was not as surprising as it may have at first sight
appeared. For though they were unlike in certain respects, they
had in common things more important than their differences:
professionalism in their approach to politics, sound political
instincts, intellectual assessments of the problems they faced and
their resolution, and shared attitudes as to the use and cultivation
of power. They had even experienced somewhat similar political
upbringings, though, to be true, Macmillan in his youth had been
much more philosophically committed than had Kennedy been
in his early political life.

Macmillan was always a much more serious figure than his
urbanity and histrionics would have us believe. He had been one

of the most progressive Conservative M.P.s in the 1930s: indeed he was the first to adopt Keynesianism. He had not only vehemently opposed Munich but had served with distinction in both World Wars. He displayed in his early political life the virtue which President Kennedy most admired in politicians: courage, that is the maintenance of self-respect, integrity, conscience—call it what you will—maintained if necessary at the expense of incurring public wrath or party disapproval. In 1936, for example, Macmillan was the only Conservative M.P. to vote against Stanley Baldwin's foreign policy, and he in fact resigned the Government Whip for a year, returning to the fold only to oppose Chamberlain. He considered it essential to preserve his intellectual independence, believing that the pledges he had made to the people who had elected him were more important than party loyalties. He was certainly not afraid to advocate drastic changes in society if he thought they were necessary, and his book, *The Middle Way*, expounded a philosophy which was both then and now revolutionary for a Conservative. His rebellious instincts were in later years to clash with his image as Tory Party leader, but he was never able, or in fact willing, fully to subdue these instincts and memories. He assumed a split personality, a political Dr Jekyll and Mr Hyde!

During the Depression, Macmillan had never gone short of food or employment himself but he was acutely conscious that many of the people had whom he was supposed to represent in Parliament. Kennedy took a similar view of his political obligations. Neither he nor Macmillan had ever had to worry about money—indeed both were really members of the much used term 'nouveau riche'—but this did not make them any less concerned for the under-privileged in Boston and Stockton.

Though both Kennedy and Macmillan were accomplished political orators, neither saw politics merely in terms of debating points. Indeed Macmillan always loathed Question Time in the House of Commons. For both Kennedy and Macmillan, politics was not an end in itself but a means towards an end, a means of ensuring their ideas could influence the course of events. Of power, Macmillan once remarked, 'when you achieve it, there's nothing there!' Nevertheless, like Kennedy, Macmillan had a strong desire to achieve something significant during his period of office, by which he would be remembered in later years. Sharing a genuine horror at the possibility of nuclear war, both Kennedy and Macmillan strove for a détente with the Soviet Union, and, as part of this end, both jointly pressed for a nuclear test-ban treaty. Macmillan in particular took what can only be described as a profoundly cynical view of politics, convinced that it was really only worth being in politics if one took epoch-making decisions. He saw himself as an arbiter, mediator or honest broker, between the United States and the Soviet Union. He put great store on the value of personal conferences. As he remarked at the outset of his diplomatic solo to Russia in 1959, which as an experiment in unilateral diplomacy, if not welcomed by his allies, was nevertheless heartily approved by the British electorate: 'personal talks and contacts are very valuable in international life today. They aren't in themselves a solution of our problems but I think they help to make solutions possible.' In reality, Macmillan, like Churchill, believed that summit meetings were in themselves considerable achievements, though the only summit meeting he actually arranged—the Paris Summit of May 1960—turned out to be an unmitigated disaster. Kennedy, however, like his predecessor, was to be sceptical about the value of summitry, and from time to time he felt obliged to discourage Macmillan's temptation to play the role of peacemaker.

The successful collaboration between Kennedy and Macmillan to achieve their more limited objective of a test-ban treaty highlighted the more genuine and positive side of Macmillan's character. Indeed it was this rather than his more flamboyant ventures which in retrospect constituted his major contribution in world affairs. His patience was infinite during the test-ban negotiations; he never failed to inject new enthusiasm when the momentum sagged, displaying real but controlled emotion. His eloquence may have given him enormous authority, but it was his persistence which produced the results.

Kennedy's approach to foreign affairs was in reality very much in the mould of traditional British diplomacy. He was very pragmatic, and very undoctrinaire. He did not seek to over-persuade a friendly nation nor did he try to impose terms on an adversary which would involve an unacceptable loss of face. His intuition was acute: he had in fact the true politician's gift for practising the art of the possible, though he was always quick to coat a disagreeable pill. He was an admirer of William Pitt and Charles James Fox in that he sought to make his foreign policy as strong as Pitt's but as subtle and conciliatory as Fox's, the supreme example of the merits of this approach being Kennedy's handling of the Cuban missile crisis. His attitude to the use of power was much more akin to Macmillan's than had ever been the case with the reformist Dulles. Both Kennedy and Macmillan viewed foreign policy objectives, and their limitations, very much in the context of the existing balance-of-power system.

That the two leaders had similar approaches to foreign affairs did not mean that they always saw eye to eye. Indeed they often had disagreements, and differences of opinion and approach. Not only was Macmillan more enthusiastic for summit meetings, but he was also much less willing to make proper preparations for the possibility of war over West Berlin. He was far from sure whether he could carry his government on McNamara's policy of increased conventional forces. Kennedy in turn knew that he could never carry his government on the British arguments for recognising Red China. He was annoyed with the British failure to restrict trade with Cuba, and he thought Macmillan's proposals for international monetary liquidity were wildly unrealistic. And where he was concerned at the apparent laxity in British security, Macmillan was on at least one occasion briefly but violently angry with the American sale of Hawk missiles to Israel, which he felt was in direct contradiction to agreed policy between the British and American governments.

But no differences of opinion and approach endangered their close personal rapport. With the exception of the Skybolt problem, both leaders as professional politicians showed acute awareness of the domestic political problems which tended to produce their disagreements. And even on the Skybolt problem, it was as brother politicians that they found a compromise.

Kennedy recognised that Macmillan was a man of great vitality, shrewdness, erudition, even ruthlessness. He knew that beneath his languid urbanity Macmillan concealed acute political acumen. When he became Prime Minister in January 1957, confronted with problems as grave as any which have confronted a peacetime Prime Minister, Macmillan had not expected his

Administration to survive very long. Yet not only had it survived, not only had the major problems been overcome, but Macmillan himself had become one of the most powerful Prime Ministers ever, dominating his Cabinet with his own political philosophy and style. Yet, however skilfully he exploited the channels of mass communication to build up his own powerful public image, Macmillan remained in many ways a most unlikely leader to be carrying Britain into the 1960s. Proud of his family tradition and heritage, Macmillan at times genuinely considered himself the last of the Victorian Prime Ministers. Certainly his mannerisms, detached wit, patrician style and aristocratic connections made Macmillan much more like a Melbourne than a Wilson.

Macmillan never claimed to be aristocratic, even though like Ormsby-Gore he was related to the Devonshire family. Nevertheless, Macmillan lived in an aristocratic world and, in the late 1950s anyway, it seems to have been a comfort to many in Britain that in an age of great change and turmoil our political leaders could govern in the way that they had always done. Despite the fact that Britain had ceased to be a great power, Macmillan was able to reassure people in Britain that at least we were civilised and that the 'special relationship', to which he attached just as much importance as Churchill, really made up for all we had lost. In the 1950s, Britain seemed to prefer the rule of patricians to the rule of plebs. By 1961, however, Macmillan's patrician image had begun to turn sour on him, and this was no doubt much influenced by the style of leadership which Kennedy offered and which appeared in marked contrast to Macmillan's. The dynamism symbolised by Kennedy in fact stimulated the growing frustration with Macmillan in Britain. 'Macmillan just sits there,' remarked one alienated Conservative voter in March 1961. 'If he would just pack up and go grouse shooting and let a younger man take over, we might get somewhere.'[3] Unhappily for Macmillan, such criticism, far from abating, only intensified as time went on.

Kennedy himself, however, far from being sceptical of Macmillan's patrician approach, was genuinely bemused by it. He enjoyed Macmillan's conversation, eloquence and sense of humour. They were both fascinated by the aristocratic life. Indeed, they had a remote family link through the late Kathleen Kennedy's marriage. The Marquis of Hartington was Macmillan's nephew by marriage and also, in passing, the cousin and best friend of Ormsby-Gore, whose own relationship with the Prime Minister was strengthened through his sister Katherine's marriage to Macmillan's son, Maurice. Not that the Kennedy–Macmillan family link was of itself very important—the two men had not met before 1961. But, in one sense, Macmillan did establish an 'avuncular' relationship with Kennedy. Indeed, though Kennedy always called Macmillan 'Prime Minister' in their frequent telephone conversations, he would at times in private refer to 'Uncle Harold'.

Kennedy always regarded Macmillan as an elder statesman: not in a derogatory sense since from April 1961 Kennedy found that at times elder statesmen have their uses! He looked up to Macmillan as a veteran, as a wise man, as a man who attached immense importance to the relationship between Britain and the United States, and as a man who wanted to be helpful in matters of common interest with the United States. He regarded Macmillan as a reliable ally, co-operative even on politically embarrassing issues like the American resumption of nuclear tests in 1962.

He never ceased to be impressed by Macmillan's wisdom and sheer experience. As one of the President's closest intimates recalled, 'he admired in Mr Macmillan his breadth of vision, the relationship he always saw between events today and past history and possible future history. This he found stimulating.' He found it especially stimulating and refreshing since it was a perspective he gained neither from his immediate associates nor for that matter from any other major ally. As a result the President greatly valued the opportunity of regular conversations on the 'hot-line' between London and Washington. Though no great decisions were ever made through this medium, these conversations proved very useful as an exchange of views, to provide the two men with the opportunity to gain at first-hand what was in the other's mind.

Both Kennedy and Macmillan were intolerant of pomposity, pretention, discursiveness and bombast, and were thus able to ensure an informality of atmosphere at their meetings, which was particularly valued by Kennedy. Macmillan's own style of conversation—the reminiscences, the raillery, the soliloquising which, though for outward effect, carried self-satisfaction, and the tongue-in-cheek—ideally suited this informality of atmosphere. Kennedy genuinely looked forward to his meetings with Macmillan. He told one of his intimates of their meeting at Birch Grove in 1963, of how he and Macmillan 'listened to their military staffs for two and a half hours, then went alone for a walk in the garden and in a couple of minutes took the decisions. He told me how refreshing this was as a way of doing business.'

It was a great comfort to Kennedy to know that he could rely on somebody of Macmillan's stature in times of crisis. 'Macmillan was a wonderful man in a crisis,' recalled one American official. He shared with Kennedy the ability to remain outwardly calm whatever the turmoil within him. He would have denied the epithet of 'unflappable', for on important occasions, such as at the Bermuda Conference of 1957, he would work himself up until he was quite ill; but his motto for his Private Office, by which he sought to model his actions, was 'Quiet, calm deliberation disentangles every knot.' Perhaps the single most important quality that Kennedy and Macmillan shared was their ability to deal with dramatic issues in a relatively undramatic way. This was of no mean importance in a period of many dramatic issues.

Yet, however valuable it was for Kennedy to be able to talk frankly with at least one of his major allies, there is little doubt that their close relationship was a great deal more important to Macmillan than to Kennedy both because the 'special relationship' was more fundamental to British foreign policy in a way that it neither was nor could be to the Kennedy Administration; and also because Macmillan's own style of diplomacy demanded that he be seen to have established a position of privilege with the United States President.

The Kennedy–Macmillan relationship was also very important to closer Anglo-American relations, for apart from exceptional circumstances personal relationships are always potential assets. Personalities of course cannot fundamentally change a situation. Kennedy could no more persuade Macmillan to change his policy on British trade with Cuba than could Macmillan in 1961 convince the United States to accept the need to recognise

Communist China. Personal relationships become more important when common ends and agreed objectives are already established. They then ensure that the two leaders are working on common paths together. During the Kennedy Presidency, there were many established common objectives in Anglo-American relations: the refusal to be intimidated by Soviet threats but the acceptance of the need to negotiate with the adversary; the need to find a solution to Laos; the need to solve the problems in interdependence and participation within NATO; the enthusiasm for a united Europe; and above all the shared conviction as to the desirability and necessity of a nuclear test-ban treaty. In this context, personal rapport becomes important in terms of enhancing the quality of the public relationship.

Close personal relationships also permit even disagreements in policy or approach to be discussed in a frank and friendly manner. There were plenty of problems in Anglo-American relations in the early 1960s but both Kennedy and Macmillan were candid with each other: they both trusted each other. Even at Nassau, their discussion in the circumstances was both informal and cordial. Because they usually understood each other's views and ideas so well, they were able to take urgent joint action when the situation demanded: it was thus that their response to the Indian appeal for military aid against China in 1962 was swift and ultimately decisive. Above all, close personal relationships guarantee that reciprocity of support which has traditionally been the basis of the 'special relationship'. Macmillan wisely counselled against American intervention in Laos at a time when the President was inclined to get involved, and, where he supported the President over the Cuban Quarantine, Kennedy responded by supporting Macmillan on the British application to join the Common Market with an enthusiasm that went far beyond the dictates of national policy. The Kennedy-Macmillan rapport was indeed the last of the great personal relationships in the Anglo-American field, and it was only paralleled, some may say surpassed, in importance by the relationship between Kennedy and Ormsby-Gore.

1. Arthur Schlesinger Jr., *A Thousand Days* (André Deutsch, 1965), p.340.
2. Arthur Schlesinger Jr., *op. cit.*, p.341.
3. Cited by Peter Webb, *Newsweek* (6 March 1961).

4

Ormsby-Gore:
A Special Relationship within
the 'Special Relationship'

No single event was of more importance to President Kennedy's relations with, and his understanding and affection for, Britain than the appointment in 1961 of Sir David Ormsby-Gore as British Ambassador in Washington. Some may be inclined to put it down to a chance of history that Ormsby-Gore just happened to have known Kennedy since they were both young men, and that he just happened also to have worked in the field of foreign affairs for the best part of ten years, and actually in the Foreign Office since 1956. Moreover, his responsibilities as Minister of State for Disarmament had meant that much of his work had been carried out in the United States, a country which has always held a special fascination for Ormsby-Gore, who became the fifth baron Harlech upon the death of his father in 1964. The Foreign Office, however, rarely subscribes to the chances of history theory and, though his proved political ability and diplomatic experience made him a leading contender as a successor to Sir Harold Caccia, it was Ormsby-Gore's known friendship with President Kennedy which guaranteed his appointment as British Ambassador. Indeed President Kennedy had taken the unprecedented step of actually suggesting to the British Government that Ormsby-Gore's presence in Washington would be a great asset to Anglo-American relations.

Many governments might have taken exception to what they would have viewed as undue interference in the selection of their Ambassador. But, with his shrewd political judgement, Macmillan quickly appreciated the obvious advantages of sending Ormsby-Gore to Washington. The appointment certainly proved to be an inspired choice and Ormsby-Gore became the pivot of the 'special relationship' during the Kennedy Presidency. His presence in Washington, and his close personal ties with both Kennedy and Macmillan, ensured the quick and informal exchange of views between Washington and London. It was a return to a style of diplomacy which obviously suited both Kennedy and Macmillan, and was in marked contrast to the rigid, and at times exhausting, way of conducting diplomatic business during the Dulles era. Ormsby-Gore was not subjected to the indignity of diplomatic 'Coventry' which Caccia had suffered in the wake of Suez in 1956. President Kennedy was as pleased with Ormsby-Gore's arrival in Washington in October 1961 as he was with the Ambassador's hand-written note of delight on his appointment.

Ormsby-Gore and Kennedy had first met in London in the 1930s though at that time neither of them had shown any inclination to make a career in politics. Both of them, however, had been encouraged by their families at an early age to take a lively interest in public affairs. Ormsby-Gore himself had been born into an established political family, his mother being a sister of Lord Salisbury, a member of the Cecil family which had been politically powerful since the reign of Elizabeth I. He was related to both the Devonshires and the Cavendishes and, despite his critical attitude to the idea of an exclusive establishment, he would undoubtedly be considered a member of the British Establishment. As a rich landed aristocrat with distinguished ancestry, he was later to be the personification of everything which American snobs like and admire about Britain. Thus was one cynic to suggest that Ormsby-Gore was 'Macmillan's special representative to the Court of King John'. Today, as Sir Alec Douglas-Home would no doubt testify, an unassuming manner and membership of the aristocracy can have positive disadvantages in British politics—this may perhaps explain Ormsby-Gore's inability to capture public imagination in Britain. But there is little doubt that his upbringing was to launch his political career—he became Member of Parliament for the family seat of Oswestry. Similarly, it was through his connections with the Devonshires that Ormsby-Gore came to establish his friendship with Jack Kennedy.

The Marquis of Hartington, Kennedy's brother-in-law, had not only been cousin and best friend of Ormsby-Gore but had also been best man at the latter's wedding to his first wife. Kathleen Kennedy was to be a very close friend of the Ormsby-Gores and was indeed invited to be god-mother to their eldest child. The Kennedys and the Ormsby-Gores thus came to meet regularly and whenever Jack Kennedy came to London he would call on Ormsby-Gore. In turn from 1954, when he first visited the United States, Ormsby-Gore would every year stay with the Kennedy family either at Palm Beach or at Hyannisport. The two friends shared a lively interest in history and public affairs and they found, as they grew older, that their attitudes towards politics matured and they followed each others' careers closely: Kennedy from Congressman to Senator to Presidential candidate, Ormsby-Gore from M.P. to junior Minister to Minister of State at the Foreign Office. They discovered that their approach to politics was very similar. Though both enjoyed the trappings of power, neither found the rough and tumble of election campaigning the most interesting aspect of politics. They went into politics because they believed that only by being in politics could they ensure that their views had some influence upon the course of events. It was not enough for them merely to be adequate: both sought professionalism, and both were equally convinced that the final decisions in the nuclear age could not be left to experts. Both men were always more interested in foreign affairs than in domestic politics. Sceptical about the clichés of the Cold War, they took a passionate interest in measures for disarmament; it was thus that when he became British Minister responsible for disarmament and test-ban negotiations, Ormsby-Gore had many long discussions with Kennedy in New York both about the British position and, as he saw it, the inconclusive and at times contradictory position of the United States. These discussions certainly made a deep impression upon Kennedy for, upon taking office, he ordered a complete review of American policy.

Kennedy greatly respected the views and advice of Ormsby-Gore, who, on more than one occasion, he remarked was the most intelligent man he had ever met. Ormsby-Gore's role, in consequence, was not only that of an Ambassador accredited to the United States but also, and perhaps of even more importance to Kennedy, as a close friend and counsellor. It was of great value to the President to be able to talk and consult with somebody apart from his own entourage in perfect confidence. He shared even his most traumatic experiences, including the Cuban missile crisis, with the British Ambassador, at times imparting more information to Ormsby-Gore than he would permit to be given to Macmillan. Kennedy knew Ormsby-Gore would not betray confidences and trusted him as much as the members of his own Cabinet. Indeed, to many observers, Ormsby-Gore was an accepted member of the Kennedy team. Certainly, very soon after his election, the President and his brother talked openly and frankly with Ormsby-Gore about possible Cabinet appointments and likely policy. It was on one such occasion, at a private luncheon in New York, that Kennedy first expressed the hope that Ormsby-Gore would come to Washington as the British Ambassador.

The President's trust in Ormsby-Gore was heightened by his lesser confidence in the other two leading Western Ambassadors, Hervé Alphand of France and Wilhelm Grewe of West Germany. He found Ormsby-Gore much less likely than either Alphand or Grewe to disclose confidential information to favoured journalists. Alphand was somewhat bedevilled by De Gaulle and Grewe by 1962 was almost *persona non grata* to the Administration and accordingly recalled.

Ormsby-Gore was a source both of new ideas and information for the President. Kennedy found the different perspective on world affairs which he gained from Ormsby-Gore both refreshing and stimulating. They had many intimate and relaxed conversations at the White House, Palm Beach and Hyannisport, in which Kennedy was not talking as President nor Ormsby-Gore as the Ambassador of Britain. They were general, free-range and private discussions such as they had had over the years of their friendship, and they were far from exclusively concerned with Anglo-American affairs. Kennedy knew that nothing he said would be construed as official policy and reported back to the British Government. Ormsby-Gore always made it quite clear to the President when he felt a point had been made which he should report back to Macmillan. These long discussions possibly gave Kennedy his best opportunity to clarify his own purposes in foreign affairs. Ormsby-Gore was as candid with Kennedy the President as he had been with Kennedy the Congressman. His advice and counsel was that of an old friend, and Kennedy himself would not have had it otherwise.

Socially, the Kennedys enjoyed no company more than the Ormsby-Gores. When they sought relaxation, they liked people around them who were amusing, informal, intelligent, stimulating and energetic and they found the British Ambassador could be all of these. Kennedy considered Ormsby-Gore a companion for every mood: at times, he was happy to be totally unserious; at times, he would enjoy sailing in Nantucket Sound or playing football in the family compound, though neither he nor Ormsby-Gore were as ruthlessly competitive as other members of the Kennedy family; at other times, Kennedy would want to brood over the horrors of nuclear holocaust and Khrushchev's brinkmanship. The Ambassador could match the President's transition from frivolity to gravity. It was as if they had powers of telepathic communication.

Ormsby-Gore was in many ways as complex a character as the President himself. There was little conventional and nothing predictable about the Ambassador. He was a strange hybrid, a split personality: at one time he would be the voice of English aristocracy, at another, he would be very much a man of the modern world, of the jet-set age. His sudden changes from polite reserve to engaging charm, from old-world courtesy to modern dynamism fascinated the President. It also went down well with the American public, and Ormsby-Gore was not unaware of the importance of the public-relations aspect of his job.

The Kennedy–Ormsby-Gore friendship was a unique relationship between an Ambassador and a President with no parallel in modern times. Yet, there was never any embarrassment or difficulty in mingling their official and social relations, and this in itself showed the true depth and meaning of their relationship, for, when discussing Anglo-American affairs, each nearly always remained the firm advocate of the policies and actions of his own government. There were times when the British Government's position and the Ambassador's position were not always identical but, as one White House aide recalled, 'we knew David well

43

enough to know when they were not identical.' Occasionally, the Ambassador's outspoken remarks got him into trouble at home as, for instance, when he expressed public agreement with much of Dean Acheson's 'played out' speech of December 1962, which in Britain caused Macmillan such acute political embarrassment.

An informal source of wisdom and new ideas for Kennedy he was, but Ormsby-Gore did not deliberately seek to use his friendship with the President to gain influence or favours. He was a man endowed not only with great intelligence but also with great integrity. He went out of his way to prevent his friendship with Kennedy provoking any resentment either in the Diplomatic Corps or in the Administration itself. That the two men were close friends could not be disguised. But they did everything possible that they could to make sure that week-end house parties did not appear in the press though this often proved difficult. Moreover, Ormsby-Gore was extremely discreet about his visits to the White House. As one Kennedy aide remarked, 'he did not advertise his presences at the White House in the way that Alphand would.' Certainly the extent to which Ormsby-Gore saw Kennedy only really became apparent after the President's assassination.

There was no pretence, deception or even embarrassment surrounding the relationship: it was just that they decided it was best to play it down as much as possible. The British Government also sought to play it down for fear that it might provoke resentment. But resentment was inevitable and it was particularly harboured by other members of the Diplomatic Corps. Ambassadors traditionally count the number of times other Ambassadors get invited to the Oval office, and Washington during the Kennedy Presidency was no exception. Hervé Alphand was especially resentful since he had been Kennedy's closest friend in the Diplomatic Corps before Ormsby-Gore moved in. And, on at least one occasion, embarrassment arose when Alphand arrived at Palm Beach for an official interview with the President only to find the British Ambassador there for a social week-end!

The close friendship between the President and Ormsby-Gore inevitably led to criticism in American papers that the Ambassador wielded too much influence. Many in Britain, however, took the opposite point of view believing that Ormsby-Gore was so much in the President's pocket that this inhibited rather than helped

Britain's position. Robert Pitman, for example, attacked Ormsby-Gore for making 'continual concessions to America. I don't think there was the slightest doubt that he was basically so close to the Kennedy family that he was a Kennedy man. He followed the Macmillan policy of doing everything the Kennedys wanted done. He is a man of an appeasing nature.'[1] Ormsby-Gore was aware of the force, if not the logic, of such charges, and in 1963, for example, he declined to lead the British delegation to the Moscow Conference for fear of being dismissed as an American stooge.

The extent to which the Ambassador meant greater influence for Britain was similarly exaggerated, not least by the Macmillan Government itself. Ormsby-Gore's advice to Kennedy at the height of the Cuban missile crisis to put back the quarantine interception line was the advice of a friend rather than as an Ambassador, however decisive it may have been. Equally, his concern with the initial scepticism of British public opinion led Ormsby-Gore to urge the President to release photographic evidence of the American claims to the press. It may well have accelerated a Presidential decision but others were also pressing for such action, and indeed the photographs of the missile installations were released first in London by David Bruce, supposedly without the President's knowledge or authority.

Nevertheless, in balancing the arguments, it is undeniable that the Ambassador had almost unlimited access to the President. 'Britain', as one American official put it, 'never had a representative in Washington who was able to reach the centre of power so quickly with fewer barriers.' The only real barriers were those which were self-imposed. Ormsby-Gore had the opportunity of talking to the President almost whenever he wanted, and he was in a position to say things to him which others would have liked to have said had they had the opportunity. His friendship with the President made it much easier for him to speak very strongly on those issues where Britain felt her interests were at stake, because he knew that Kennedy would not take offence. When he was in Washington in February 1961 for discussions on the test-ban negotiations, Ormsby-Gore saw the President, and, speaking with the bluntness of a friend, offered a caustic picture of American policy in Laos. The British Government, he told the President, could never understand how Laos could ever become a bastion of

Western democracy, as Dulles had envisaged. The best hope lay in a truly neutral Laos under Souvanna Phouma. Yet, he went on, the United States had done its best to destroy this single hope by pushing Souvanna into alliance with the communists. Kennedy was clearly impressed with the soundness of the British policy so forcefully and persuasively put by Ormsby-Gore.

Since President Kennedy could and did enjoy political discussions while relaxing, the Ambassador was never embarrassed to raise matters which were of concern to the British Government even when he was spending a social week-end with the Kennedys. It was impossible for President Kennedy not to listen to what Ormsby-Gore had to say. This did not mean that Kennedy would do something because of his friendship with the Ambassador, but it did mean that Ormsby-Gore was able to present the British point of view in a language that would have been very difficult for a normal Ambassador. A case in point was the misunderstanding which arose over the size of the British contribution to the further research costs of Polaris as envisaged in the Nassau Agreement. Kennedy and Ormsby-Gore had originally agreed on a formula whereby Britain would be expected to pay both for the missiles and a small share of the additional research costs related as a percentage of the total British investment. Macmillan had told the House of Commons of this arrangement, but then Kennedy found that he had misunderstood McNamara and that the actual contribution demanded was much higher. Ormsby-Gore took the first opportunity of impressing upon the President the impossible position Macmillan would be put in if the arrangements were changed, and a compromise was thereby reached in the best Anglo-American tradition.

Perhaps with the single exception of the political implications of the cancellation of Skybolt, Ormsby-Gore knew what matters were of sufficient importance to bring to the attention of the President, and what not to bother him with. Of course, most of the diplomatic business was conducted through the Secretary of State with whom he established a close relationship. If Rusk ever harboured resentment at occasionally being by-passed, he never showed it. In part this was due to the careful attention the Ambassador always gave to informing Rusk and Bundy of his conversations with the President. In large part, however, this was due to the ease with which Ormsby-Gore could get on with people. His charm, courtesy and unassuming manner made him a very personable individual who could make his way around the State Department with great ease. And his obvious diplomatic ability was quickly recognised, with his valuable contribution in the four-power ambassadorial meetings on Berlin.

A lucid conversationalist and persuasive debater, Ormsby-Gore offered counsel only when he considered it was relevant and useful. He approached his job with no preconceptions or prejudices but as essentially a pragmatist. All the time, his advice was governed by a delicate but positive balance in his own mind between what was desirable and what was feasible. He was fully aware that as Ambassador he had two primary functions. First, he had to know what his own Government's policy was and which direction it was likely to lead to, so that he could represent the British views and inform the Administration where his Government stood and where in certain circumstances it would move. Second, he had to familiarise himself with American policy so as to keep his own Government informed both of existing policies and future direction. To do his job effectively, Ormsby-Gore recognised the obvious importance of getting to know the minds of the key principals. He was of course fortunate in that many of them he already knew. But with those whom he did not know, who included Bundy and McNamara, he set out to establish a relationship of confidence and friendship. He knew that the formalised structure of the American government did not necessarily give a true or accurate picture of the actual way in which policy was formulated and determined. He understood very well how decisions were taken in the Kennedy Administration and in consequence when and where to make British representations. It is always very difficult to consult with the American government because, with the enormous and elaborate procedures of decision-taking, once a conclusion is reached it is very difficult to change it. This means that the time to consult with the United States is at a very early stage, and, as one American official remarked, 'Ormsby-Gore had a knack of getting in the British views at the early stages so we took them into account *before* we came to a final conclusion.'

When there is a close relationship between the Prime Minister and the President, as was the case with Macmillan and Kennedy, the Ambassador is the bearer of a special responsibility. He must not only advise right and represent right. He must also give the government to which he is accredited the feeling that, if something is said to him, somebody at the other end will listen. An Ambassador can be extraordinarily able but totally ineffective if he fails to hold the confidence of his own government. There was, however, never any doubt in Washington of Ormsby-Gore's standing with his own government. The same was true of the standing in Washington of the extremely competent and experienced American Ambassador in London, David Bruce. Macmillan was in no doubt that whatever he said to Bruce, formerly Ambassador to both France and West Germany, would receive the attention of the President. Kennedy in turn found Ormsby-Gore much more likely than either Alphand or Grewe to know what was in the mind of his principal.

Knowing both Kennedy and Macmillan so well, Ormsby-Gore was able to ensure that the two understood each other and were on the same wavelength. He was ideally equipped to interpret or even predict Macmillan's and Kennedy's reactions to the other's proposals. When Kennedy was concerned about Macmillan's possible reaction to the Cuban quarantine, Ormsby Gore could assure him of the Prime Minister's support, which was indeed forthcoming if somewhat belatedly. And following the initial scepticism in Britain, the Ambassador volunteered to return to London to ensure the Government knew exactly the President's thoughts and intentions. It was a matter of two-way confidence and, again with the single exception of the Skybolt crisis, it operated perfectly. The confidence which Kennedy and Macmillan bestowed on Ormsby-Gore and Bruce guaranteed that misunderstandings and conflicts were kept to a minimum. There has never been a time before, or since, when the respective representatives of Britain and the United States have been so competent. The close understanding between the two countries during the Kennedy Presidency was both a justification for Ormsby-Gore's appointment and a reflection on his own ability.

1. Quoted in *The Sunday Times Magazine* (9 June 1968), 'Peer Of All Trades'.

5

Kennedy, Khrushchev and Macmillan

Kennedy's initiation in the Presidency was anything but easy. He had never entertained any illusion about being able to avoid or postpone decisions, but the international horizon exploded about him in one storm after another. Each day the problems multiplied, each day the solutions to them became seemingly less obvious, seemingly more intractable. In January 1961 the communist world was riding on the crest of a wave, and their offensive was pursued on every front in the ensuing weeks: in Laos, the Pathet Lao threatened to overrun the Government forces; in the Congo, the Soviet Union threatened new intervention following the assassination of former Prime Minister Lumumba; in the test-ban negotiations, the Soviets in March blandly abandoned positions which they had previously agreed; and in April they dramatically demonstrated their superiority in the Space race by sending the first man into orbit around the earth. Even his own country's initiatives, the new President found, seemed destined to failure, the C.I.A.-inspired invasion of Cuba ending up as a humiliating fiasco. Things were not only as bad as he had said in the campaign they would be: they were in fact to get worse! He had gloomily predicted in his first State of the Union address that there would be 'further setbacks before the tide is turned': but he could never have foreseen that world tensions in the following months would necessitate a unique second State of the Union address in the spring, and that even greater dangers would appear both in the summer and in the second year of his Presidency.

Kennedy had campaigned vigorously to reassert American prestige in the world, which he considered had declined relative to that of the Soviets. His supreme challenge thus lay not in Havana, nor even in Paris, Bonn or London: the great test was his ability to deal with Moscow, and in particular Nikita Khrushchev. Certainly the Soviet Chairman himself, having adamantly refused to negotiate with Eisenhower after the U-2 incident the previous May, awaited the arrival of the new President with more than just a passing interest. He immediately extended the hand of friendship in a warm congratulatory telegram on Kennedy's Inauguration and, as a further move to bring about a thaw in Soviet-American relations, he released the two RB-47 fliers who had been shot down over the Arctic six months before. As a response to Khrushchev's good-will gesture, Kennedy removed restrictions on the importation of Russian crab-meat and proposed a pact on more consulates. He further made it clear that U-2 flights over Soviet territory were not to be resumed. Later Khrushchev was to release U-2 pilot, Gary Powers, in a direct exchange for Soviet Master-Spy, Rudolf Abel. Small steps they may have been: at least they were steps in the right direction. But as usual Khrushchev's was a double policy, for the velvet glove only barely concealed the iron fist. Indeed, even before Kennedy's Inauguration, the Soviet leader on 6 January had delivered a blood-curdling speech in which he came out strongly in support of 'wars of national liberation'. He had, moreover, in reference to Berlin, vowed to 'eradicate this splinter from the heart of Europe,' before the end of the year.

Ever since his first ultimatum of November 1958, which Dulles had rejected the day it was received, Khrushchev had insisted that a peace treaty be signed which recognised both East and West Germany, and which transformed West Berlin into what he called a 'demilitarized city'. Not surprisingly the West had strongly opposed an arrangement which effectively would have terminated at a stroke all the rights of the occupying powers. Khrushchev had, however, further insisted on his right to conclude a separate treaty with the G.D.R. which, at least in his opinion, would produce substantially the same result, the end of allied rights in the city. But the crises over Berlin have never been just about the rights of access or indeed the status of the city; the fundamental issue in Berlin, as later in Cuba, has essentially been in the nature of a direct super-power struggle over the determination, on the one hand to shift, on the other to preserve, the existing balance of power. Berlin has since the War been a symbol of America's continuing determination to defend Western Europe, and American prestige has thus been deeply involved; whatever has happened in Berlin has become of immediate concern to both the national security interests and international obligations of the United States. Thus, while Khrushchev's threat of a peace treaty was not new, his insistence on a deadline immeasurably heightened the chances of nuclear war in 1961, since the United States could not afford to allow its commitment to seem wanting.

President Kennedy himself rejected entirely the kind of moral crusade which Dulles was apt to undertake. He did not believe that the world could be seen in terms of absolutes of capitalism versus communism, of good versus evil. Sceptical of such Cold War rhetoric, Kennedy was nevertheless under no illusion about the character of Russian polity and purpose. He knew that the chances of nuclear holocaust were high if Khrushchev persisted in his policy on Berlin. He was, above all, concerned about the dangers of miscalculation in the nuclear age, and worried that the Soviet leader would underestimate his determination to defend vital interests. He thus sought an early meeting with Khrushchev, in the conviction, as Walt Rostow once put it, that 'an awful lot of life on this planet is one man's assessment of the other.'[1] Kennedy was only too aware that many wars in history owed much to men's mistakes and miscalculations of their adversaries. Kennedy wanted an early opportunity to try to ensure that neither he nor Khrushchev made such a miscalculation.

Kennedy did not share Rusk's doctrinaire opposition to the idea of summitry. 'It is far better,' he had observed in 1959, 'that we meet at the summit than at the brink.' It was the experiments in summit meetings during the Eisenhower years which made him sceptical of their value. He knew that on occasion such a meeting might be necessary if war appeared imminent—though, as President, he never seriously entertained the possibility of a summit meeting to resolve either the Berlin or the Cuban crisis. He further recognised that a summit might possibly be of value as a place where agreements or treaties, achieved through the normal diplomatic channels, could be officially and publicly approved. But he never shared Macmillan's belief that a summit could also be a useful beginning. Not wanting to be a party to another Paris fiasco, Kennedy resisted attempts to put him in a position where he was supporting and attending a summit, which was only serving a politician's vanity or electoral chances. He knew that a summit was likely to inject considerations of personal prestige and face-saving into grave international conflicts: he was well aware that Khrushchev, for propaganda opportunities, and Macmillan, for personal and political motives, were much more enthusiastic about summitry, both believing that there was nothing like personal contacts. Kennedy, however, argued that a summit would raise undue hopes and public attention and would produce unjustified tensions and dis-appointments. He thus strongly opposed attempts by both Khrushchev and Macmillan to call a summit. Khrushchev pressed particularly hard for a summit in 1962, when he proposed that heads of government should attend the opening proceedings of the Eighteen-Nation Disarmament Conference in Geneva: it was a proposal which, so he argued in a letter to Kennedy and Macmillan, 'you will agree . . . is quite justified by the greatness of the aim.' Kennedy at least did not agree, recognising all too clearly that it would give Khrushchev an unrivalled opportunity for propaganda speeches. In probability, had Kennedy agreed, Macmillan would willingly have attended the opening of the Conference: he was certainly not opposed on principle to Khrushchev's suggestion. His disappointment arose more from the fact that, as he saw it, a circus of eighteen heads of government was no real substitute for a meeting of the Big Three! Kennedy nevertheless stood fast, refusing to agree to a summit unless there had been positive results achieved at a secondary level. It was, of course, precisely on these grounds that Macmillan in April 1963 again pressed hard for a summit meeting, which so he argued would be the means to achieve a real break-through in the test-ban treaty negotiations. Kennedy did instruct his negotiators to the Moscow Conference in July that they could commit him to a summit if it were absolutely necessary to secure a treaty: in the end it proved unnecessary, and in fact there never was a summit meeting as such during the Kennedy Presidency.

Kennedy's objections to summitry were numerous, but one at least stemmed from his embarrassment at Macmillan's attempts to play the role of 'honest broker' between East and West. Macmillan had very quickly to recognise that his influence would inevitably decline, for under Kennedy direct communications between Washington and Moscow were re-opened. The new President simply did not need a go-between, as was later to be confirmed in 1963 with the establishment of the 'hot-line' telephone between the two super-powers, which obviously by-passed London. Macmillan was thus confronted with the harsh reality that, while Kennedy was willing to consult with Britain and France both before and after meetings of the Big Two, they would not actually take part in them. Certainly, Macmillan's position was not even raised when in February 1961 the President met with his Soviet experts to review the possibility of a meeting with Khrushchev.

Kennedy clearly distinguished between a 'formal' summit and a personal, informal, meeting with the Soviet leader: yet even then he saw no sense in meeting Khrushchev unless something real was likely to result and the omens in February were far from encouraging. It was only after he was given to understand that progress was quite possible on both Laos and the test-ban treaty that he agreed to arrangements being made for a tête-à-tête in Vienna in June.

Possibly out of resentment at being left out, the British Government was far from happy about the Vienna confrontation. Macmillan urged that the new President proceed cautiously and not be taken in by Khrushchev's offensive; and Douglas-Home, for one, later confessed his disquiet that the new President 'instead of giving himself time to play himself into international affairs . . . launched into a meeting with Mr Khrushchev.'[2] Both the Prime Minister and his Foreign Secretary were disturbed with the advice which Kennedy received, particularly from the hard-line school within his Administration. Eloquently if not always rationally led by Acheson, they tended to take the view that the Cold War had hardly changed since its beginning, and that the only language which the Russians understood and respected was that which came from the end of a gun, tank or missile! Opposed to this view were not only the British Government but also many respected members of the Administration, including Stevenson, Harriman and Finletter, who argued that the world had indeed changed since Stalin's death, and that military might, far from being the only answer to world problems, was insufficient unless exercised within the context of a dynamic economic and political programme. But Acheson clearly wielded influence on Kennedy at that stage, for the President was encouraged to play it tough with the Soviet leader. It was not surprising therefore that those who advised such belligerency should also suspect that Macmillan was completely the wrong type of person to deal with Khrushchev. As one American Kremlinologist put it, 'Macmillan was a little too urbane and civilised to deal effectively with a man like Khrushchev.'

Certainly keen to seize any opportunity for increasing the dialogue with the Soviet Union, Macmillan was nonetheless fully conscious of the dangers of concessions always being one-way. He knew that on occasion it was necessary to call Khrushchev's bluff, though he did not agree with De Gaulle that Soviet threats should never be taken seriously. In fact Macmillan was quietly confident of his own ability to deal with the Soviet leader, whose character was such an unpredictable combination of genuine threats and histrionics. Macmillan was a past-master at probing the mind and motives of individuals, to comprehend better their true personality. Indeed, his very urbanity and civility, which others claimed was a liability, Macmillan could use to almost invaluable advantage. 'Premier Khrushchev,' he once jibed in a tête-à-tête with the Soviet leader, which rapidly broke the tension in the atmosphere, 'you ought to have elections in Russia [then, after a seemingly interminably long pause]—you'd win them!!' Certainly few politicians have more brilliantly and successfully dealt with their adversaries as did Macmillan with Khrushchev. He could with justification claim to know how best to approach a man like Khrushchev: indeed it was because of his very depth of knowledge of the make-up of the Soviet leader that he was disturbed at the way Kennedy set out for the Vienna confrontation. Kennedy never again over-estimated himself or underestimated his opponent but at

Vienna, as Home put it 'he made . . . a very bad mistake from which it took a lot of time to recover.'[3]

Considered by Kennedy as useful, by Khrushchev as necessary, the Vienna meeting was neither a victory nor a defeat for either of the two leaders; but it was a harrowing and rather traumatic experience for the young President. It may well be, as later reported, that Khrushchev was quite unconscious of the depressing effect which the encounter had on Kennedy: it may even be possible that he genuinely thought that he was doing the West a great favour on Berlin! But undeniably Kennedy seemed easy game to Khrushchev who set out to brow-beat this inexperienced President. His presentation, particularly on Berlin, was brutal: it was only just short of a tirade. The decision to sign a peace treaty with the East German Government before the end of the year, he declared, was irrevocable! If the President thereafter still insisted on occupation rights, and if the East German border was thus violated, then war, in Khrushchev's opinion, was almost inevitable and both super-powers might just as well recognise this and start to prepare for it. 'I want peace', he said, 'but, if you want war, that is your problem.' Then did Kennedy observe that it was going to be 'a cold winter!'

In fact the cold winter was to be preceded by a very hot summer, in which Khrushchev alternated between reasonable and threatening postures, one day menacingly describing the devastation which would result from a nuclear war over Berlin, the next day, reasonableness itself, when he would calmly suggest that token forces remain in Berlin under United Nations auspices. As Macmillan, much more than Kennedy, clearly perceived, Khrushchev had created the Berlin crisis for his own purpose, which was to try to create disarray in the Western alliance, to undermine American prestige in Europe: it was because he was able to increase and decrease its gravity at will that he was able to put the West on the defensive the whole time. He decided in the end to support Ulbricht's erection of the infamous Berlin Wall because he concluded that it would confront the West with a *fait accompli*, which would arouse their ire but which would not risk provoking a nuclear confrontation. Khrushchev was no more prepared than Kennedy to risk nuclear war. But President Kennedy, as Macmillan feared, over-reacted to Khrushchev's threats. Persuaded by Acheson that Berlin was not a problem but a pretext, Kennedy responded to the Soviet belligerency with a supplementary military budget of over three billion dollars. It was only through the substantial strengthening of America's armed forces, Acheson had argued, that Khrushchev would know America had so irretrievably committed itself to Berlin that to back down would be impossible. It was thus that Kennedy demanded an increase of over 200,000 men in the strength of American forces and requested sweeping call-up powers. His response to Khrushchev's threats was certainly belligerent: in fact it was too belligerent, for it directly influenced the increased flow of refugees out of East Germany which in August compelled the erection of the Berlin Wall.

1. Quoted in Hugh Sidey, *John F. Kennedy: Portrait of a President* (André Deutsch, 1964), p.168.
2. Sir Alec Douglas-Home's Statement for the Kennedy Library (17 March 1965).
3. *Ibid.*

6
Britain and the Berlin Crisis

If Khrushchev had really meant what he had said at Vienna, Kennedy mused, then the possibility of nuclear war was very real, for he, Kennedy, had also meant what he had said. Berlin was the touchstone to American honour, an essential foundation in the structure of the Atlantic Community, and Kennedy recognised all too clearly that he could not give in. His resolve to defend the rights of the city could not be seen wanting. He was thus determined to take all the necessary preparations for the eventuality of war before the end of the year. Nevertheless, he was just as determined to find agreement both within his Administration and within the alliance for a swift and effective response to the *aide-mémoire* on Berlin which Khrushchev had presented at Vienna. In it, the Soviet leader had insisted that, once a peace treaty had been concluded with the G.D.R., any attempt by the West to reach Berlin without obtaining the permission of East Germany would provoke a military conflict with the Soviet Union. He gave but six months' breathing-space and even then his deadline caused confusion. The *aide-mémoire* referred to a six months' period during which the two Germanies could discuss their differences but otherwise omitted the previous references to 'freeing' West Berlin by the end of the year. Khrushchev himself, however, continued to make perfectly clear in public his intentions. And his East German puppet, Walter Ulbricht, went even further. He boldly declared that a peace treaty would enable him to close Berlin's refugee centres, its radio station, perhaps even its Tempelhof Airport! It was widely believed that Khrushchev would call a German peace conference immediately after the Communist Party Congress in October. The West was thus left with very little time to determine what action should be taken to avert a crisis. Yet the weeks went by and there was still no response to Khrushchev's *aide-mémoire*. In fact six weeks were eventually required before a reply was sent, which tends to illustrate the great divisions within both the Administration and the alliance on how best to handle the Berlin issue. This in itself represented an achievement for Khrushchev, who continually probed the West's will to resist, and, by a variety of means, tested the weaknesses of the alliance.

Dean Acheson had warned that Khrushchev would be only too eager to exploit the seemingly hopeless divisions of the West and that a Berlin crisis was imminent in view of the obvious unpreparedness of the alliance effectively to counter a major Soviet ground offensive in Berlin. With the West lacking both the desire and the capability to wage a conventional war on the ground, Khrushchev was unlikely to take any Western military response as an indication of serious intent. As Kennedy himself was forced to admit, 'if Mr Khrushchev believed that all we have is the atomic bomb, he is going to feel that we are . . . somewhat unlikely to use it.' Kennedy thus agreed with Acheson that the greatest priority must be given to increasing both the strength and readiness of Western combat troops in Berlin. 'We shall not surrender,' he sombrely told an audience. He was conscious that West Berlin's importance might compel the United States to use all-out force to uphold the three basic American objectives: the freedom of West Berliners to choose their own system, the continued presence of Western troops in the city for as long as they were wanted, and the assurance of unimpeded access to the city.

The Administration agreed on the need for a large and immediate build-up of conventional forces, as reflected in Kennedy's sweeping requests of 25 July 1961. But there was much disagreement both on whether to declare a state of national emergency, which Acheson had recommended, and also on whether an offer to negotiate should accompany the build-up, which the former Secretary had just as vehemently opposed. Eventually Kennedy overruled Acheson. 'We have nothing to fear from negotiations,' he said, 'and nothing to gain by refusing to take part in them.'

President Kennedy took personal charge of the discussions, constantly reviewing and revising the contingency plans, appraising the actual requirements for the build-up, proposing and all the time challenging the purposes of diplomatic and propaganda initiatives. He was prepared to consider any arrangement for Germany so long as it safeguarded the legitimate security interests of all nations concerned. Yet before new proposals could be put before Khrushchev the West had first to come forward with new ideas, which would recognise those interests, and then agree upon them, and neither had occurred by mid-August. 'The French', as Sorensen put it, 'were against all negotiations, the British were against risking war without negotiations; and the Germans, as their autumn elections drew nearer, were against both of these positions and seemingly everything else.'[1] In retrospect the very failure of the Western Ministers in August to agree upon concrete proposals may well have influenced the timing of the erection of the Berlin Wall, that ugly concrete and barbed-wire reminder of the inadequacy of communism. Certainly the hesitancy of the West and the belligerency of Kennedy's actions had an unsettling influence on East Berliners who, fearful of the imminent closure of the border, were fleeing as refugees to the West in unprecedented numbers. By August their number had exceeded a thousand a day! On the night of 13 August, to the scream of sirens and the rumble of tanks, the infamous Wall was erected.

Perhaps the most surprising aspect of the Berlin Wall is that it should have taken the West quite so much by surprise. It had been obvious at least a month before that the Ulbricht regime would be compelled to take drastic action to halt the flow of refugees, for the East German economy was bleeding to death. Yet, despite all the sheaves of emergency measures dreamed up for every other crisis, incredibly the West had no plan to counter the East German action. West Berliners stood shocked as the West stood silent. Not one of the Western allies correctly assessed the nature of the crisis and in particular the reaction of West Berliners to the Wall. Adenauer received news of the Wall while on a train returning from a vacation in Caddenabbia; Kennedy was vacationing in Hyannisport; Macmillan was grouse-shooting in Scotland. Indeed the Prime Minister took his unflappability to almost embarrassing lengths. Willy Brandt, West Berlin's courageous mayor, demanded counter-measures, declaring that if nothing were done, the people would feel betrayed. Macmillan, in contrast, merely observed that the crisis was 'all got up by the Press', a statement which he only retracted on the insistence of Douglas-Home. Macmillan's remarks, however, reflected the general failure of the West to estimate the crisis correctly. The psychological opportunities quickly passed, and neither Adenauer nor Macmillan could see any point in going to Berlin. They took the view, shared by the Kennedy Administration, that there should be no panic and that the situation should not be exaggerated. The people of Berlin meanwhile wondered at the inaction.

'It was not necessary to have permitted the Wall to have been built,' recalled one senior American official. 'If allied trucks operating that night had gone back and forth across the streets connecting the two sectors of the city—which they had every right to do—I doubt if the Wall would have been built.' In probability only a reliable and properly evaluated intelligence report, which indicated a complete closure of the border, could have brought the allies together in time for concerted action to have prevented the Wall from being built. But there was no such report, and even had there been, what really could the West have done? It was admittedly a problem exacerbated by the lack of decisive authority vested in the allied commanders in the city, compounded by their poor co-ordination and their lack of confidence in each other's ability under stress. But not even Brandt advocated the destruction of the Wall while it was still weak and incomplete. General Watson, the American Garrison Commander, did briefly consider this possibility and had General Clay, from September Kennedy's personal Berlin Representative, been in the city at the time then perhaps the tanks would have rolled. But a military response really ignored the military realities of the situation. Politically and psychologically important as they were, nevertheless the presence of Western troops in Berlin was militarily untenable. There were then but a mere 11,000 allied troops in total, of which 6,000 were American and 3,000 British. In contrast the Soviets had at least twenty-two divisions in

East Germany alone! The Western sector could have been over-run within an hour. Moreover, had the Wall been torn down, the communists could just have built another, ten or twenty or more yards back inside East Germany, and then the West would have had to decide whether it was prepared to fight a war over extending its interests into East Berlin. A few brave individuals, including Sir Christopher Steel, the British Ambassador to Bonn, did make public their protest at the violation of allied rights by undertaking somewhat futile excursions into the Eastern sector. But the Wall remained.

Whether its erection should have been anticipated or not, there was in fact precious little the West could do about the Wall. It was a superbly executed *fait accompli*! The refugee problem had never been considered by the allies as central to the Berlin problem and that Ulbricht had selected what was to be an effective means to stem the haemorrhage did not in itself con-stitute enough difference in the existing situation to resort to military action. The chances of nuclear confrontation, moreover, would have been immeasurably increased had the Soviet Union been compelled to conclude that its vital national interests were at stake, and East Berlin had never been seen by the West as a *casus belli*. The alliance was thus compelled to limit its response to the normal protests at the violation of the quadripartite agreement, which carried their normal lack of effect.

West Berlin demanded political action, not protests. Instead, the four-power ambassadorial group, which had been established in Washington as the necessary machinery to co-ordinate the orders to the Commanders on the field, met and decided against retaliation. They merely agreed to send a strong protest to the military commander of the Soviet sector. The British Government did propose the limited retaliatory action of caging-in the Soviet War Memorial which happened to be situated in the Western sector. Later the British refused to allow the Soviets to bring their guards to the War Memorial in armoured carriers via Checkpoint Charlie, insisting instead that they use the shorter Sandkrug bridge border post. Kennedy sent Vice-President Johnson and General Lucius Clay (the hero of the Berlin Blockade) to restore the morale of West Berliners. He also increased the American garrison by a further battalion which was dispatched down the Helmstedt autobahn to test communist intentions and to demonstrate his own. Alone of America's allies, Britain increased her strength in Berlin with the dispatch of eighteen troop carriers and a further sixteen scout cars to the city.

Both the British and American Governments, nevertheless, vastly underestimated the nature of the reaction of the West Berliners and the West Germans, who were first frightened and then angry: the negative allied response came as a great shock to West Germany, which had seen the strengthening of the Western alliance as the means to achieve the ultimate goal of German reunification. Kennedy thus became the obvious target for German anger and frustration. West Berlin students even sent him an umbrella as symbolic of Chamberlain and appeasement.

Confidence in Berlin was in the circumstances surprisingly swiftly restored, no doubt helped by the measures which Kennedy and Macmillan adopted, especially those aimed at increasing both military strength and investment in the city. The incredulity provoked by the negative response of the West to the Wall, however, made the American task of establishing a common Western negotiating position even more difficult. Yet the tension created by the Wall and the coincidental reopening of the arms race, with the Soviet resumption of atmospheric tests in September, made, as both Kennedy and Macmillan concluded, much more urgent the need for a dialogue with the Soviet leaders. 'The events and decisions of the next ten months', President Kennedy told the United Nations in September, 'may well decide the fate of man for the next ten thousand years. There will be no avoiding these events;' but, pledged the President, while 'we shall never negotiate out of fear . . . we shall never fear to negotiate.'

Kennedy shared Macmillan's hope that the explosive nature of the Berlin issue would be 'defused' gradually through prolonged and intricate discussions. But their joint efforts to prepare for such discussions remained frustrated by the now vehement opposition of France and the uneasiness of West Germany, which the French fanned for their own purposes. 'It is vain to wish for a satisfactory settlement of the German problem,' De Gaulle declared at his Sixth Major News Conference. The United States can do what it likes, he went on, 'as for ourselves, we consider it much more preferable to maintain an attitude of reserve.' Not merely satisfied with such an attitude of reserve, De Gaulle in fact created an atmosphere of quiet desperation within the Alliance. He was somehow able to recognise the Soviet position on the Oder-Neisse and to accept the division of Germany yet at the same time persuade Adenauer that he was really a greater friend of Germany and far more militantly anti-communist than other allies! It soon became very evident that if the United States was to conduct negotiations with the Soviet Union it would have to do so without the blessing of the French President. And with Germany also uneasy, though this compelled closer Anglo-American collaboration, Britain had to bow out of the proceedings gracefully, leaving the United States to jaw-jaw on behalf of the alliance in bilateral talks with the Soviets. These talks, held in Moscow, New York and Washington, were themselves only exploratory to determine if serious negotiation was possible. But France took exception even to these limited terms of reference, thus causing at the NATO Ministerial Meeting in December 1961 the first split communiqué (14 to 1) in the history of NATO.

Even though they were only exploratory talks, they served also to confirm the apprehension of the Adenauer Government that negotiations were being limited to a discussion of the status of Berlin and the rights of access, rather than the wider context of German reunification. Berlin was in actuality sensitive, not because the city was physically vulnerable but because all of Germany was psychologically so vulnerable. The tension which the Berlin debate provoked was almost inevitable given, on the one hand, the German desire for national unity and, on the other, the quest for stability on the part of its allies, for which the acceptance of a *de facto*, if not a *de jure*, division of Germany may have seemed a small price to pay. Kennedy himself was later to acknowledge that one of the principal errors in his policy was to put forward proposals which caused great uneasiness within the alliance yet which were anyway unacceptable to the Soviets. There was in reality no alternative to Khrushchev's peace treaty, yet not one senior allied official advocated the recognition of East Germany. Many varied, and at times conflicting, proposals were put forward as solutions to the Berlin problem: a revised version of the Western peace plan of 1959, adjudication by the International

Court at the Hague, Western and communist peace conferences, an all-Berlin free city, the use of Berlin as a United Nations headquarters, Berlin as a nation on its own, a Central European security plan, an International Access Authority, even a *modus vivendi* of agreed duration. In the spring of 1962, Dean Rusk obtained the agreement of his allies to discuss with the Soviets a four-point plan which was concerned with questions likely to arise if a peace treaty was indeed signed. The four elements comprised an agreement on nuclear non-proliferation, designed to allay the genuine Soviet fear that some day Germany would acquire nuclear weapons of its own; an exchange of non-aggression declarations between NATO and the Warsaw Pact countries; the possibility of establishing an international authority, composed of the representatives of the four occupying powers, the two Germanies and several other governments, to supervise travel between West Germany and Berlin; and, finally, a proposal to set up joint committees to handle 'technical contracts' between the G.D.R. and West Germany. This plan, in effect a *modus vivendi*, was prepared by the State Department Berlin Task Force in consultation with Britain, France and West Germany. It was fully supported by Britain, which was no surprise, and even received qualified endorsement by France, which was a surprise. Unfortunately, it proved to be unacceptable to Adenauer, who, much to Kennedy's annoyance, adopted the simple, but effective, expediency of deliberately leaking the details of the plan in order to kill it. In May Adenauer finally came out in open denunciation of the talks which he declared 'have not been crowned with success ... and I don't see why they should be pursued.' Those Berlin proposals which did survive copious allied study rarely survived deliberate French and West German leaks. The result, as Macmillan described to Kennedy, was that there was little specific to offer Khrushchev, 'hardly the soup course and none of the fish!'

The very unpredictability of Khrushchev's belligerency put the West on the defensive the whole time, virtually making impossible any Western initiatives. Yet those proposals which were followed up were usually initiated by the American Administration and generally supported only by the British Government. Britain, alone of America's principal allies, was reliable in her support of American policy; yet, even then, there were some in the United States who were inclined to be critical of Britain as troublesome, and worse, soft on Berlin. They saw Britain as dragging her feet and certainly the Macmillan Government failed to follow the United States in military preparations. The Government considered, however, that it was already pulling its weight and that Britain's balance of payments problems made it impossible to contemplate increasing Britain's ground forces in Germany.

The British Army on the Rhine (hereafter referred to as B.A.O.R.) since 1945 has been a symbol of Britain's commitment to peace in Europe. It has given Britain an important voice in matters affecting European security. It has also served the political function of appearing to counter the Prussian boot, of which even today some allies remain nervous. Most importantly, B.A.O.R. has been a reflection of Britain's continuing willingness to play a substantial military role in the ground defence of NATO: and, since it is an integrated element of NATO forces, its role has been much determined by the changing nature of NATO strategy.

B.A.O.R.'s deployment in the early 1950s clearly reflected the then current strategy of a planned withdrawal, or orderly retreat, to the Rhine in the event of a major Soviet offensive, which in 1954 (under West German pressure) was superseded by a forward strategy which provided for the defence of Germany as far to the east as possible. This strategy, however, based on a plan to defeat any offensive by purely conventional means, envisaged the totally unrealistic force levels of ninety-six NATO divisions. Even a Britain with conscription and with an annual defence budget of £3,500 millon was unable to maintain the force level demanded of 300,000 men! The increasing possibilities of nuclear weapons led NATO in 1956 to reduce its target to thirty full divisions, of which four were to be British. The downgrading in importance of conventional combat undoubtedly suited a British Government whose defence policy was much motivated by domestic political considerations. Accordingly, conscription was abolished in 1957 and between that year and 1960 the size of B.A.O.R. was reduced from 77,000 to 55,000 men, since which time it has settled at about 50,000 men.

Praised by a former American Secretary of Defence as 'one of the best elements in NATO forces', B.A.O.R. in 1961 was organised as a corps of three divisions, each with two brigades plus corps troops including artillery brigades and armoured reconnaissance. Thus even then it was all of one division below the level stipulated under the Paris Agreements which were supposed to be binding on Britain until 1998. But the Agreements had an escape clause which Britain has been able to invoke in the event of either 'an acute overseas emergency', such as Cyprus in 1958, or because of 'too great a strain on the external finances of the United Kingdom'. McNamara was certainly unimpressed with the British Government's arguments on its inability to meet the force level requirements. For he genuinely believed this was something within Britain's capabilities. But, far from contemplating any increase in British ground forces, the Macmillan Government in 1961 seriously considered reducing its force levels still further, following West Germany's decision to end its contribution to the support costs of allied troops in Germany. It was ironically on the very day when Kennedy was demanding huge increases in America's defence budget, on 25 July, that Selwyn Lloyd, in his famous 'pay-pause' statement, argued that the cost to the Exchequer of B.A.O.R. was no less than £65 million, warning that, in view of Britain's acute balance of payments problem, the Government would be compelled to reduce the number of troops unless West Germany reimbursed a figure of about £25 million. No doubt there was a large element of bluff in Lloyd's statement though at least one senior Minister sincerely believed that a reduction of B.A.O.R. to 40,000 men 'could have been made without affecting Western security at all.' Certainly Lloyd was quick to assure that no decision would 'affect our determination to stand by our NATO obligation in the defence of West Berlin.' Much as they annoyed McNamara, Lloyd's remarks did at least tend to indicate the extreme difficulties for Britain in meeting her full commitments to Berlin.

The related criticism of Britain's role in the Berlin crisis was that, in contrast to De Gaulle who was convinced that Khrushchev was bluffing, the British, as Sorensen expressed it, 'let it be known that they were only too eager to make major negotiating concessions ... and this simply encouraged Khrushchev to be tougher, in Kennedy's view.'² Macmillan was in actuality never as keen to grant concessions as was suggested: he certainly recognised that negotiations could not be undertaken on the basis of what's mine is mine, what's yours is negotiable! He knew that it was necessary on occasion to stand up to Khrushchev, and, indeed, according to one American official, it was Kennedy who was 'extremely jittery' about the British action in preventing the Soviets from henceforth travelling to their War Memorial via Checkpoint Charlie: that the President 'agreed reluctantly, only under pressure from his own people in Berlin who insisted that the tough British position was the right one and would work.' Nevertheless Macmillan was equally convinced, as he had told the United Nations in 1960, that a Berlin settlement could be reached only 'by the gradual acceptance of the view that we can all gain more by agreement than by aggression.'

The differences in the British and American approaches to the Berlin issue tended to be placed in sharp relief by the fact that there was a tendency in Washington to differentiate between allies who were 'soft' and 'hard-liners' on Berlin, where in the United States there was no such division or distinction: it was hard, harder, hardest! Even Kennedy, who would be considered highly restrained in comparison with some of his advisers, on at least three separate occasions contemplated the use of nuclear weapons over Berlin. It was thus hardly surprising that the alarmists within his Administration should both fear that Macmillan, because of the role he occupied during the Eisenhower years, still wanted to act as a kind of middleman and also be convinced that the Prime Minister was merely following the path which Chamberlain took!

If a 'soft-liner' was one who rejected brinkmanship then Macmillan was 'soft', for he never shared General Clay's enthusiasm for such alarmist tactics. But then even President Kennedy himself was caused much uneasiness by his personal representative, who was prone to take rather violent initiatives. It was Clay, for example, who in October 1961 initiated, and then with great glee directed, the tank confrontation at the border: American and Soviet tanks moved up to the border, faced each other eyeball-to-eyeball, as for three days the world tottered on the brink of nuclear war. Much to Clay's anger, (which he once gave vent to at a dinner with Delacombe, the British G.O.C. in the city), Britain neither agreed with nor supported this initiative, though British tanks were moved up to the Brandenburg Gate. To Macmillan such brinkmanship, reminiscent of the very worst of Dulles, served no purpose other than to escalate an already highly dangerous situation: and was, moreover, simply not justified in the centre of a vital sphere of Soviet power. Eventually (and much to Britain's relief), Clay was retired though by then President Kennedy, himself anxious to avoid any escalation in the situation, had put rigid limitations on the discretionary powers which the American military command in Berlin had previously enjoyed.

That Macmillan wanted to apply an emergency brake on American actions owed much to the very different climates of public opinion to which Kennedy and Macmillan had to play the crisis. In Britain, as *The Guardian* reported as late as August 1961, 'Berlin seems to be the crisis in which no-one believes.'[3] Public interest was much greater on Selwyn Lloyd's Little Budget and on the Common Market than on Berlin. In the United States, in contrast, Kennedy's actions had geared American opinion to the acceptance of the imminence of a crisis in Berlin. Moreover, there was in the United States a much greater degree of public acceptability to stand by Berlin if necessary by risking war. No less than seventy-one per cent of an American sample expressed a willingness to fight for Berlin, where the corresponding figure for Britain was only forty-six per cent, and for France but a mere nine per cent.[4] These opinion surveys conducted between July and September 1961 did little to increase the Administration's confidence that any action which it decided to take would be backed up by its allies. Yet, in Britain's case, more conciliatory as she was—and, since she did not bear the overall responsibility for the security of the West, as she could afford to be—there was nevertheless, as even one of her critics conceded, 'never any doubt where Britain would be in the end.'

Britain's contribution in essence was, as in Laos, to strengthen Kennedy's position relative to his more extreme 'hard-liners', to restrain the wilder ideas advocated by some Americans and by many West Berliners. It was a role which inevitably assumed more importance for Kennedy in view of the attitudes of France and West Germany, for the alliance had to stand firm and, of more importance, be seen to be standing firm in its determination to defend its rights in Berlin. 'If there had been in the summer of 1961', recalled a former British Minister, 'complete disarray in the Western alliance, and a lack of determination to stand by commitments, then Khrushchev might well have gone ahead and signed the Peace Treaty.' Instead the confrontation which was expected never came. The deadline of December 1961 passed without a treaty having been signed. The Soviets of course relentlessly kept up the pressure in 1962: incidents were sparked off at the Wall, such as the brutal gunning-down of Peter Fechter in August 1962; the Russians tried to upset allied radar in the air corridors through the dropping of chaff. They tried by every means possible to harass the alliance into disunity and disarray, though they were equally careful to avoid serious incidents. The West, however, stood firm, and slowly, but perceptibly, the crisis receded. Khrushchev did eventually in June 1964 sign a kind of peace treaty with East Germany but its form clearly indicated the Soviet acceptance of the status quo, and Khrushchev's recognition that the West was not going to concede on non-negotiable rights. Its only reference to Berlin was the brief statement that 'the high contracting parties will regard West Berlin as an independent political entity.'[5]

If the West had stood firmer in Berlin 1961, so it has been suggested, the Cuban crisis might never have occurred. Certainly, in retrospect, though there were to be further incidents in Berlin in the ensuing years, with the Soviet backdown in the missile crisis the battle for Berlin had essentially been won.

1. Theodore Sorensen, *Kennedy* (Hodder & Stoughton, 1965), pp.590-1.
2. Theodore Sorensen, *op. cit.*, p.597.
3. *The Guardian* (4 August 1961).
4. British figures quoted in *The Daily Mail* (21 July 1961) which called the British survey 'the gravest and most important poll this newspaper has ever undertaken'.
5. 'A Treaty of Friendship, Mutual Assistance and Co-operation' was signed in Moscow on 12 June 1964.

7

The Cuban Missile Crisis—
Britain Pawn or Power?

'Within the past week', President Kennedy declared of Cuba on American television on Monday 22 October 1962, 'unmistakeable evidence has established the fact that a series of offensive missile sites is now in preparation on that imprisoned island. The purpose of these bases can be none other than to provide a nuclear strike capability against the Western Hemisphere.' This was the way the world first learnt of the Cuban missile crisis. It was thus that President Kennedy publicly declared his determination to halt Khrushchev's clandestine action by means of a quarantine, or blockade, of Cuba. For seven days, and more, the whole world held its breath: Cuba was many people's Armageddon, the long predicted nuclear holocaust became reality. The crisis carried momentous implications for the Cold War, both sides retreating from the brink only just in time. It also told much of the relationship between allies in the nuclear age, and in particular the limitations on the ability of lesser powers to influence the course of events in a super-power confrontation. For Britain's contribution in the Cuban crisis, valuable as it may have been, was nevertheless limited to a role of support and to the mobilisation of unanimity, and was made effective not through mediation in world affairs nor through her ownership of nuclear weapons, but through her close relationship with the United States. The supreme paradox in this context, therefore, is that British support for the American blockade was neither immediately nor in fact obviously forthcoming! Indeed the reaction in Britain to the American action was highly sceptical.

The Daily Express of 23 October was confident in its pre-diction that 'in Britain there will be full understanding of Mr Kennedy's initiative, full backing for his warning and sympathy with his effort to seek a solution in Cuba.' Yet in actuality there was little understanding, backing or sympathy. Instead Kennedy was accused of having plunged the world into another war without having even bothered to consult his allies, of overriding his obligations to the United Nations, and of initiating a perilous chain of events which too easily could get out of control. *The Daily Herald*, for one, saw 'no valid excuse for "going it alone" and imperilling peace'; *The Daily Worker* condemned 'the crazy action of the wild men of Washington'; and even *The Daily Telegraph*, while sympathising with the President's refusal to condone a military build-up on his back door, enquired whether it would not have been wiser to have stated his case 'to the United Nations and to the Organisation of American States before, instead of after, so far-reaching a pronouncement?' Many in Britain frankly refused to believe the American accusations. Others, like *The Guardian*, which within a week was demanding that Britain actually vote against the American action at the U.N., suggested that if Khrushchev had, as Kennedy claimed, put offensive missiles into Cuba, then he had done so 'primarily to demonstrate to the United States and the world the meaning of American bases close to the Soviet frontier.'

If the British press reaction to the crisis was weak, even pacifist, it was nevertheless only a reflection of the widespread scepticism in Britain of the American claims and a general condemnation of the American action. Trade Unions were particularly hostile, two of them, the Amalgamated Union of Foundry Workers and the South Wales area of the National Union of Miners, openly condemning Kennedy's quarantine. Thirty-seven left-wing M.P.s signed a Commons motion demanding that the West should actually increase its trade with Cuba and urging that 'Britain should resist all proposals for an economic or shipping boycott.' C.N.D. sympathisers and others demonstrated outside the American Embassy in London, where on one day alone 126 persons were arrested and charged. 'Viva Fidel, Kennedy to Hell' was the cry that went up from Grosvenor Square. The Oxford Union passed a motion (by 325 to 304) for the adjournment of the House as a protest against the American action; the Cambridge Union also passed a motion (by 130 to 118) refusing to support 'the present powers assumed by America'. A Cuba Committee was set up at Oxford, a No War Over Cuba Committee at Cambridge, and Hands Off Cuba Committees established at other universities including Leeds and Liverpool. The University of London Socialist Society called for a one-day strike in protest. A group of intellectuals, including A.J.P. Taylor and A. J. Ayer, publicly attacked the quarantine and insisted that Britain be neutral in the confrontation. Bertrand Russell, the pacifist-philosopher, appealed to Khrushchev's 'continued forebearance as our great hope', while at the same time, condemning Kennedy's action as 'desperate . . . No conceivable justification. We will not have mass murder . . . End this madness.' The left-wing *Tribune* went as far as to suggest a possible connection between Kennedy's action and the then imminence of the mid-term Congressional elections: 'It may well be that Kennedy is risking blowing the world to hell in order to sweep a few Democrats into office.' For the official Opposition, the Labour Party National Executive doubted the legality of the quarantine, regretted that the decision had been taken without consultation with America's allies, and declined to accept as proven that long-range missiles of an offensive capability had in fact been put into Cuba. During those early days in the crisis the persistent theme of the British debate was the need for evidence, the photographs, on which the American action was based, having initially been withheld for security reasons. 'In judging whether President Kennedy is right in militarily blockading Cuba', remarked *The Times* on 24 October, 'almost everything depends on the accuracy of the evidence . . . Past American mistakes in coping with Cuba, the violent emotions . . . the wrong information which was served to the President before the invasion fiasco eighteen months ago, and even the President's sudden display of toughness . . . all these things were bound to make people in Britain extremely wary on first hearing the news.'

Kennedy's action would undoubtedly have carried more credibility had the United States not sponsored the ridiculous Bay of Pigs venture. Having appeared to represent the hope of imaginative but responsible foreign policy, Kennedy, by that one mistake, seemed for many in Britain but a continuation of the Dulles past. Moreover, despite Foreign Office assurances to the contrary, Britain had in fact never shared America's preoccupations with the cancer festering ninety miles from American shores: indeed the British Government had long considered America's policy towards Castro as clumsy and inept. And since Cuba was something uniquely harmful to the United States, it was hardly surprising that Britain's refusal to join in bringing Castro down should be regarded by many Americans, as *The Observer* of 17 October 1962 remarked, as 'a gross act of betrayal'. One indignant American went as far as to suggest, in a letter to *The Times* of 5 October, that 'We Americans have been accused of being naïve and politically unsophisticated. The present Cuban situation proves this. . . . After having poured our sons' blood and our resources twice in one generation to save England we had assumed, like children do, that the English people would support us in our present crisis. Being innocent in diplomacy, we had foolishly expected gratitude!' Kennedy had not expected gratitude but he had hoped that his allies would support his trade embargo on Cuba. Instead, unimpressed by American arguments and inclined to consider Cuba an American obsession, Britain refused to agree to new restrictions on British trade with the Castro regime. After all, it was argued, British exports to Cuba had since the Revolution already plummeted to a mere £1,300,000. Thus, so Lord Home told Kennedy as late as 30 September, while the grave Cuban situation merited the continued attention of the British and American Governments, there was no chance of Britain applying an economic boycott against Castro.

Throughout 1962, however, the Kennedy Administration spoke sternly of those members of NATO, and in particular Britain, who allowed their shipping to be involved, even if only indirectly, with supporting the Cuban regime. It took special exception to the fact that British tankers were being chartered by the Soviet Union to carry oil from the Black Sea ports to Cuba, and even more exception to the fact that the British Government seemed unwilling to do anything to prevent it. For as the situation in the Caribbean rapidly deteriorated, Greece, Denmark, Italy and West Germany agreed to advise their shipping not to get involved in Cuban trade. Even in Norway, though the Government refused to intervene, the Norwegian Shipowners' Association advised its members not to send ships to Cuba. In contrast, Britain, as the staunchest defender of the freedom of the seas, and with the tradition and interests of a sea-trading nation, refused to do more than advise shipping to weigh up the risks involved. The Government, inclined to take umbrage less at the relative caution of the American Administration than at the insults levelled against Britain from the American right, refused to be intimidated by the veiled American threats of retaliation. 'We pushed very much harder on Britain than we had any right to do', admitted one Kennedy official referring particularly to George Ball's ultimatum of 4 October, to refuse the use of American ports to ships of countries which traded with Cuba. The threat was very embarrassing for Britain since it was known at that time that China wanted to charter ships through the Baltic Exchange in London, provided that they could make stop-overs in Cuba. For many Americans, Britain was putting self-interest before idealism and since her actions were obviously threatening America's very security she must be treated accordingly. The possibility of sanctions caused indignation in Britain, though no British company in the end took the chance of the Chinese charters. But Britain did protest, though this was to be quickly overtaken by the missile crisis. Certainly, as the Americans in 1956 had failed to share Britain's preoccupations with the threat posed by Nasser, so in October 1962 Britain failed to recognise immediately the new, and more dangerous, dimensions created in the Cuban situation.

Britain's cautious response to Kennedy's quarantine may similarly have derived much from the realisation, if not resentment, that Britain's closest ally had taken a decision, carrying the gravest of repercussions, without once having consulted its allies. The 'special relationship' had counted for little: of even less account had been the influence of Britain's nuclear deterrent. 'We are told', wrote Richard Crossman in *The Guardian* on 26 October, that Britain's nuclear weapons 'do give us a place in the councils of the nations. And in particular make sure that the Americans will listen to us more than to any other ally. Well, after last Monday night, that little myth is exploded!' Britain had seemingly been drawn into a crisis which directly threatened her

75

with nuclear devastation, yet in which she had had no say, exercised no control, had been powerless to prevent and which—on the surface at least—carried no obvious implications for the Cold War in Europe! The crisis in fact posed in the most dramatic form the difficulty in reconciling the desire on the part of allies for genuine consultation, as almost a condition for unanimity, with the clear need for prompt and positive action on the part of the United States to prevent the completion of the offensive missile installations. Of course the problem was neither posed in that way nor resolved: for once again Britain found herself reduced almost to the role of an onlooker in a great international confrontation. 'In common with the rest of the world,' lamented one Cabinet Minister, 'we were by-standers.'

If Macmillan was shaken and upset by Kennedy's apparent failure to consult him, he gave no hint of it in public. 'I was consulted', he insisted on television in 1969, 'two and often three times a day on the telephone . . . before the final decisions were made.' Yet, as one of his own colleagues remarked, 'this was a very loose use of the phrase "consultation". We were kept fully informed—more fully informed than anybody else. But we were not really consulted about the actual decisions as they affected Cuba itself.' The Kennedy Administration took its own decisions on the actual handling of the crisis, the operation of the quarantine, even the crucial selection of the appropriate American action. And until a definite course of action had been decided, Kennedy was not willing to discuss the affair outside his immediate entourage. All the time his fear was that, his one trump card, the secret that the Americans knew of the missile sites, would be prematurely leaked.

It was this need to maintain absolute secrecy more than anything else that precluded any consultation between the Administration and its allies. To find, and more important, within a week to agree upon a definite course of action proved so difficult within the Administration itself that it is conceivable that had there been true consultation it would have been impossible. Even the very gesture of informing allies, in the view of some officials, could not have occurred any earlier. As one Kennedy aide put it, 'I would not have wanted to have seen either De Gaulle or Macmillan informed any sooner than they were, because both of them would have wanted to get into the act.'

The secrecy of the American deliberations was almost complete. As late as the day of Kennedy's television speech, much respected journalists, observing the presence at the White House of Martin Hillerbrand, concluded that the crisis must be over Berlin! Not even Bruce in London knew fully the details of the crisis until a mere twenty-four hours before Kennedy's speech. He had received instructions to go, alone and armed, to the American SAC base at Greenham Common near Newbury, where, late on that Sunday night, he met Dean Acheson, who was on his way to Paris as Kennedy's special emissary to explain the American action to De Gaulle. The former Secretary made a brief stop-over in England to give Bruce a set of the aerial photographs taken of the missiles, an expert interpreter, Sherman Kent of the C.I.A., and an armed escort. It was by all accounts an episode full of the cloak-and-dagger stuff of which even James Bond would have been proud!

Only Kennedy's closest national security advisers knew definitely of the erection of offensive missile installations in Cuba. But, during that first week of the crisis, journalists and others, whose business it was to detect clues, were well on the way to finding out. By the week-end, a premonitory excitement had all but engulfed Washington. A delegation of British intelligence officers, led by Sir Hugh Stephenson, a Deputy Under Secretary at the Foreign Office, and a Major-General Strong, happened to be in Washington at the time for a long-scheduled conference with the C.I.A., and their suspicions were aroused by the diminishing attendance of key American officials at their joint meetings, and by the movement of beds inside the Pentagon! The two men alerted Ormsby-Gore of their observations and, by a process of elimination, the three 007s had decided by the Friday that an international crisis, probably over Cuba, was imminent. One British official later recalled the possibility that he might even have been told of the nature of the crisis by his American opposite number. Be that as it may, the Ambassador's telegram of warning, dispatched to London on the Friday, was only speculative. He had certainly not been officially informed of the crisis by the American Government. It was thus by sheer chance, or good detective work, that the British Government became—by at least thirty-six hours—the first of America's allies to learn of the crisis! In fact, the Government would have known even sooner, and with a great deal more confirmation, had not the British Ambassador in Havana, fearing that his communication system with London was too vulnerable to tapping, rightly refused to pass on the information about the missile installations which he himself had already acquired!

If Kennedy was going ahead with the quarantine regardless of allied reaction, he was nevertheless conscious of the need to carry his allies with him. He thus wanted them to be informed at the earliest opportunity. And, whatever else, Britain was officially informed before any other ally: indeed the Ambassador was called to the White House at lunchtime on Sunday 21 October, and was told of the crisis, with all its detail, by Kennedy within half-an-hour of the final decision having been taken. The President outlined the major courses of action open to the United States, as he saw them, and then, very characteristically, rather than tell his friend which course had been chosen, invited instead the Ambassador to select from the alternatives. Ormsby-Gore, after a couple of minutes' thought, elected on the blockade as the bare minimum necessary to impress upon Khrushchev that he was risking nuclear war: a selection which Kennedy immediately (and happily) confirmed. The Ambassador then returned to his Embassy and dispatched a telegram to London, which noted in general terms only the facts as related by the President.

President Kennedy phoned the Prime Minister that same evening to explain personally why he had found it necessary in the interests of both security and speed to take the crucial first decision on his own responsibility. He nevertheless assured Macmillan that he expected to maintain close touch with his allies. Macmillan was later to give the impression that he was Kennedy's right-hand man from the start but it took him a little time. The President was in fact surprised by Macmillan's initial reaction. His unflappability, to be of great value in the ensuing days, was taken too far in that first conversation. 'Well, these missiles are in Cuba a few miles from the United States,' Macmillan was later to recall as his first reaction, 'but so were all the missiles in Russia a few hundred miles from Britain, and we don't want them!' Macmillan even remembered jibing in that first conversation, 'I won't attack you before the Assembly of the United Nations. I hope that whatever you do we will be able to carry through as we weren't able to do at Suez.' The Prime Minister was further insistent that close attention would have to be given to public opinion, because, always living close to the threat of nuclear devastation, they might not see what all the fuss was about—and how right he was!

He was given a more detailed account of the crisis by Bruce on the Monday morning, and, like De Gaulle, he waved aside the need to verify the American claims: 'I take it,' he told the Ambassador, 'that the statements made by your Government are unchallengeable.' But he was much more concerned than De Gaulle about the scepticism of public opinion. Indeed Dean Acheson was later to contrast their different attitudes, De Gaulle remarking ' "You may tell your President that France will support him in every way in this crisis." He didn't say I will, or the French Government will . . . He was France.' Macmillan, however, according to Acheson, was concerned that 'We must publish these [photographs] right away . . . we must get these in the papers . . . no one will believe this unless they see them.' De Gaulle 'didn't care whether anyone believed it or not. He did. This was enough for him!'[1] If Bruce did indeed leave Macmillan as *The Observer* later suggested, 'angry depressed and uneasy', it certainly owed more to the Prime Minister's concern to convince his public than to any disappointment he may have felt at not being consulted sooner.

Was Britain then a pawn or a power in this great international conflict? The Macmillan Government was to be many times attacked and ridiculed for its deplorable role in the crisis, and its deterrent policy was inevitably challenged, since the assumption behind it was that Britain's nuclear weapons gave her the power to influence the course of events. Instead Britain seemed a small and rather insignificant island during the Cuban confrontation. Yet, for all this, Macmillan in June 1963 was to refer to the crisis as 'the week of most strain I can ever remember in my life!'

What was for Kennedy a two-weeks' crisis, was only a week's crisis for Macmillan, which began on the Sunday: it was on that crisp, sunny, autumn day that one Cabinet Minister, walking along the Embankment, wondered whether the moment of truth for all had now arrived. A series of small meetings were held on the Sunday, and a tense Cabinet meeting arranged for the Monday; but the Government quickly discovered that there was very little it could do about the crisis. Military support was never offered by Macmillan, nor indeed requested by Kennedy, but Bomber Command was placed by Thorneycroft in a state of readiness. Unlike France, which moved not a plane nor a soldier, the Government did take action to deploy certain elements of the armed forces, a move which, at least in the view of *The Daily Telegraph*, 'may well have been a critical factor in [Khrushchev] deciding that an attack on the West was not worthwhile.' But it was all played down at a pretty low level because, as one Minister conceded, 'we were all incapable of doing anything about it. We were as fully informed of events as possible, but what could we have done?' Since Britain's contribution was limited to a role of support, it is ironic that the Government was slightly less forthcoming than other allies in its public backing of the President's action. Macmillan called the quarantine measures 'studiously moderate' and 'extremely limited' in an 'unprecedented situation', but he did not immediately publicly endorse the blockade. 'We should have come out sooner in support of Kennedy,' insisted one Minister, further lamenting, 'as it was, the French—the "disloyal", "anti-NATO" French—beat us by several hours.'

Macmillan phoned his support through to Kennedy on the Monday evening, though he again expressed 'his interest in a summit talk on disarmament and an interim suspension of activity on both sides.'[2] He also reiterated his concern with public opinion. Detecting an element of reserve, Kennedy assured Macmillan that this was not merely a squabble with Castro but a major showdown with Khrushchev. Then, after assurance that the United States would not stand aside in the event of a Soviet retaliatory move on Berlin, Macmillan did not falter and, in Schlesinger's opinion, 'his counsel and support proved constant through the week.'[3]

Few people do not remember their own private thoughts and fears in those dramatic days, when each development in the crisis seemed to follow on from its predecessor, with ever increasing gravity. It is only in this context perhaps that one can fully appreciate the extent to which, as a Kennedy Cabinet Minister put it, 'experiences like the Cuban missile crisis tend to draw people together, and,' as he went on, 'Kennedy took the Prime Minister completely into his confidence over Cuba.' Macmillan's role was in fact substantial. He first avoided the moralistic-legalistic warnings of the kind Dulles dished out liberally to the British over Suez, the only effect of which was to infuriate and egg Eden on to even greater fiasco. More important for Kennedy, Macmillan was separate from the hawks and doves surrounding the President to whom the latter could and did talk. Kennedy was glad every day to have a frank conversation with somebody outside his immediate circle, glad to test out his latest thoughts on others, particularly on a man of Macmillan's stature and experience. The President of course viewed the situation in the light of a stream of information coming in, which he knew the Prime Minister did not have: it was thus not always possible for him to explain everything he had in mind, all the pressures being exerted upon him, all the factors that had to be taken into account. It was, therefore, as a Kennedy aide concluded, 'on the broad issues of the general reaction of the Soviet leaders to what he was doing, and the possible repercussions in Europe, and of course over Berlin, which he was glad to test out on Macmillan with his experience and knowledge, which Kennedy recognised as more intimate than he had as yet acquired.'

Macmillan may have been neither resentful nor indeed surprised at his role being limited to that of support, but he was clearly embarrassed by his inability to demonstrate publicly his influence on the course of events. 'It is not true,' he told the House of Commons on 30 October, 'that we in this country played an inactive role in this great trial of strength.' The United States, he said, had, in the circumstances, 'maintained the closest possible co-operation with its allies.' He had told the House on 25 October that Britain 'would always be ready to take an initiative at the moment at which I thought it valuable and would serve a useful purpose.' Yet his only known initiative was a letter to Khrushchev, dated 29 October, in which he declared that the time was now 'right . . . to make a public intervention;' and, by the time the letter was received in Moscow, Macmillan had already learned from Kennedy of Khrushchev's climb-down!

On 23 October, Lord Home had assured the National Committee of the International Chamber of Commerce that 'the Prime Minister and myself, upon whom the main burden of decision must fall, will, once we have checked the present fever, play our full part in an attempt to end the Cold War.' But two days later he told the Soviet Chargé d'Affairs, Loginov, that the Government had 'no intention of seeking to mediate' in the Cuban confrontation. He had thus rebuffed Soviet advances, formal and informal, which sought to persuade Britain to intervene by inviting an immediate summit meeting in London. Macmillan himself was to recall this curious Soviet diplomacy in June 1963, during the censure debate on the Profumo affair. For, of the many Soviet approaches in London to diplomatic missions and to other people, a particularly persistent source of activity was the Soviet military attaché, Captain Ivanov. On 24 October, he contacted a West-End osteopath friend, Dr Stephen Ward—about both of them, the world was to hear a great deal later! Ivanov persuaded Ward that Britain should prove that she was no American pawn by immediately inviting Kennedy and Khrushchev to a summit in London to resolve the Cuban conflict. Taken in by Ivanov's claim to have a direct line to the Kremlin, Ward agreed to spread the word among his influential friends. He even went to the extent of having his conversations with Ivanov related to Sir Harold Caccia, the Permanent Under Secretary at the Foreign Office. He contacted Lord Arran, the widely-read columnist of the *London Evening News*, whom he knew, and convinced him of Ivanov's importance. Ward also convinced one of his patients, a Tory M.P., Sir Godfrey Nicholson, who met Ivanov and then tried, in vain, to arrange a personal meeting between Ivanov and the Foreign Secretary. Ward also wrote to Harold Wilson, whom he did not personally know and, for that matter, did not convince. Neither the Government nor the Opposition was in fact deceived by the Ivanov channel, which, since it did not openly commit the Soviet Union, could so easily and quickly be disavowed if things went wrong. Indeed the final message to emanate from Ivanov, still pressing for a summit, came after Macmillan had already learnt of Khrushchev's climbdown! 'The Russians', as one British expert put it, 'had triggered Ivanov off and forgot to pull him back.'

The Soviet pressures, not altogether unusual in a crisis situation nor in fact limited in scope to London, were spotted very quickly as splitting operations 'to drive a wedge between ourselves and the United States at this very critical moment', as Macmillan himself told the House in 1963: 'Ivanov's approaches . . . were a natural part of the Soviet attempt to weaken our resolution.' This was indeed admirable restraint and foresight exercised by a man so long an enthusiast for summitry. Yet equally, had nuclear war seemed imminent, Macmillan in probability would have taken almost any initiative to try to find some solution before the abyss. Both he and Home were in fact more prepared to intervene than was publicly known at the time. Home, for example, clearly intimated at his press briefing towards the end of the week that he had definite proposals which he would put forward if there was still deadlock over the week-end, though in the end they proved unnecessary. But a proposal for a summit could have been very dangerous, for Khrushchev would have seized the opportunity to get off his impossible hook and to orchestrate world opinion as best he could to bring enormous pressures to bear on the President. It was thus of great importance to Kennedy that Macmillan should not want to call a summit, indeed, that he should not even be seen to want to do so. 'The best role that the British could play', in the view at least of one senior Minister, 'we did play: which was just not to fool around, not to demand summit conferences, not to try to run the show ourselves.' 'A febrile, excited nervosity, which expresses itself in frantic demands that somebody ought to do something or other, is', as Macmillan himself put it at the time, 'not always the most useful contribution.'

Britain's role in the Cuban crisis was thus limited to assurances of support for the President's policy and, equally important, the mobilisation of support to try to ensure the unanimity of the West. Without this unanimity, Khrushchev might well have been tempted to conclude that, as one official put it, 'he could have got away with it, if he only stayed steady in the boat!' Britain's attitude to the crisis was especially important in that the American Administration feared that certain allies might get cold feet. Had this happened it would have rapidly undermined Kennedy's position, in that it would have made almost impossible the maintenance of

83

a tough line. As it was, Sir Patrick Dean's contribution, for example, at the United Nations was widely acclaimed by his American counterparts: for he not only gave categorical assurances of support but also tried hard himself to reassure nervous governments. 'Several European delegations came to us,' a member of the British team at the U.N. recalled, 'because they said that we probably knew more about the facts and the issues at stake than they did.' And what happened at the United Nations also occurred at NATO headquarters. What Kennedy required was an assurance from Britain that his tough policy would be supported. He was given that assurance by Macmillan, and in the end the alliance held.

The only person other than Macmillan and Home who could be said to have played a decisive role in the crisis was Ormsby-Gore, the Ambassador and intimate counsellor of the President. With events moving so rapidly, he was Britain's main influence in Washington: indeed, concerned that his Government had not fully understood Kennedy's actions and motives, the Ambassador at one stage offered to return to London, but he was wisely told that he would be of more value remaining in Washington. But much of the information which was given to him, especially as to the details of the quarantine, he was required to respect as confidential. The British Government was in fact never given detailed information about the implementation of the quarantine—'we had to get that information ourselves,' remarked one British Intelligence official.

The quarantine was set to come into effect on the morning of Wednesday 24 October and it so happened that the Ormsby-Gores had a long-standing invitation to a dinner-and-dance at the White House on the previous evening. In the circumstances, the dance was cancelled but the Ormsby-Gores still dined with the Kennedys. Cuba was hardly mentioned at the table, but after dinner the President beckoned Ormsby-Gore to join him in the long central hall, where the two friends were shortly joined by the Attorney-General, Robert Kennedy. Since the President trusted Ormsby-Gore implicitly, his brother openly related his conversation that evening with the Soviet Ambassador, Dobrynin, who was obviously shaken by events and equally obviously had not received any instructions from his Government.

It looked, therefore, as if there would inevitably be a clash when the quarantine was imposed. The three friends discussed, but quickly dismissed, the idea of a summit with Khrushchev. It was then that the Ambassador recalled a conversation which he had had with Pentagon officials, who had stressed the importance, as the Navy saw it, of halting Soviet ships as far as possible out of range of Cuban MIG fighters. To the Ambassador, this was no real reason why the quarantine line of interception should be as far away as eight hundred miles, which would mean a probable clash within a very few hours of its implementation. The Cuban jets could be shot down if they tried to interfere, Ormsby-Gore argued. Much more important was the fact that Khrushchev had some very difficult and searching decisions to take and that every extra hour the West could give would allow more time for him to analyse his position and then climb down gracefully. Kennedy immediately accepted the Ambassador's argument, called McNamara and, overruling the Navy's protests, ordered the interception line to be re-drawn at five hundred miles. It was a decision which, in Schlesinger's view, 'was of vital importance in postponing the moment of irreversible action.'[4] The blockade came into effect on the following morning, and within hours the news was received that some Soviet ships, heading for the reduced interception line, had been stopped!

Ormsby-Gore also took the opportunity of his after-dinner conversation with the President on the Tuesday evening to mention his concern about the scepticism of British opinion, which genuinely surprised both men. The Ambassador had sought to impress upon the British Press corps in Washington how very cautiously, in the circumstances, the President was in fact handling the situation. But even those who believed in the threat— and the press had been shown the photographs but were not allowed to use them—considered that Kennedy had probably over-reacted. Americans were prepared to support their President but, in the continued absence of evidence, British public opinion was beginning to believe the worst of Kennedy. He thus agreed to Ormsby-Gore's suggestion that certain photographs should be published, and indeed, sending for a file of them, the two friends selected those photographs which they considered most convincing to the non-expert eye. The President then authorised their release though in fact, no doubt in part because of the time differences, they were released first in London, on instructions from Bruce.

'They were released,' remarked one Kennedy official, 'and everyone immediately believed the American story.' An exaggeration perhaps, but Stevenson's dramatic presentation of the American case at the United Nations, and Home's appearance on television with the photographs, combined to produce a marked change in the climate of British opinion. The photographs 'enormously strengthen the American case', declared *The Daily Express*. 'President Kennedy's evidence has been published', commented *The Daily Herald*: 'It has convinced the British Government—and will convince most of the world—that the Russians ARE building missile bases in Cuba.' Lord Altrincham, who in *The Guardian* at the outset had written that 'Mr Kennedy has committed the gravest and most far-reaching American blunder since 1945,' but a week later, as the worst of the crisis had passed, admitted that he had 'misjudged the situation, and . . . seriously underestimated President Kennedy [for which] I would like to apologise—wholeheartedly and unreservedly.'

The Cuban missile crisis may only have lasted two weeks but its implications and repercussions were to be felt for years. Its impact went wider than Cuba, wider even than the Western Hemisphere. For to the world, Kennedy's handling of the situation displayed the ripening of an American leadership unprecedented almost in its responsible management of power. Everything that the Bay of Pigs had proved wrong in 1961, the missile crisis was to prove right in 1962. If the Bay of Pigs was Kennedy's greatest mistake, his handling of the missile crisis was without doubt his greatest single triumph. It may have been comprised, as Kennedy himself was to observe, of three fortunate features: it took place in an area where the United States enjoyed local conventional superiority, where Soviet national interests were not directly engaged and where the Russians really lacked a case which could be plausibly sustained before the arena of world opinion. Had any of these elements been different, then the resolution of the crisis might have come out very differently. Kennedy might even be considered lucky in his handling of the crisis. But his almost total control of events and their repercussions, his determination to ensure that the missiles should be removed if possible by peaceful means, his gradual but continual application of the pressure, his preparedness to allow Khrushchev time to reflect on his position, his insistence that the Soviet leader should be allowed to withdraw gracefully, even his refusal later to claim a victory: combined, these qualities were universally acclaimed. 'In Britain,' declared *The Daily Express* of 29 October, 'there is unqualified admiration for the force of character and steadiness of nerve which President Kennedy [displayed] throughout the crisis.'

But if Cuba was a personal triumph for Kennedy in his career as a statesman, for Macmillan, it merely gave further ammunition to his critics. Moreover, in so far as it was the making of Kennedy in foreign affairs, Cuba inevitably augured a decline in Macmillan's influence within the alliance. The crisis may have highlighted the great strength of the Anglo-American relationship, especially as to the manner in which one ally can clarify, understand and then respond to the other's claims. Indeed, the Cuban crisis surely proved that Macmillan, to his eternal credit, lived up to the ultimate threat of nuclear annihilation: for, had the United States become involved in a nuclear war over Cuba then so would have Britain. Nevertheless, the experience of acting without his allies left its mark on Kennedy. Henceforth he became much more confident of his own ability to give strong leadership. He was not always able to impose his policy hopes on his alliance partners but equally Cuba proved that in the nuclear age it is impossible to share certain decisions with one's allies.

Cuba not only made its mark on Kennedy, Macmillan and the Alliance: undeniably, it made a lasting impression upon Khrushchev. If it was poker by Kennedy, it was even more dangerous poker by Khrushchev. Even today there is still complete astonishment that the Soviet supremo should have allowed himself to be jockeyed into such brinkmanship, that he should have shown such profound ignorance of the American President. 'We hope that Chairman Khrushchev has not made a miscalculation,' Adlai Stevenson told the United Nations General Assembly. But Khrushchev had miscalculated and badly: he had deluded himself into concluding at Vienna that in any future crisis Kennedy would lose his nerve!

In his reputed memoirs, and certainly in keeping with his character, Khrushchev was to claim the Cuban crisis as 'a great victory for us . . . a triumph of Soviet foreign policy, and a personal triumph in my own career as a statesman. We achieved, I would say, a spectacular success without having to fire a single shot!'[5] But Khrushchev had wanted much more than the promise which Kennedy gave that the United States would not henceforth invade Cuba. To be true, his reputation could not have afforded an invasion of Cuba, but he saw a great deal further than this. For, by 1962, things had been going sadly wrong for Nikita Khrushchev. His boastings had become almost a joke, his threats on Berlin had achieved nothing, and his recklessness had created a widespread mood of frustration within the communist world. The movement, which but twenty months before was riding on the crest of a wave, was rapidly disintegrating. A bold initiative was thus required of Khrushchev, whose prestige and position were much dependent upon the success of his policy. He saw in the Cuban plan an effective and quick means to redress the strategic balance which, had it been undertaken either by conventional means or by the build-up of an inter-continental ballistic missile system, would have meant an intolerable postponement of his ambitious ideas for the Soviet economy. The daring plan which, had it succeeded, would virtually have doubled Soviet striking capacity against the West, bore the trademarks of the classic Khrushchev tactic: the sudden, bold initiative, designed to put opponents off their balance. But it also went wrong. Khrushchev had gambled for high stakes—the highest stake—and lost.

The consequences of the Cuban missile crisis were, however, to be far more beneficial than had seemed possible in its immediate wake. It was in fact to be Khrushchev's last kick against destiny. Henceforth he attached the highest priority to East/West détente. The two Ks learnt much of the power of decision at Berlin and Cuba. At Cuba, Kennedy made the point which he had hoped, but failed, to make at Vienna: that neither side could afford in the nuclear age to be careless in upsetting the equilibrium of world power. Khrushchev now came to appreciate this point and he thus sought a closer relationship with the United States, which of necessity demanded a redefinition of Sino-

Soviet relations. It was no coincidence that the winter of 1962 witnessed the first public Soviet attacks on China. And paradoxically the recognition of the growing rift between the two Communist countries greatly improved the chances for the test-ban treaty. For in the treaty Khrushchev saw an instrument that would further isolate the Chinese in the world. And it was for this reason, as much as for any, that the Soviet Union eventually agreed to a treaty in 1963.

1. The Kennedy Library Oral History Interview of Dean Acheson.
2. Theodore Sorensen, *Kennedy* (Hodder & Stoughton, 1965), pp.705.
3. Arthur Schlesinger Jr., *A Thousand Days* (André Deutsch, 1965), p.698.
4. Arthur Schlesinger Jr., *op. cit.*, p.699.
5. Nikita Khrushchev, *Khrushchev Remembers* (André Deutsch, 1971), pp.500, 504. Its authenticity has yet to be convincingly proved.

8

The Nuclear Test-Ban Treaty—
Success for Kennedy and Macmillan

At the height of the missile crisis, Macmillan sent a letter to Khrushchev, suggesting that the resolution of the Cuban situation would open the way for a test-ban agreement. 'I therefore ask you,' he wrote, 'to take the action necessary to make all this possible. This is an opportunity which we should seize.' The opportunity was to be seized and the Cuban crisis was to prove one of the great turning points in history. For, within a year, the Partial Test-Ban Treaty, which symbolised the new détente, was signed. To be true, it seems little reward for more than five years' intensive negotiation at the three-nation test-ban conference, at the ten-nation and eighteen-nation disarmament conferences and in the United Nations. It was initialled neither in Geneva nor in New York but in Moscow, and it came about primarily because Khrushchev concluded that the cessation of atmospheric tests was in the interest of the Soviet Union. Even then, the treaty did nothing to resolve the fundamental problem of underground nuclear explosions: it covered only those tests in the three non-controversial environments, in the atmosphere, underwater and in space. Two of the five nuclear powers (China and France) refused to sign it. And, above all, it relied for verification not on an international basis but on systems of national detection. The treaty was nevertheless a significant step forward in East/West détente. It was also the major achievement of the close collaboration between President Kennedy and Mr Macmillan. Though neither country's national interests were directly at stake, their partnership was made both effective and fruitful by their equally assigned importance to a specific, if only limited, objective. Yet this collaboration between Britain and America had not always proved possible. Indeed the advent of the Kennedy Administration represented a very considerable improvement in Anglo-American co-operation in the disarmament field. With Kennedy sharing Macmillan's conviction as to the desirability of a test-ban agreement, there was none of the vacillation and hesitation which had characterised his predecessor's policy and which, in the British view, had made the task of securing positive results all but impossible. 'The Eisenhower Administration', recalled one British disarmament expert, 'would not make the most obvious concessions, without which there was no hope whatever of a treaty.'

Disarmament had indeed had a melancholy history. Prior to 1957, not even Britain had shown much interest in the cessation of tests. And even when, under Macmillan's premiership, Britain gave a lead, there was very little progress while the United States was preoccupied with the dangers of a surprise Soviet attack and the Soviet Union in its turn refused to accept control and inspection. A disarmament subcommittee, convened in London in 1957, had met for five months without reaching agreement. Hopes for a test-ban were perhaps at their highest in August 1958 when, following the unilateral Soviet suspension of atmospheric tests, a conference of experts at Geneva had concluded that with an extensive control system all nuclear tests could be monitored. Macmillan had then persuaded Eisenhower to accept a Soviet proposal to consider a test-ban separate from general disarmament, and a three-power test-ban conference (comprised of Britain, America and Russia) opened in October with the task of drawing up a treaty. Further taking the initiative, Macmillan ordered the suspension of British tests, as did Eisenhower though against the advice of many of his Administration and also it seems to his later regret.

The Americans were never happy with the unpoliced moratorium for they feared that underground tests could be conducted in big caverns and were thus beyond detection. This 'big hole' obsession, as it came to be called, was to hang over all the discussions and frustrate Macmillan's efforts to get a united Anglo-American position on a test-ban agreement. Even when American experts reported that the problem had been exaggerated, American suspicions remained and, indeed, in March 1962 Macmillan was to remember in the Commons 'certainly two occasions on which I pleaded with ... President Eisenhower to hold his hand and to continue the voluntary unofficial moratorium when I am bound to say his advisers were taking a rather different attitude.'

The indeterminate nature of the American contribution made very difficult the establishment of a joint Anglo-American front but Macmillan was still determined to keep the talks going. And, in the opinion of Britain's chief negotiator, Sir Michael Wright, 'if it had not been for his active interventions the test-ban negotiations would almost certainly have broken down early in 1959 and again in the spring of 1960.'[1] In the first instance, Macmillan concluded that the Soviet Union, having demanded a veto on all inspections, would never agree to the American demand for all suspicious events to be inspected. He thus put forward his proposal for an annual quota of veto-free inspections. Ultimately it was to have no practical effect on the outcome of the negotiations for the Soviets really refused to talk seriously of any inspection. And at least one American expert considered Macmillan's proposal was 'the biggest hurdle that we had all the way through': certainly from that time, the Soviet Union regularly argued that on-site inspection was peripheral rather than central to a test-ban treaty. Yet Macmillan's proposal did break the dead-lock in 1959. Against the advice of the Americans, he raised it during his visit to Russia and Khrushchev received it well. So well in fact that in May he put forward the proposal himself before the conference. Within nine months it also became official American policy.

In February 1960, the Americans proposed a phased treaty which accepted the quota system for underground events above a certain magnitude but which excluded those below. It was again Macmillan who intervened to persuade Eisenhower to agree to the Soviet demand for a continued moratorium on events below the specified threshold. This thus opened the way to final agreement, which Macmillan at least hoped could be achieved at the Paris Summit. 'We hope that it may be the pioneer scheme,' he said in a speech prior to the Summit; 'that is why I attach so much importance to it, why I have tried myself to do everything possible to further it.' But, neither for the first nor the last time, Macmillan's hopes were to be dashed, on this occasion by the collapse of the Summit. The test-ban talks did continue but the Soviets were much less ready to discuss international verification. 'If only we could recover the spirit that seemed to be at work even a few months ago,' Macmillan lamented at the U.N. in September 1960, 'we could make a new start.' But Khrushchev was now much more suspicious of American designs, for which Macmillan was inclined to blame the American 'big hole' obsession.

This then was the position in the talks in January 1961, and Macmillan's contribution in retrospect had been substantial. 'He kept the talks going through the last dreary years of the Eisenhower Administration,' was how one columnist put it, 'when it was feared that the Americans might lose interest in a treaty.' Any such fears about the incoming President were quickly dispelled. 'Let both sides, for the first time, formulate serious and precise proposals for the inspection and control of arms,' Kennedy declared in his Inaugural Address, further eloquently proclaiming the need to 'bring the absolute power to destroy other nations under the absolute control of all nations.' Made conscious by Ormsby-Gore among others of the indecisive role played by the United States in the past, President Kennedy immediately requested a six-week postponement in the reconvening of the three-nation conference to permit a complete review of the negotiations and, within a week of taking office, he set up a panel of experts to study the possibilities for a treaty. It was thus that, when they went to Washington in February for preliminary discussions, Ormsby-Gore and Wright, leading the British delegation, found to their surprise the extent to which the Americans gave favourable consideration to long-held British positions. Indeed the modifications to the American position which the British had urged for two years were now more or less accepted. Instead of demanding watertight arrangements, the new Administration settled for reasonable safeguards against illegal tests. Thus, when the three-nation conference opened on 21 March, Britain and America jointly put forward what *The Times* called 'sweeping concessions designed to meet Russian objections'.

All the West's proposals centred on the question of the

prevention and identification of breaches in the agreement. The United States proposed that the already agreed moratorium on small underground explosions be extended from twenty-seven months to three years, which went nearer the Soviet demand of five years. The Americans also agreed to a reduction in the number of control posts on Soviet territory to nineteen, which again went closer to the Soviet position of fifteen such posts. Kennedy further agreed to request from Congress authority to allow Soviet scientists to inspect nuclear devices exploded by America for peaceful purposes, as long as similar facilities were granted by the Soviet Union to American scientists. Another significant concession, subject to agreement on an adequate control system, was the acceptance of the Soviet proposal for East/West parity of representation on the Control Commission. The Anglo-American plan was for a three-tier system of control, at the top of which was to be an annual conference of signatory states. Beneath that was to be a Control Commission, now enlarged from seven to eleven states, four of which would represent the West, four the communist bloc, and three the 'non-aligned' states. At the bottom was to be a single executive office, 'The Administrator', to whom the operation of the detection and identification system was to be entrusted. The West even accepted the Soviet demand that the original parties to the treaty—Britain, America and Russia—should each have the right of veto over the total budget of the control organisation. Last, but not least, on the controversial issue of on-site inspection, the West agreed to an identical number of Soviet inspections in Britain and America as Western inspections in Russia, which in effect allowed the Soviets twice as many inspections as the West. And, in May, the West proposed a sliding scale to determine the annual quota of inspections (to a maximum of twenty) related in a ratio of 1:5 to the number of seismic events in any given year. Combined, these important concessions would two years before have all but secured agreement. But, of course, by March 1961, the Soviet position had totally changed, their chief delegate, Tsarapkin, blandly going back on already agreed points. In an extremely negative speech, Tsarapkin suggested that any more than three on-site inspections meant that the West was only interested in espionage, and he rejected the idea of a single 'neutral' Administrator, arguing instead for a

Troika, or three-man directorate, which Khrushchev was at the time also demanding for the office of the U.N. Secretary-General.

In the ensuing months the Soviets obstinately refused to enter into any serious negotiation. They rejected the Western proposal of parity on the staffing of nuclear test control posts and also the very idea that such parity could be ensured by a neutral Administrator. In his *aide-mémoire* presented at Vienna, Khrushchev insisted that if a treaty on the basis of the Soviet proposals was impossible then the question of a test-ban treaty should thereafter be considered within the wider context of general and complete disarmament. Not only did this run counter to the original Soviet proposal of 1958 but it was clearly a retrograde move for it made the chances of a treaty even more remote. In July, Britain and the United States put the whole issue before the United Nations but this achieved nothing. And in August, as a last desperate attempt to keep the talks going, the Anglo-Americans, in a new set of proposals, offered to yield decisive powers to the 'neutrals' on the Control Commission to dismiss any administrator whom either side found unsuitable. But again the Soviets were totally negative in their response. Writing in *The New York Herald Tribune* on 30 August, Don Cook remarked 'If ever a negotiation has reached a state of futility, it is the nuclear test-ban talks.'

The reason for this charade becomes quite clear in retrospect. 'The Soviet representative at Geneva', Adlai Stevenson explained at the U.N. in October, 'had . . . long ceased to negotiate in good faith, for while he had been fighting his delaying action at Geneva, Soviet scientists, engineers and military experts had been secretly laying plans for the resumption of testing in the atmosphere.' The Soviets announced their decision to end the three-year moratorium at the end of August but such a series of tests as that undertaken, culminating in the explosion of a fifty-megaton bomb on 30 October, obviously required many months of detailed preparation.

An embittered Macmillan talked in the Commons of 'the cynicism and brutality of what the Russians have done'. It was a personal blow to the Prime Minister who had long sought that the West should go to the last mile before being the first to resume nuclear tests. Now, with the American President under increased pressure to permit an American resumption, it seemed all Macmillan's efforts had been in vain. He and Kennedy jointly appealed in a letter to Khrushchev of 3 September that their three Governments agree, effective immediately, not to conduct tests that produce radioactive fall-out. But Kennedy equally considered it necessary on 5 September to authorise the American resumption of underground tests. And, with Khrushchev's rejection of the Anglo-American proposal on the grounds that 'cessation of one kind of test only—in the atmosphere—would be a disservice to the cause of peace', the arms race had seemingly reopened. Macmillan's 'rogue elephant' had seemingly been unleashed, though, ironically in that very same month progress was made on the disarmament front through the joint American-Soviet statement of agreed principles. Both sides agreed to resume negotiations within a disarmament committee comprised of eighteen states, of which five were to represent the West, five the communist bloc and eight the 'non-aligned' nations.

On the test-ban front, the Soviet Union agreed to return to the three-nation conference in November but the renewed talks achieved nothing new. Indeed, by declaring in December that the 'old basis' was no longer valid, the Soviets in effect buried all the eighteen draft treaty articles which had so painstakenly been drawn up in the previous three years. Hardly surprising, therefore, that *The Observer* of 4 February 1962 should comment that 'the conference on nuclear tests at Geneva has been dying for so long that its actual demise has passed almost unnoticed.'

The total lack of progress in the test-ban negotiations inevitably increased the pressures exerted on President Kennedy to permit a resumption of American atmospheric tests. The Pentagon had never been in favour of the moratorium. Nor had the Atomic Energy Commission. Indeed, as early as January, in its annual report to Congress, the latter had attacked the moratorium as 'a threat to the security of the free world', which prevented America from making 'major advances' in nuclear weaponry. Nearly all of Kennedy's principal advisers favoured an early American resumption of tests: in February in fact the Joint Chiefs of Staff had urged the President to allow a resumption if agreement on a test-ban could not be reached within sixty days of negotiation, (though, in so arguing, they implied that their support of his test-ban proposals was conditional on his agreement to their demand). President Kennedy resisted all the pressures but the Soviet series of tests made an American resumption seemingly even more imperative. 'Had the Soviet tests of last fall reflected merely a new effort in intimidation and bluff,' as Kennedy himself was to put it on television on 2 March 1962, 'our security would not have been affected. But in fact they also reflected a highly sophisticated technology, the trial of novel designs and techniques and some substantial gains in weaponry.' Dr Jerome Wiesner and Sir William Penney, respectively the President's and the Prime Minister's chief scientific advisers, reported as much to Kennedy and Macmillan at their Bermuda meeting in December. But they did not consider the Soviet advances actually amounted to a security risk to the West and, indeed, but a few days before America resumed tests, McNamara, at a lunch with Rusk and Bundy, all but admitted they were not really necessary!

If Kennedy's decision was not militarily essential, it was nonetheless politically necessary. He had staved off a decision for as long as possible but, with the Soviets totally unresponsive to the West's initiatives, all the pressures built up from within his Administration, from Congress and from the military establishment. He really then had no option but to agree to an American resumption. And, having so decided, he looked to Macmillan both for support and also for permission to use Christmas Island, part of the Gilbert and Ellice Group, as a logistics base for the American tests. But at Bermuda Macmillan proved reluctant. 'The nightmare of nuclear holocaust,' as Schlesinger put it, 'stirred more than ever underneath Macmillan's Edwardian flippancies, and he opened the talks by evoking the awful prospects of an indefinite arms race.'[2] Impressed by Macmillan's sincerity, Kennedy nevertheless rejected the Prime Minister's suggestion of a summit. Macmillan urged that a final decision await another try for disarmament but, Kennedy argued, the Soviets would only stall. Again he asked the Prime Minister to agree, if the situation did not change, to the American use of Christmas Island. In the end, Macmillan secured a postponement of a decision pending a Cabinet discussion, but this was only really a technicality. For, just as Kennedy's domestic political climate compelled him to authorise an American test resumption, so Macmillan in direct contrast caused him acute embarrassment if the Americans did resume!

Ignored, even mocked, by Macmillan, the Campaign for Nuclear Disarmament nevertheless was a reflection of the very definite British views about the arms race. Nor was it just a matter of satisfying British public opinion. The British Government had anyway come to believe that a controlled test-ban would prove the key to the advantages which genuine disarmament would subsequently bring. The underlying theme of Britain's attitude was that the Anglo-Americans should be at least as forthcoming in political negotiation as the scientific assessment of the risks warranted, for the contrary risk of an unlimited arms race was considered infinitely more dangerous.

It was in the context of this theme that on 7 January 1962 Macmillan wrote a deeply personal and moving letter to Kennedy in which he noted the irony that he should have spent Christmas Day pondering how to commend to his Cabinet the American use of Christmas Island. He warned that if the Americans resumed tests then so too would the Soviets and then a supreme effort would be necessary to rescue all the work. 'If this capacity for destruction ended up in the hands of dictators, reactionaries, revolutionaries, madmen around the world, then sooner or later, possibly at the end of the century, either by error or folly or insanity the great crime would be committed.' Macmillan proposed that the three leaders convert the impending eighteen-nation Disarmament Conference into one final try for general disarmament and/or a test-ban treaty. He did not, however, make explicit whether the use of Christmas Island was conditional on American agreement to a final initiative or whether the resumption of American tests was conditional on the failure of the forthcoming conference. And certainly some Administration officials, noting this ambiguity, urged Kennedy not to be swayed by what they thought was Macmillan's 'emotional blackmail'.

Kennedy's reply to Macmillan's letter (dispatched after much revision by Bundy) was an affirmation of equal concern, but it rejected any link between the use of Christmas Island and a new disarmament initiative. Kennedy, did not, however, want to forego Macmillan's suggestion and indeed, when he announced his decision on 2 March (an announcement postponed by twenty-four hours in response to a Macmillan appeal), he suggested that the American resumption would be unnecessary if Russia would agree to a comprehensive treaty, sign it before the latter part of April and then apply it. He even hinted that it would then be fitting if he, Macmillan and Khrushchev met at Geneva to sign the final treaty.

Clearly preparing both his Government and his public opinion for the imminence of an American resumption, Macmillan told the Commons in February that 'it is clear now . . . that there is a military need . . . to have some tests . . . we have reached agreement in principle about the moral justification for making further tests.' He was nevertheless embittered and distressed by the American decision which, he said, 'would shatter the hopes of millons of people.' But, with no Soviet response to Kennedy's initiative, as Macmillan told the House on 10 April, the American tests would have to go on. And on 25 April, three years after their last nuclear test, and to world-wide condemnation, the Americans resumed atmospheric tests. 'We have done everything we possibly could,' Macmillan declared in the House. 'We worked as hard as we could. We made proposal after proposal. We are discouraged but not defeated.' It meant, however, that Macmillan's efforts had seemingly come to nothing: and, if that were not enough, there was now the further humiliation of having agreed to the tests being carried out on British territory!

The American decision was also predictably condemned by Khrushchev, who represented it as 'a new expression of the agressive course in international affairs.' 'No matter how much you may try to prove the contrary,' he wrote in a letter to Kennedy dated 3 March, 'the shock wave from the American nuclear tests in the Pacific Ocean will reach to the Palais des Nations at Geneva!'

In a joint message of 7 February Kennedy and Macmillan had told Khrushchev that 'a supreme effort must be made and the three of us must accept a common measure of personal obligation to seek every avenue to restrain and reverse the mounting arms race.' The forthcoming Disarmament Conference, they declared, 'must not be allowed to drift into failure. Accordingly, we propose that we three accept a personal responsibility for directing the part to be played by our representatives in the forthcoming talks, and that we agree beforehand that our representatives will remain at the conference table until concrete results have been achieved, however long this may take.' For reasons already noted, Kennedy and Macmillan rejected Khrushchev's proposal that heads of government should open the conference proceedings. Instead they had urged that each nation should send its Foreign Minister 'as a symbol of the importance which we jointly attach to these negotiations.' And in fact those nations attending the opening proceedings of the conference were all represented by their Foreign Ministers. The noticeable absentee was, of course and again, France. 'We . . . do not see any reason to increase the size of the honourable assembly,' declared De Gaulle, in one of his more pontifical moods at his Sixth Major News Conference, 'which . . . can do nothing but moan a little, like the chorus of old men and women in ancient tragedy: "Insoluble difficulty. How to find a way out?"' And, with France refusing to have anything to do with the conference proceedings, the West's position even more relied on the effectiveness of Anglo-American collaboration.

The Disarmament Conference duly opened on 14 March 1962 and within a day the Soviets presented their sweeping draft treaty for General and Complete Disarmament. The American draft treaty was not presented until a month later, on 18 April, which did lose them some mileage with the neutrals on the Committee. Both the American and Soviet treaties envisaged the process of disarmament being undertaken in three separate stages and both also envisaged obligations not to transfer the control of nuclear weapons to non-nuclear powers. But in almost all other respects, even in the timetable of the stages, the two drafts varied! Nevertheless the 'non-aligned' nations quickly expressed greater interest in further test-ban negotiations and the Soviets as a consequence grudgingly agreed to tripartite discussions being renewed under the guise of a sub-committee of the eighteen-nation conference.

On 16 April 1962, the eight 'non-aligned' nations submitted a joint memorandum, which contained suggestions and ideas commended to the three nuclear powers in their discussions. The eight nations expressed their confidence that 'possibilities exist of establishing by agreement a system for continuous observation and effective control on a purely scientific and non-political basis.' The memorandum was in fact accepted by all the nuclear powers as a basis for negotiation but there were unfortunately important differences of interpretation, particularly over the operation of the neutral control commission. The Americans considered the memorandum justified compulsory on-site inspection in the case of unidentified underground events; the Soviets, in contrast, claimed that the memorandum provided for on-site inspection only at the invitation of the party concerned. Not unnaturally, Britain and America held that this interpretation gave no assurance that any invitation would ever be extended! In fact the Soviets still hedged on the fundamental issue of inspection and verification, without the resolution of which there was no real hope of progress.

Meanwhile, however, significant advances had been made in the detection and, of much greater importance, the identification of suspicious events. British scientists had always been inclined to question the need for elaborate inspection, on which the Americans were then so insistent. Indeed British statements on the subject were, on occasion, of considerable embarrassment to the United States. Macmillan himself had in March 1962 suggested that scientific advances had made the control of a test-ban easier when, at that time, the American Defence Department and Disarmament Commission were stating precisely the opposite viewpoint, though an ad hoc committee, sponsored by the Arms Control and Disarmament Agency, did conclude that the prospects for a partial treaty were good. But developments in seismology increased American confidence in their methods of detection and identification. The Air Force Technical Applications Center made two particularly important discoveries: they found that there had been a wrong estimate as to the number of earthquakes in the Soviet Union which could be confused with a nuclear test; and also that third-zone detection (monitoring from a distance) was in fact considerably more accurate than they had originally thought possible. It was as a result of these discoveries, made public in July, and also conceding to British pressure, that the United States in August agreed to the submission of two draft test-ban treaties: the first, a comprehensive treaty,

which envisaged a ban in all environments but with a considerably reduced number of both control posts and on-site inspections;
the second, a partial treaty, which contemplated a test-ban in the
three non-controversial environments with no international
verification. The United States was still clearly reluctant to
accept an uncontrolled moratorium on underground events. This
double opportunity, however, no more appealed to the Russians
than earlier proposals. They rejected the comprehensive treaty
because it did not depart from the principle of on-site inspection
and the partial treaty because it excluded underground tests.

With deadlock seemingly as complete as ever, the Soviet
Union in November began to advance the proposal of unmanned
automatic seismic recording stations, commonly nicknamed
'black-boxes', as an alternative to on-site inspection. In December
they even listed three sites in Russia at which such stations
could be established. Britain and America considered that 'black-
boxes', if used in sufficient numbers and if properly operated and
located, would be a useful adjunct. But they did not eliminate
the need for some on-site inspection. The talks thus again ended
in failure, but there remained considerable optimism in both
London and Washington about the prospects for a test-ban
agreement.

This optimism arose in the wake of the missile crisis, for
Khrushchev did indeed seize the opportunity which Macmillan
had seen. 'It seems to me, Mr President,' he wrote in a letter
of 19 December which Kennedy received at Nassau and showed
Macmillan, 'that the time has come now to put an end once and
for all to nuclear tests, to draw a line through such tests. The
moment for this is very, very appropriate.' By this letter Khrushchev had again accepted the principle of on-site inspection but
with one important qualification. He suggested that American
experts, and specifically Arthur Dean and Jerome Wiesner, had in
private discussions with Soviet experts indicated that Kennedy
would be prepared to accept a treaty based on only two to three
on-site inspections. Dean and Weisner were both later adamant
in their denial of having mentioned specific numbers: both
claimed that their only intention was to get the Soviet Union to
accept on-site inspection as a principle. Whether specific figures
were mentioned or not, Khrushchev in his letter pursued the

impression he had been given that without nominal on-site inspection the Senate would never ratify a treaty. 'If this is the only obstacle to agreement,' he wrote, 'we are prepared to meet you on this point.'

Kennedy's reply of 28 December was very carefully worded, challenging the Soviet leader on the Dean–Kuznetsov and Wiesner–Federov conversations, and denying that the requirement of on-site inspection was merely to placate the American Senate. It was, he wrote, at 'the heart of a reliable agreement'.

Kennedy also suggested in his letter that on-site inspection should be permitted in areas of little or no seismic activity as well as in those areas of regular activity, a suggestion which Khrushchev agreed to on 7 January 1963. Indeed, by the time the Disarmament Conference was reconvened on 12 February, there were three areas of agreement between the West and the Soviet Union for a test-ban treaty: on the use of nationally-manned and nationally-controlled stations for detection and identification of seismic events, on the use of 'black-boxes' as a check on the proper functioning of nationally-manned stations, and on the need for a quota of on-site inspections as a means to identify suspicious underground events. Small wonder, therefore, that *The Guardian* of 13 February should remark, 'The gap remaining to be crossed seems negligible in comparison with the distance already covered.'

Yet the intransigence seemed to be as great as ever, even though the difference seemed only one of numbers, of four to five on-site inspections and four 'black-boxes'! On 1 March Canada challenged the nuclear powers to stop pretending that such differences would constitute a risk to their security comparable to the risk of an unchecked arms race. 'It is hard to find common-sense arguments to justify this intransigence', remarked *The Guardian* of 8 March. 'If seven inspections a year represents safety, it is hard to believe that three represents disaster; if three annual inspections will not endanger the secrecy surrounding Soviet military establishments, it is hard to see that another four can make much difference.'

It was not long before the British press demanded, as *The Times* put it, that Britain give notice that 'at least one nuclear power is exasperated by the endless and apparently fruitless discussion. . . . It can do no harm and it might achieve much to make clear to the Americans that to continue to reject the offer of three inspections is to fly in the face of military and scientific logic.' Had the decision been purely one for the British Government, there is little doubt that Macmillan would willingly have seized on Khrushchev's offer, especially since the treaty which was eventually secured provided for no on-site inspection whatsoever. 'All we ask for is the bare minimum of verification,' Lord Home declared. And the then British Minister in Geneva, Joseph Godber, was at the time working hard to find a compromise between the Soviet and American positions on the basis of five on-site inspections. But, and for valid reasons, Kennedy refused to budge.

In less than three years, the American demand had been reduced from the inspection of all suspicious events to an annual quota of seven or eight inspections, and the President was thus neither prepared nor in fact in any position to go further. In Britain, political parties were pressing Macmillan to go as far as possible to secure an agreement and were thus unlikely to blame him for having been too conciliatory. The reverse was the case for President Kennedy. There was in the United States no widespread support for a test-ban agreement. American opinion was much more suspicious of Russian intentions and thus, as also the bearer of the major responsibility for the security of the West, much less ready to take a chance. Moreover, an attitude of reserve was far from unjustified in the context of the obvious doubts as to Soviet sincerity and the history of Soviet retractions and contradictions. And even American scientists in favour of the test-ban treaty would have been compelled, if called to testify before Congressional hearings, to admit that three on-site inspections were no effective deterrent to the Soviets' cheating. Kennedy clearly did not want the Senate to reject his treaty, as they had in 1919 rejected Woodrow Wilson's Treaty of Versailles. Indeed, in the end, Congress ratified the test-ban treaty with the Administration taking the line that it did not matter anyway: that all important tests could still be conducted underground!

From the distinct perspectives with which Britain and the United States viewed the requirements for the treaty can be

derived the differences in the British and American positions.
'It was purely a political decision of how many inspections it was
necessary to have as a random check,' recalled one British
official. 'We felt that possibly the very knowledge that there would
be some checks—even a relatively small number—was sufficient.
We were prepared to take that chance, but the Americans were
not.' And even Macmillan recognised that the ultimate decision
must rest in Washington, not London. But the negotiations
eventually failed not over the matter of numbers but over the
fact that, when it came to the crucial decision, the Soviets were
simply not prepared to discuss a test-ban treaty in scientific
terms at all.

With the realisation that a comprehensive treaty, conditional
on a requisite number of on-site inspections, was proving impossible to achieve came in the spring of 1963 increasing interest in a
partial treaty, the advantages of which Britain had long been
emphasising. And, despite the apparent deadlock, Kennedy and
Macmillan had not given up trying. After exchanging drafts in
March and April, they sent a joint letter to Khrushchev suggesting
both that the quota of inspections might possibly be spread over a
number of years, and also, to by-pass the politicking in Geneva,
that senior representatives might be sent to Moscow. There is no
doubt that this initiative emanated from London for Kennedy's
own advisers were inclined to consider it ill-timed and likely to
carry unfortunate political side effects for the Administration.
The suggestion was even made that it might not be unconnected
with British domestic politics. Be that as it may, Macmillan,
against the advice of his Ambassador in Moscow, concluded
that the time was ripe for another offer to Khrushchev of a
partial treaty and Kennedy agreed. This gave real meaning to the
phrase 'special relationship'. For, having listened to the arguments of his own advisers and to the views of London, Kennedy
overruled his own advisers and agreed with Macmillan that
another offer of a partial treaty would be worthwhile.

Khrushchev's initial response to the Kennedy–Macmillan
initiative was anything but hopeful. His rejection of the suggestion
to spread the quota of inspections over a number of years in
fact led to an acrimonious debate between Washington and
Moscow. But, sometime between April and June, the Soviet

leader changed his mind about a partial treaty, and he grudgingly agreed to receive British and American representatives in Moscow. Kennedy appointed Averell Harriman, the much experienced Ambassador-at-large, to lead the American team. Macmillan sent Lord Hailsham (to amuse Khrushchev, as he put it to journalists!), though he agreed that Harriman should head the joint delegation.

When the Moscow conference was announced on 10 June it was hailed, at least by *The Observer*, as 'the most important diplomatic event for a decade'. But *The Daily Telegraph* expressed a caution which even Kennedy shared: 'We know too well that the Russians can have a test-ban treaty whenever they want one. From experience at Geneva, what are we to conclude but that they do not want one? What can be expected from new talks in a new place with new talkers?' Harriman at least was confident of getting agreement on a partial treaty, and his confidence ultimately proved justified: for the treaty was initialled on 25 July, only ten days after his arrival in Moscow.

The Western delegations first saw Khrushchev on 15 July when the Soviet leader immediately ruled out a comprehensive treaty. It was then that Harriman pressed hard for a partial treaty and was particularly insistent on a clause which permitted any nation to withdraw from the treaty in the light of 'extraordinary events'. His inflexibility, however, much distressed the flamboyant Hailsham, who cabled his concern to Macmillan. Indeed Ormsby-Gore was asked to express Britain's apprehension to President Kennedy though in the end this proved unnecessary. For it was while Ormsby-Gore was with the President that they learnt that the Soviet Union had come up with acceptable new wording on the two controversial clauses, and the treaty was then initialled. Almost immediately Macmillan himself came on the telephone to explain personally why he had sent Ormsby-Gore to see Kennedy. It was at that stage that, with a broad smile on his face, the President interrupted the Prime Minister thus, 'Well, in fact I've got David sitting beside me. We've just been on to Moscow. We've initialled the Treaty!'

Signed in August and ratified in October, the Partial Nuclear Test-Ban Treaty was almost universally hailed as a great personal achievement for Macmillan. *The Daily Mail* called it 'Mac's Hour of Triumph'. *The Daily Telegraph* commented that it was 'a considerable triumph for the world's leading statesmen, not least for the British Prime Minister, who has worked long and hard for this moment.' 'Over the years', declared *The Daily Express*, 'Mr Harold Macmillan has prepared for it by tireless diplomacy. He would never be discouraged. Not all the rebuffs and all the setbacks made him falter on the way. His pertinacity is rewarded . . .' Macmillan was given a standing ovation by his Parliamentary supporters in the Commons, where he expressed his own personal satisfaction thus: 'The House will, I know, understand my own feelings at seeing at last the result of efforts made over many years and of hopes long deferred.'

The confusion of Macmillan's political and statesmanlike motives has always been difficult to disentangle, but he was always both consistent and persistent in his efforts to get a détente. Fear and suspicion, for Macmillan, were the causes rather than the effects of the arms race, and nations therefore required more than words as an assurance of safety. 'The key of it all is faith,' he had told the U.N. in 1960, 'and in the present state of the world faith cannot grow on its own. It must be strengthened, fortified, buttressed by practice.' It was because he considered that the test-ban treaty could do all these things, and more, that he never let an opportunity pass. 'Is there no hope?' he enquired in the House of Commons in 1958. 'Are we to live for ever in this sort of twilight between war and peace?' Essentially an optimist, Macmillan believed that there was a way out and that the hopes of millions demanded that the world's statesmen should find it. The partial test-ban treaty symbolised for Macmillan 'the détente which everyone knows has taken place but which it is difficult for any of us to grasp, until there has been one solid achievement.'[3]

Under Macmillan, British policy showed none of the vacillation of Moscow or the hesitation of Washington: his single-minded determination was indeed of immeasurable importance in the shaping of the course of the negotiations. He spared no effort to try to ensure that the talks, if they did not always reap results, at least continued. The lack of progress in 1961 and 1962 was, as Macmillan himself observed in March 1962, 'not for want of trying'. 'Without his sustained exertions and repeated initiatives', recorded Wright, 'there would not have been the successive

Anglo-American treaty offers in March 1961 and in August 1962 in the form they were made, the Western position on disarmament would not have been as forthcoming as it was and there would have been no partial test-ban signed in 1963.'[4]

Macmillan was not always able to claim credit for his interventions, for this would have damaged his position, since many of his efforts were undertaken behind the scenes. 'The initiative', as one British negotiator put it, 'was in forcing the issue in private with the other two. We looked at Britain as being in the position of being able to bring the two sides together.' That British initiatives took place behind the scenes, however, 'increased rather than diminished their effectiveness in a highly sensitive field of international action.'[5]

Differences both of scientific assessment and political appreciation frequently arose between Britain and the United States but both Governments acted in a manner designed to minimise their differences. Certainly neither delegation sprang a surprise upon the other at the conference table. Indeed, during the Kennedy Presidency, there developed a real working partnership between the two countries, and the treaty owed much to the joint determination of Kennedy and Macmillan and to their intimate understanding of each other's problems and objectives. But, while Britain provided a valuable single-mindedness of purpose, her contribution was nevertheless made effective through her close relationship with the United States. And it was not until Kennedy took office that the United States gave the essential leadership. The test-ban agreement would never have occurred without Kennedy's interest, his conviction of its desirability, his skill in negotiation and, above all, the influence of his office. Kennedy's special contribution was to emphasise the need to respect each other's interest and to accept honest differences. But that did not mean that he did not value British support and pressure for the treaty. British efforts were indeed nearly always to reinforce the President's inclinations and to support him in a direction which he wanted to take but for which he found little enthusiasm at home.

Kennedy was to express his gratitude in a private letter to the Prime Minister, dated 8 October, which, when he heard of Macmillan's illness, he suggested should be published:

Dear Friend,

This morning, as I signed the instrument of ratification of the Nuclear Test-Ban Treaty, I could not but reflect on the extent to which your steadfastness of commitment and determined perseverance made this treaty possible. Thanks to your never flagging interest, we were ready with our views when the Soviets decided they were ready to negotiate.

If humanity is to be spared further radioactive contamination of the atmosphere, if the nuclear arms race is to be slowed down, if we are to make more rapid progress towards lasting stability in international affairs, it would be in no small measure due to your own deep concern and long labour.

History will eventually record your indispensable role in bringing about the limitation of nuclear testing; but I cannot let this moment pass without expressing to you my own keen appreciation of your signal contribution to world peace.

With warm regards,

Sincerely, JOHN F. KENNEDY

But, however indispensable was Macmillan's role, the treaty eventually came about because Khrushchev decided to negotiate and Kennedy was ready to agree to a treaty. Signature of the treaty in fact represented a conjunction of American and Russian policies. Britain was in Moscow as a third man. That is not to underrate the part played by Macmillan. But no amount of prodding by Britain (which has the bomb) or by the other nations on the Disarmament Committee (which do not) would have had much effect, had not the moment for agreement seemed ripe in both Moscow and Washington. The power of decision even more now relies on the actions of the two super-powers, as Cuba so dramatically—and almost disastrously—demonstrated. The Moscow Conference was thus not to be the first of a new series of Big Three gatherings. It was actually the last of the old series, begun exactly twenty years before at Teheran. Henceforth, as far as summitry is concerned, the principle of the 'higher the fewer' has been well and truly established.

1. Sir Michael Wright, *Disarm and Verify* (Chatto & Windus, 1964), p.136.
2. Arthur Schlesinger Jr., *A Thousand Days* (André Deutsch, 1965), p.430.
3. Quoted in *The Daily Express* (12 June 1963).
4. Sir Michael Wright, *op. cit.*, pp. 136-7.   5. *Ibid.*, p.130.

9
Kennedy and Macmillan's 'Independence to Commit Suicide'

The Kennedy Administration presided over one of the most complete reorganisations ever of both American and NATO defence policies. For as long as the United States had maintained an obvious nuclear supremacy over the Soviet Union, neither the condition of America's defences nor really the purpose and logic of American strategy had been seriously challenged. But by 1961 the Soviet Union had not only acquired a significant nuclear capability. It had, or so it was then widely believed, actually surpassed in strength the nuclear power of the United States. And, as a leading contender for the Presidency, Kennedy had in February 1960 called for 'an investment in peace that we can afford and cannot avoid. . . . We should be willing to gamble with our money rather than our survival.' Thus, on taking office, he was determined to preserve and if necessary strengthen America's capacity to restrain potential aggressors, a determination which he so forcefully averred in his Inaugural Address. 'We dare not tempt them with weakness,' he declared, 'for only when our arms are sufficient beyond doubt, can we be certain beyond doubt that they will never be employed.' Seeing defence policy as essentially an instrument of his foreign policy, President Kennedy demanded a military capability strong enough to give his foreign policy a solid foundation but versatile enough to 'liberate diplomacy from the constraints imposed by a rigid military strategy.'[1] Accordingly, he ordered his Secretary of Defence, Robert McNamara, to conduct a thorough investigation into the state of American defences.

The tough, intellectual, and at times ruthless technocrat, who was determined to bring order into Pentagon planning, found from his investigation that, although the state of American nuclear power was not as bad as had been anticipated, the condition of American conventional forces was much worse. Of the seventeen Army and Marine divisions, McNamara discovered only about half which were ready to fight a limited war and none in a full state of readiness. Within weeks of taking office, the President himself was to be shocked to find that if he sent 10,000 men to South-East Asia he would have virtually nothing in reserve for other emergencies. Indeed in the Laotian crisis he was faced with the agonising dilemma of either holding back or almost at once unleashing the horrifying power of the Strategic Air Command. 'We couldn't prepare for everything,' recalled one Eisenhower official. 'Our forces had contracted to the point where we simply couldn't be ready for everything!' Both Laos and the Bay of Pigs venture demonstrated all too clearly to the new President the impotence of American nuclear power. It was seemingly powerless in a situation where the communists went on a bold, but limited, offensive.

The new Administration thus authorised a huge increase in expenditure on both American conventional and nuclear programmes. Kennedy ordered more Polaris missiles and accelerated both the Minuteman and Skybolt programmes. To improve and protect the bomber deterrent, provision was made for one-eighth of the force to be placed on airborne alert at any one time and for half to be on ground alert. The Midas satellite-borne system and the early warning ballistic system were both accelerated. American capacity to deal with guerrilla wars was also greatly increased. An extra 129 modern transport aircraft enhanced American airlift capacity, and sea-lift capacity was similarly expanded. The Army and Marine Corps was strengthened by the addition of 13,000 men: and all of this was before the Berlin crisis necessitated in July a further $3247 million on the defence budget and before a new joint command, Strike Command, was established which was eventually to comprise eight full divisions.

Yet of even more importance than these actual increases in American capability, and at the same time reflecting the versatility in defence which the President demanded, was the redefinition of defence strategy which, so it was believed, would permit a selection of suitable responses to various forms of aggression. Both Kennedy and McNamara were profoundly sceptical of the previous Administration's reliance on the deterrent value of nuclear weapons. Indeed, as a Senator, Kennedy had in 1958 attacked the policy of massive retaliation as producing almost a Maginot-Line mentality, '[a] dependence upon a strategy which may collapse or may never be used but which meanwhile prevents the consideration of any alternative'.

Refusing to accept the simplicity of massive retaliation (the inherent limitations of which by 1960 even Eisenhower had begun to recognise), but equally rejecting the defeatism of disengagement, Kennedy and McNamara came to formulate a new defence doctrine which was commonly referred to as 'flexible response'. The whole conception of graduated deterrence, which was central to this doctrine, emerged from a careful, if at times exacting, process of strategic analysis, initiated by McNamara, to which no European Defence Ministry, let alone Government, had previously been exposed.

Convinced of the value of scientific management in defence planning, McNamara sought to apply the techniques of systematic quantitative analysis to strategic decisions. Ingenious new methods were introduced whereby problems could be formulated and broken down, alternatives established and the effects of different decisions distinguished and analysed. McNamara insisted on a definition of options which would facilitate choice. 'Bob McNamara seeks his options', as one friend was to observe, 'as Parsifal sought the Holy Grail!' Ridiculed it may have been, it was nevertheless in this way that McNamara expounded a more precise definition of what was meant by, and more important what was needed for, 'deterrence': specifically, a nuclear force sufficiently strong to discourage a pre-emptive strike but one sufficiently secure to provide for a second-strike capacity. Nuclear capabilities which failed to meet these requirements were, in McNamara's view, not credible and indeed it was on these grounds that he later publicly attacked the British and French nuclear deterrents. What McNamara sought above all else was a balance between capability and strategy, and this requirement, he considered, applied equally to NATO as well as to American defence policy. It was thus that he urged NATO to attach the highest priority to the strengthening of its conventional forces which would thereby permit greater choice in defence planning. 'We called upon Europe', as one senior Pentagon official put it, 'not to increase their budgets but to increase their real strength in NATO. It was out of balance in terms of strategy and capability, particularly in the nuclear area: the strategy was a nuclear strategy, but there was no nuclear capability.' America's allies were, however, to be as unconvinced by McNamara's strategic arguments as they were to be unimpressed by Kennedy's baiting of a NATO nuclear force. By the end of 1961 in fact the combined non-American contribution to the ground defences of NATO had been increased by a mere three divisions to a total of twenty-one divisions.

European scepticism of 'flexible response' was neither wholly surprising nor in the circumstances without justification. The Americans had after all been preaching the opposite doctrine for years! Ideas of conventional combat, which but three years previously had been derided, were now suddenly resurrected. The belief, first taken up by the Americans, that the deployment of tactical nuclear weapons could off-set Soviet superiority in manpower was now directly refuted. And the many devices introduced to assure political control over nuclear weapons in Europe were taken now as designed to prevent their use altogether. For, despite President Kennedy's repeated assurances to the contrary, the new emphasis on balancing capabilities, which then in effect meant increasing conventional strength, was read in Europe, and especially in Britain, as undermining the credibility of America's nuclear resolve. It did not seem reasonable to suppose that the need for strong conventional forces had arisen precisely because this had already happened! Instead, it was feared that any strengthening in conventional forces would only further discredit the nuclear deterrent. Indeed it was argued that the Soviets would be deterred more effectively if they knew that America had no alternative but massive retaliation. This was certainly the view of Franz Joseph Strauss, West Germany's Defence Minister, a view which earned qualified endorsement from Harold Watkinson, his British opposite number. The very discussion of the limited value of nuclear weapons seemed for many Europeans to reduce that value still further.

Much of the apprehension in Europe stemmed from a genuine confusion as to exactly what was meant by 'flexible response'. When he was Supreme Allied Commander in Europe, General Lemnitzer felt compelled to forbid use of the term in SHAPE since too many of his staff thought it was synonymous with conventional response, when what McNamara meant by it was an appropriate response! European Governments were, moreover, unlikely to welcome the more equal sharing of the burden of defence which McNamara demanded, when it so obviously called for increased national defence expenditure. And finally, even if the doctrine itself had been generally accepted, its chances of implementation were made more remote by the tactlessness shown by McNamara and other Kennedy officials in the manner in which they demanded that everyone should pay more, and do more, for their own defence. As Lord Hailsham remarked in 1963, in an attack on the American monopoly of advanced technologies, 'Occasionally it is the very qualities which make for efficiency which undermine the political and sentimental ties of a friendship.' Never one to claim tact as his cardinal virtue, McNamara only angered governments by his pressure to get them to increase their conventional strength. His efforts to get Britain to restore the equivalent of one division to B.A.O.R., for example, earned him only a cold shoulder and a rebuke from *The Times* of 30 July 1961, which declared that Britain 'has no intention of calling up men simply to show willingness as an ally.' A visit to London by McNamara's deputy, Roswell Gilpatric, in October 1961 similarly provoked ill-mannered comment, even if he was, by his own admission, perhaps a little too candid in an 'off the record' press conference. 'Every new Administration brings in new men who think they are able to tackle problems earlier than they actually are in terms of judgement,' was how one veteran American official put it. 'I saw some of the young lads rush to Europe and start lecturing the Europeans on the subject of their defence strategy. I regret our ineptitude but I still think the doctrine was sound.'

The logic of the new American defence thinking did have its impact on NATO policy. For in the summer of 1961 preliminary planning began on a new defence directive to cover the five years from 1962 to 1967, and as such to replace the then current NATO planning document, code-named MC-70. The new directive, code-named MC-96, envisaged a substantial increase in conventional forces and significant increases in the armament of forces with tactical nuclear power, though it also attacked the role and importance which Britain among others had attached to such weapons in favour of the permanent build-up of ground forces in Europe. But it was still widely believed in Europe that flexible response would only be playing about with a few hours, or at most a couple of days. Indeed it was not until 1967 that NATO formally adopted the flexible response doctrine, and even then the British Defence Minister, Denis Healey, considered it all but synonymous with a nuclear response. As he said in his Munich speech of February 1969, 'Nuclear escalation would be the only alternative to surrender in the case of a major Soviet attack.'

If President Kennedy's determination to make the West less dependent on nuclear weaponry, and thus less likely to suffer a nuclear miscalculation, should have been supported wholly and without equivocation by any British government, the sad truth is that it was not. While not actively opposing the new doctrine, the Macmillan Government nevertheless refused to accept the McNamara strategy in either of its two major aspects. A counter-force strategy was almost meaningless in British terms. And for a country where defence policy has traditionally been influenced and shaped by political and economic circumstance, a ground strategy, resting on the build-up of conventional forces in Europe, was similarly political and economic lunacy. The importance which NATO had attached to tactical nuclear weapons had ideally suited the British Government, enabling it in 1957 to abolish conscription; and any official admission that British combat troops might after all become involved in a protracted conventional war could have carried major repercussions for the whole concept of a small, professional army. It was in this context that *The Observer* was inclined to conclude of British hesitation over flexible response that 'British policy is based simply on the degrading fact that we cannot produce the soldiers to man our armed forces.'[2] Be that as it may, the new American strategy was embarrassing for Macmillan in that it tended, if not to vindicate, then at least to validate, the arguments put forward by the opposition to his deterrent policy. For, ever since the War, British Prime Ministers have been disposed to rely upon the deterrent value of Britain's nuclear arsenal, and perhaps none more than Macmillan, who personally regarded Britain and America as holding the deterrent in trust for the free world. 'We must rely on the power of the nuclear deterrent,' he had declared in 1957 in the wake of the revelations of Sandys's White Paper, 'or we must throw up the sponge!' For Macmillan, it would have been an act of consummate folly for Britain unilaterally and gratuitously to discard a weapon which, in his opinion, had given Britain both a voice and an authority in determining the great issues of the world. It was thus that, with flexible response attacking the previous reliance on nuclear weapons, Macmillan feared an emergence of a further debate on the credibility of the British deterrent and worse, of the American willingness to sustain it.

Yet, despite all the British reservations, flexible response was quickly recognised as more sensible for Britain than massive retaliation. A strategy which relies on the deterrence of aggression rather than on defence against it is inclined to put the victim of aggression in a great predicament if his deterrent threat in fact fails to deter! For a British Government this meant that if it ever became necessary to carry out a threat of retaliation the choice would be between surrender or suicide, neither of which was a suitable, acceptable or for that matter credible alternatives.

The advantages to Britain of greater flexibility in defence were thus obvious. Less obvious is the extent to which British policy was directly influenced by the new American doctrine. Anyway by 1962 the guide-lines of British defence planning, as laid down in the Government's White Paper, were very different from massive retaliation, the dominant theme of the 1957 White Paper. In part it was no doubt due to changes in personality and thinking, in part no doubt due to a natural change with the times: whatever the reasons, the 1962 White Paper all but refuted the crudities of the Sandys Paper. 'We must continue to make it clear to potential aggressors . . . that we should strike back with all the means that we judge appropriate, conventional or nuclear. *If we had nothing but nuclear force, this would not be credible.*' (Author's italics)

Accepting the need to balance capabilities with strategy, the British Government nevertheless refused to be swayed by what it considered unreasonable and unrealistic pressures to get B.A.O.R. increased. The Government refused, as the Defence Paper made explicit, because it did not believe that 'major war could long continue without one side or the other resorting to nuclear weapons. It is therefore the prevention of war that is vital rather than preparations for long-drawn-out conventional war.'[3] A veiled if firm rebuttal of McNamara's strategic arguments.

But, despite his repeated pressures, it is in fact doubtful whether McNamara really expected Britain to increase the strength of B.A.O.R., though equally this was genuinely something which he thought she could, and should, do. Indeed, inclined to believe that Britain's inability to meet her force level requirements owed much to the maintenance of the nuclear deterrent, and totally rejecting British 'excuses' as long as Britain indulged in the luxury of no conscription, McNamara showed very little sympathy for Watkinson's efforts to get a financial contribution from West Germany to offset the costs of British troops stationed there. He stolidly refused to pool the question of the costs of British and American troops in Germany, insisting that both Governments should conduct separate negotiations. He was to be, however, more successful than Watkinson in securing a satisfactory arrangement, not least because he could exert much stronger pressures on West Germany to purchase American defence hardware to ease the foreign exchange drain for America. The very success of the American negotiations in fact made the chances more remote of any really satisfactory arrangement between West Germany and Britain. 'When the bigger partner went in and made an offset agreement,' as one American negotiator admitted, 'it made it much more difficult for the smaller partner to get anything really equivalent.'

It was a problem never finally settled but ultimately McNamara was compelled to accept Britain's unwillingness to increase her troop strength in Europe. And he was compelled to accept this primarily because he attached greater significance to Britain's commitments outside the European theatre. He was particularly anxious that these commitments should not be jeopardised because in an emergency he knew that the United States would not always be able to replace British troops in these areas.

Referring to Britain's refusal to meet her NATO force-level requirements, *The Times* of 9 December 1961 reported that 'the United States and many of the European allies make no secret of their belief that Britain is not paying a full subscription to the club.' In fact Britain's many commitments around the world assured her a continuing special position in the defence planning of the West. McNamara may have considered British civilian leadership in the defence field of a superficial, even a dilettante, nature; Watkinson, and later Thorneycroft, may in turn have found McNamara politically inexperienced. But, when it came to the practical relationship between the Defence Ministries of the two countries, British and American officials talked more frankly, more intimately, and over a greater range of issues, with each other than they did with anybody else. It was a relationship in part reliant on the still keenly felt heritage of war-time alliance. It was also reinforced by their strategic connection in nuclear weapons, a relationship which was anterior to NATO and which at least until 1957 represented a more powerful response to the Soviet challenge than did the then total military strength under NATO's control. Anglo-American friendship is what after all really made feasible the coalition strategy of the West. Yet of much greater importance than these factors was that Britain was in a unique position to support and complement American policy world-wide. And the Americans genuinely valued British support and, more important, Britain's presence especially in the strategic areas East of Suez.

Since 1945, with the obvious decline in her capabilities, the effectiveness of Britain's defence role has very much been emphasised within the context of a sea-borne mobile police force, and in this she has (with the exception of Suez) been remarkably successful: the Malaysia campaign in the 1950s, the Cyprus Emergency of 1958, and the quashing of the rebellion in Brunei and Sarawak in 1962 to name but a few instances. So successful has Britain been in containing bush-fire incidents that the United States itself had much to learn from British experience. Where they learnt most from Britain was in the priorities to be attached to defeating communist insurgency, the optimum scale of operation required, the demands of training, the requirements of political initiatives, and the need to campaign vigorously against political as well as military subversion.

Waning as her power may have been by 1961, Britain still exercised a decisive influence in the Indian Ocean, in the Persian Gulf, in the Middle East, in Australasia and in the Caribbean. She still retained many of the air and naval bases, like Gibraltar, Malta, Aden, Hong Kong and Singapore, which originally had been established to support the Empire. Combined, these influences and strategic commitments, in so far as they were of value to the United States, led in 1961 to a joint agreement being drawn up between the British and American Defence Ministries, specifying each other's obligations and defining each other's spheres of influence. The Americans undoubtedly considered Africa, India and to an extent Australasia and Indonesia as British spheres of influence which, in purely military terms, were of a great deal more importance to the United States than Britain's European commitment. As one British Minister commented, 'The Americans might have felt that we ought to do more, but I don't think that they felt we were doing it in the wrong places.' Illustrative of this is the immediate (and lasting) effect on Anglo-American relations of the Labour Government's decision of 1967 to end the British presence East of Suez, a decision which Rusk and McNamara at first refused to accept, and which made Britain appear to be opting out of her responsibilities.

But if the United States generally approved of Britain's defence commitments around the world, in one area there was profound disagreement. In fact no Anglo-American difference was more bitter or intractable than that over the role and importance that each Government assigned to the nuclear deterrent. For what has commonly been called the nuclear 'special relationship' has in actuality been fraught with friction ever since Churchill in October 1941 agreed to the pooling of the British and American efforts in the atomic field. Under the agreement reached with Roosevelt, which was so obviously governed by the exigencies of war, all the research on the atomic bomb was to be conducted in the United States and largely financed by the Americans, but all the information acquired would be pooled, and all the results shared with Britain. This understanding between the principals unfortunately never penetrated far down the American chain of command. In fact one American official, General Groves, was later to admit 'I was not responsible for our close co-operation with the British. I did everything to hold back on it.'[4] On two or three occasions, Churchill and Roosevelt were compelled to intervene personally to define the limits of co-operation. What they never clearly defined (not even at Quebec) was the precise nature of the relationship between the two countries over the exchange of information in the post-War developments of atomic energy. The passing of the McMahon Act in 1946 of course effectively deprived Britain of any information at all, and as such led Britain to embark upon her own nuclear programme.

A *modus vivendi* of January 1948, commonly known as the Blair House Agreement, did establish nine areas in which the United States was prepared to exchange information, but none was concerned with the military uses of atomic energy, and indeed the deprivation to Britain resulting from the McMahon Act was complete. It was in consequence that its repeal in 1958 meant, at least for Macmillan, that 'for the next decade Britain's problems in this immensely expensive and complicated area of scientific development of weapons were resolved.'[5] But by 1958 the British programme had already fallen so far behind those of the super-powers that, far from problems being resolved, the McMahon amendments only created new tensions with the Americans. And in fact Britain was to be the first major casualty of McNamara's new defence policy.

European apprehension about America's nuclear resolve (already great) was in 1962 heightened when McNamara began to talk about a strategy designed to 'control' general war. A strategy that exposes a limited territory to the fluctuations of conventional combat, however sound, does little to assure security for the territory concerned. It will be recalled that this was the primary motive for the German advocacy, and consequent acceptance by NATO, of a forward strategy. Since Europe was likely to be the battleground for any conventional war between the super-powers, it was hardly surprising that Europeans would have preferred a strategy which would magnify the risks of aggression rather than minimise the losses of the defender. It was thus that paradoxically McNamara's new ideas tended to encourage rather than discourage European Governments in seeking their own national nuclear programmes.

In an effort to clear up misunderstandings and thereby to reassure his allies, McNamara declared, first in private at the NATO Ministerial Meeting in Athens in May 1962, and then in public at the University of Michigan, Ann Arbor, in June, that American vulnerability to Soviet missiles did not make the United States a 'less willing partner in the defence of Europe'. But instead of reassuring his allies, the effect of McNamara's Ann Arbor speech was to give any American effort to secure closure co-operation within NATO the appearance of an assertion of hegemony, an appearance which was really to seal the fate of the multi-lateral force. And it was an effect made even worse by McNamara's scathing attack on the national nuclear forces of America's chief allies, Britain and France.

If the Kennedy Administration was more hostile to the French nuclear programme, and in June 1962 the President himself attacked it as 'inimical to the community interest', it nonetheless conducted a vigorous intellectual campaign against the British deterrent. On more than one occasion, President Kennedy himself warned Macmillan that the British deterrent exacerbated Anglo-French relations. His military aide, General Maxwell Taylor, came to London in March 1962 to try to win the British over to the new doctrine, and Under Secretary of State, George Ball, in April criticised the British deterrent as effective only in leading to a reduction of British commitments elsewhere. Not everyone in the Administration shared the strong views of Ball about the British deterrent, and certainly McNamara's objections, such as they were, were almost wholly military. With the United States already spending the vast sum of $15 billion on nuclear weapons, it seemed to McNamara totally unnecessary for European Governments to duplicate the American effort. Limited national nuclear forces were, moreover, unlikely to perform the function of deterrence: indeed he argued that if an adversary believed that a national force could be used independently then that force was merely inviting a pre-emptive strike. In the event of a war, its use against a major nuclear power would be tantamount to suicide, without having had any effect on the outcome of the conflict. Meanwhile its very existence, in McNamara's view, only encouraged others to seek their own programmes, thus immeasurably increasing the dangers of miscalculation. 'In short, then,' declared McNamara at Ann Arbor, 'limited nuclear capabilities, operating independently, are dangerous, expensive, prone to obsolescence and lacking in credibility as a deterrent.'

Sound defence strategy it may have been, but McNamara's attack was undeniably poor alliance politics. No doubt as a diplomatic nicety, he did refrain from referring to any country by name. But if, as both American and British officials were to insist, his primary target was De Gaulle's policy, it was nevertheless hardly surprising that it should also have been read in London as an attack on the British deterrent. And this being so, the recollections of British Ministers seem disconcertingly nonchalant. 'Ann Arbor was frightfully interesting to the defence correspondent of *The Times*, but not to us,' was how one Minister recalled the Government's reaction. 'I think we felt that Robert McNamara was rather the kind of chap who was inclined to say these things.' In probability, however, it was in response to wails from London that on 23 June McNamara publicly declared that he had not been referring to Britain in his Ann Arbor speech. Whether or not the British Government sought such a public assurance, and at least one Minister directly refuted this suggestion ('We had our policy. We didn't have to ask Mr McNamara's permission!'), McNamara's exoneration did nothing to clarify the political controversy which developed in Britain as to the 'independent' nature of the British deterrent. For, if Ann Arbor applied directly to France, it equally applied to Britain. 'If the emperor doesn't have any clothes,' as one McNamara aide put it, 'it is very difficult to say that he does!'

The Kennedy Administration in fact considered neither the French *nor* the British deterrents credible: neither were strong enough to survive a pre-emptive strike and neither had any second-strike capacity. They were both, in the American view, unnecessary and a waste of limited resources. If it represented an investment of only ten per cent of the total British defence budget, the deterrent was nevertheless considered as leading to a reduction in other commitments. Moreover, in so far as they gave the two countries status, the British and French deterrents were considered as encouraging other countries to seek their own nuclear forces. And herein in fact lies the key to the difference between the American attitude and the attitude of its allies to nuclear ownership.

The debate within the alliance over the ownership of nuclear weapons has essentially been one of two-way confidence. Dr Kissinger described the issue thus: 'The United States tends to ask those of its allies possessing nuclear arsenals: if you trust us, why do you need nuclear weapons of your own? The allies reply: if you trust us, why are you so concerned about our possession of nuclear weapons? Since the answer must inevitably emphasise contingencies in which either the goals of the allies or their strategy would be incompatible, the debate on nuclear control within NATO has been inherently divisive.'[6] The essential truth of the British deterrent is that its justification is more than merely emotional or sentimental. If it was obvious military foolishness, it was nevertheless a political weapon of some importance, as too was the French deterrent. Neither Macmillan nor De Gaulle would (or could for that matter) have seriously claimed that their nuclear power was likely to deter a determined Soviet offensive. Nor was their ownership of nuclear weapons dictated by any mistrust of what in the future the Americans might do, however much this may have motivated Attlee in 1946 to initiate a British nuclear programme.[7] The issue of nuclear control was not military: it had become symbolic of status. For both France and Britain, the deterrent was an instrument for wielding influence: and in both cases the primary aim was less that of dissuading an adversary than that of persuading an ally.

The United States could no more than the Soviet Union permit a major advance by the other side into an area whether that area was formally protected or not. And, not reaping any obvious benefits of a special relationship with the United States, De Gaulle decided that in virtually no circumstances was the American commitment likely to be jeopardised. He saw little to be lost and much to be gained from intransigence. He may even have concluded that the only way for France to exert influence was through withholding co-operation. How else can we possibly explain the apparent naïvety, not to say arrogance, of his declaration at the Ecole Militaire in 1959: 'The defence of France must be in French hands . . . if a nation like France has to make war it must be her war; it must be her effort. The defence of France might in some circumstances be inter-connected with the defence of other nations. But in our own affairs it is indispensable that France should defend herself, by herself, for herself and in her own way'?

In contrast Britain decided that influence was best exercised through her close relationship with the United States. The only stipulation seemed to be that she should retain an 'independent' deterrent to sustain her great-power pretensions, to wield influence over American actions, and as a means for British Prime Ministers to pursue the kind of personal diplomacy in which they all seemed to revel. But, in accepting American assistance in the procurement of nuclear weapons, as reflected in the abandonment of Blue Streak in April 1960 and its replacement by the American-developed and American-financed Skybolt, Britain put herself in an unnecessarily dangerous and ambiguous position. Blue Streak was no doubt an addled egg of gigantic size, but should Britain so readily have opted for Skybolt, thereby increasing her dependence on the United States?

National prestige can become a major preoccupation of Governments when they seem less and less free to employ their national power, and this has increasingly been the case for Britain. British dependence on the United States has made the need ever more urgent for Britain to demonstrate her independence and uphold her value as an ally. The primary argument for British nuclear weapons after all has been that to be without them would mean total diplomatic dependence upon the United States. The frequent stains in Anglo-American relations have indeed tended to result from diminutions in effective British power, even when at times those diminutions have stemmed from the pressures of American policy. It is just that every British decision that reduces Britain's autonomous power also reduces British influence within the alliance and makes for potential conflict. And this is what unfortunately happened in the relationship between Britain and the United States over the issue of nuclear weapons. For, in accepting American assistance to maintain her deterrent policy, Britain clearly made herself dependent upon the continuing willingness of the United States to perpetuate a state of affairs about which many Americans held strong views. And, just as the British and French deterrents were retained with a view to increasing their influence over an ally, rather than as weapons to dissuade an adversary, so American opposition to them was due less to their ineffectiveness than to America's determination not to be dragged into a nuclear war against its will. Kennedy took more exception to De Gaulle's nuclear policy precisely because in fact he exercised less influence, indeed less control over its use than he did over the British deterrent. It was not just that the target plan of Bomber Command was completely integrated with that of the American Strategic Air Command. Much more important was the fact that the very existence of the British deterrent depended upon the Americans, the eventual recognition of which was to prove very painful for the British Government, when the Kennedy Administration decided to cancel the ill-fated Skybolt missile.

1. Arthur Schlesinger Jr., *A Thousand Days* (André Deutsch, 1965), p.288.
2. *The Observer* (4 June 1961).
3. Cmnd 1639, 'Statement on Defence 1962. The Next Five Years'.
4. *U.S. Atomic Energy Commission.* In the Matter of J. Robert Oppenheimer: transcript of hearing before Personnel Security Board.
5. Harold Macmillan, *Riding the Storm* (Macmillan, 1971), p.323.
6. Henry Kissinger, *The Troubled Partnership*, *A Reappraisal of the Atlantic Alliance* (McGraw Hill, 1965), p.14.
7. Attlee recalled in Baron Francis Williams, *A Prime Minister Remembers* (London, 1961), pp.118-19: 'We couldn't allow ourselves to be wholly in their [American] hands . . .' We had to 'bear in mind that there was always the possibility of their withdrawing and becoming isolationist once again.'

10
The Skybolt Crisis

'Like the final twitching of the tail of a dead lizard'.[1] This was how Henry Brandon described the final, and perhaps most bizarre, act in the Skybolt story. It was three days before Christmas 1962. An unusually tired President Kennedy had gone from Nassau with Sir David Ormsby-Gore to Palm Beach for what they both hoped would be an undisturbed week-end. Robert McNamara was on his way to Aspen, Colorado, for a short holiday. Macmillan was seeing John Diefenbaker, the Prime Minister of Canada. And a triumphant Thorneycroft had returned to London and announced that Skybolt was thought to be a failure. Then it happened: the news came through that at the sixth attempt the Skybolt missile had proved a success! The U.S. Air Force was jubilant, Macmillan was embarrassed, Kennedy was furious. 'I can't understand them doing this,' he remarked; 'they must have been tired.' They were all tired, desperately so, for in the previous week they had preserved the Anglo-American alliance. Nothing less. Macmillan's government had been given a new, but as it turned out all-too-short, lease of life. Relations with France had been overturned, overnight. The entire course of history was soon to change as a result.

'It is more shameful', Rochefoucauld had written in *Les Maximes*, 'to distrust one's friends, than to be deceived by them.' The Skybolt story was certainly a crisis compounded of drama and deceit, of uncertainty and distrust, of muddled perceptions and disappointed expectations, of high political stakes both won and lost, of miscalculation and misjudgement, at times carefully concealed from the public eye, at times skilfully exposed for the public's benefit. But it was also a phoney crisis. It should never have been allowed to happen. Like the Suez débâcle of 1956, the crisis over Skybolt brought the Anglo-American alliance to its knees, producing as it did an almost complete breakdown in transatlantic communication which remains even more of a mystery given the close relationship between the two governments. But, like all the best dramatic plays, the opening act in the Skybolt story gave no hint of how events were to unfold. It was as it should have been, as it could only have been, in Anglo-American relations: a meeting between Macmillan and Eisenhower at Camp David in March 1960 for one of their periodic reviews of world affairs.

As expected, and in the best tradition of Anglo-American friendship, the atmosphere was serene and informal: the two leaders knew each other too well for it to have been otherwise. But it was at the luxury Presidential retreat in the Maryland hills that the seeds were sown for the Skybolt story. It was there that Eisenhower agreed to keep Britain in the nuclear club after the mid-1960s with his promise of a new air-to-ground missile, Skybolt, the development of which had only been given the go-ahead one month earlier. For Macmillan it was essential to obtain a satisfactory alternative from the Americans for the now doomed Blue Streak, the last serious attempt at a truly independent British deterrent. Without such a substitute, his deterrent policy, on which much of the credibility of his government relied, would be in ruins. Given the spirit of that Camp David meeting, Macmillan could in probability have had the rival Polaris, the U.S. Navy's dream child. His Minister of Defence, Harold Watkinson, however, advised against Polaris. It would be too expensive, he said. It may possibly have strings attached to it. The Navy weren't keen for it. Only Skybolt, he argued, would keep Britain's deterrent independent. Certainly Skybolt appeared to offer distinct advantages. To the R.A.F., always keen to be one up on the other services, it presented a means of extending the life of the V-bomber force, then the mainstay of the British deterrent but expected to become obsolete by the mid-1960s. It was also a very cheap way of retaining a politically necessary deterrent. The United States, as Mr McNamara himself admitted in 1963, 'undertook to bear the entire cost of the Skybolt development.'[2]

Under the agreement formalised in June the British Government was committed to pay only for the number of missiles it wanted (up to a maximum of one hundred, all, of course, without warheads), and for the minor adaptation costs on the V-bomber.

Thus, when Skybolt was cancelled, the British Government had certainly no valid cause for complaint on the financial loss to Britain. The costs to Britain had in fact been minimal. Indeed, no doubt anxious to repay Eisenhower for his generous offer, Macmillan proved agreeable to the establishment of an American Polaris base at Holy Loch in Scotland. It most certainly was never referred to as a 'bargain', and any suggestion that this was the case was suitably played down by the gentlemanly diplomacy that had come to be expected of Eisenhower and Macmillan. Both parties, however, considered each others' commitments morally binding. Indeed it was the American government which first reminded Macmillan of this fact. Mr Douglas Dillon, then Under Secretary of State, complained to the British Ambassador in Washington, Sir Harold Caccia, about the delay in London arising from the expected political embarrassment that the announcement of American nuclear submarines being harboured in a British port was certain to produce.

Macmillan returned to London excited by the prospect of a new dimension in Anglo-American friendship. Had he not, he charged his critics, proved that the alliance works both ways? But unfortunately for Macmillan the British press did not seem to share his enthusiasm. No doubt lamenting the demise of the British deterrent, *The Daily Express* posed questions which in less than two years were to cause some soul-searching within the Government itself: 'Will it work? If it works, will the American Government go ahead with it? Will it be ready in 1965? Can she afford it?'[3] An extremely advantageous arrangement for Britain, it nevertheless lacked one essential ingredient: certitude. The Government was simply riding piggy-back on an American project, the consequence of which was that, as Ronald Steel remarked, 'when the driver decided he had gone far enough, the hitchhiker had no place to go.'[4]

Even at the outset there were strong sceptics about Skybolt, including both the Secretary of Defence, Thomas Gates, and his deputy, James Douglas. Though they had approved the project against the recommendation of the Fletcher Committee, a review body inside the Pentagon, they had done so because at that time only the Atlas missile was fully operational: no prediction could have been made with confidence as to which of the competing systems—Skybolt, Polaris or Minuteman—would eventually prove successful. Gates was dubious about any basic need for Skybolt and pessimistic about the extreme costs likely to be incurred in overcoming the technical difficulties of an incredibly complex and hitherto untried experiment in ballistic systems. Leading scientists in both countries shared these doubts, including Sir Solly Zuckerman, the British Government's Chief Scientific Adviser. But as the issue became more and more political, so scientific advice carried less and less weight.

Gates's doubts about the project were matched only by his impatience with the poor management of Douglas Aircraft, the contractors for the Skybolt missile. Accordingly, he insisted in September 1960 that a detailed termination clause be inserted, whereby either Government could contract out at any time but that neither would do so except after prior consultation with the other. Gates was fully aware that the British Government had taken up Skybolt for political reasons, and on at least two occasions he felt obliged to warn his opposite number not to exclude the possibility of failure, not, as one official put it, to 'go too far overboard for it'. But this is precisely what the British Government proceeded to do, making the whole credibility of its deterrent policy dependent upon the outcome of an uncertain research project. Watkinson's reasoning was as simple as it appeared obvious. As he told the House of Commons in February, 1960, 'We have to pick the winners out of a stable. We are not like the Americans who have an enormous stable and pick the winners as they come down the course.' Neither Watkinson nor Macmillan apparently had a good eye for form, since far from finding a winner, they picked a non-starter!

To be fair, the enthusiasm of the United States Air Force for Skybolt seemed in 1960 sufficient to guarantee that the project would be carried through to completion. 'It is impossible', *The Times* of 9 June suggested, 'to conceive of the United States

Air Force dropping a project designed to keep it in business after the mid-1960s.' But it only appeared impossible because no Secretary of Defence to date, and certainly not Gates, had succeeded in imposing his will on the Pentagon, which had acquired a frightening momentum of its own. A co-ordinated defence policy seemingly took second place to inter-service rivalry where success was dependent upon lobbying techniques and internal intrigues. One of the ironies in the Skybolt story is that the project was originally conceived by the Air Force to offset the growing enthusiasm in the Pentagon for Polaris!

In one respect, however, Gates refused to be either intimidated by the pressures within the Pentagon or swayed by the repre- sentations—and at times veiled threats—of the British Govern- ment. Convinced that Skybolt would never work, he sharply cut back funds for the project in Eisenhower's final Budget in December 1960. While it would not have meant the abandonment of Skybolt, the cutback in funds was viewed with consternation in London. In consequence there is little doubt that McNamara's decision in early 1961 not only to restore the funds but marginally to increase them was met with profound relief in Whitehall. This action, British Ministers reasoned, showed that the new Administration shared their confidence in Skybolt and accepted certain obligations towards Britain. In actuality, their confidence was ill-founded for there was nothing in McNamara's reasoning which was likely to comfort the British Government.

In restoring the funds for Skybolt, McNamara overruled the advice of both the Budget Bureau Director, David Bell, and his own Assistant Secretary for International Affairs, Paul Nitze. He was persuaded that the reduced rate recommended by his predecessor would have proved Skybolt neither one way nor the other, and he was under pressure from the Air Force to give it a chance. Not that he needed much persuasion: McNamara was not the kind of man who settled for half-measures or makeshift compromises. Moreover he was conscious at that stage of the election commitment of President Kennedy to end the 'missile gap', which was shortly found to be illusory. As far as Britain was concerned, as a senior American official recalled, 'we knew of course the arrangements with Britain but they didn't influence us.'

Of the many striking qualities which McNamara brought to his office of Secretary of Defence, two were to carry significance for the Skybolt story. His determination, and indeed success, in asserting the primacy of civilian leadership in the Pentagon was to be continually disbelieved by the British Government, which mistakenly put its faith in the power of the U.S.A.F. to resist any opposition to Skybolt. After all, it was argued, no Secretary of Defence had ever controlled the Pentagon before! But there the reasoning stopped, for no Secretary of Defence before had displayed McNamara's single-minded purpose and resolute determination.

Of even greater significance to Skybolt's fate was McNamara's introduction of the techniques of large-scale management into Pentagon planning. His critics derided his 'whiz-kids', and his 'intellectual jargon': they scoffed at McNamara's options! He was widely caricatured as the ruthless technocrat who believed in the omnipotence of the slide-rule. In fact, as Arthur Schlesinger wrote: 'He knew that abstractions were different from realities and that the tolerances of calculation on the great computers were refined beyond the precision of the assumptions. But the quest for control required in his judgement two things: the use of analysis to force alternative programmes to the surface and the definition of the "options" in quantitive terms in order to facilitate choice.'[5] In effect this meant that Skybolt was henceforth to be judged both on its own cost effectiveness and also in comparison with the competing systems of Minuteman and Polaris. And the omens were not good. Both the latter projects were proceeding well whereas the estimated costs of the development and procurement of Skybolt had more than doubled in under two years.

Another determined effort was thus made to get Skybolt cancelled in the Autumn of 1961, this time led by Bell and Jerome Wiesner, the President's Scientific Adviser. But again McNamara resisted the pressures, settling instead for a typically American compromise with his Secretary of the Air Force, Eugene Zuckert. It was a marvellous arrangement in every respect except one—it was totally unrealistic! A ceiling of $500 million was placed on the development costs of Skybolt for 1962. The project, it seemed, was reprieved again. But in actual terms this compromise allowed for a margin of less than $10 million for any further revision in the estimates for the whole of one year, a figure wildly unrealistic even discounting inflation. Nevertheless, as one senior British official recalled, while 'there was always the danger it was going to be scrapped, the reverse of that is that the President and the Secretary of Defence were determined to make it work.'

In January, 1962, however, President Kennedy thought it right to tell a visiting British Minister, Julian Amery, of the growing doubts about Skybolt. At a luncheon in the White House given for Amery, the President casually wondered aloud whether Skybolt would ever work, urging the British not to bank too heavily on it. Amery apparently reacted very strongly to Kennedy's remarks. 'Skybolt must be made to work,' he declared. 'The political consequences on Anglo-American relations if Skybolt is cancelled do not bear thinking about.' Genuinely surprised at Amery's outburst, Kennedy sought to reassure him: 'Well I have told you that there are these doubts, but I hasten to add that we are anxious to make it work and fulfil our commitments.' Just as Kennedy was later to forget Amery's angry outburst, so the British Government refused to attach too much importance to Kennedy's remarks, believing as they did that the President had not been properly briefed and was merely offering the advice of a layman.

But as 1962 wore on the prospects for Skybolt worsened. Minuteman was but a few months from the production line and the Polaris trials indicated that it was obviously going to be fully up to expectations. It soon became apparent to all except the British Government that on any conceivable calculation a third means of delivery, which was proving to be both the least satisfactory and the most expensive, was unlikely to be required by the Americans. It had the lowest accuracy, reliability and yield of any of the American strategic missile systems. It was unsuitable as an American first strike weapon since it would take hours to reach its target whereas in contrast a Minuteman would take only thirty minutes. Nor did Skybolt have any place in the American arsenal as a weapon for controlled counter-city retaliation. Aside from its relative vulnerability to anti-ballistic missile defences, it had the great disadvantage that its carrier—the B-52—had to be committed to its target, if at all, early in a war, otherwise it would have been vulnerable on the ground to enemy missile attack. As Mr McNamara summed up the case against Skybolt in 1963, 'Common sense requires that we do not let ourselves be inflexibly locked in on such a matter . . . [which] is unnecessary when we have systems like Polaris whose missiles can be with-held for days if desired.'[6] The only function that Skybolt could have performed for the Americans was as a tactical weapon for 'defence suppression' and this would only have been valuable if cheap to do. Yet, by the time it was scrapped, McNamara had estimated that Skybolt would have been a three-billion-dollar programme. And even then Skybolt failed to meet the require-ments of precision in targeting which were essential for a role of 'defence suppression'. In short, therefore, Skybolt was both unsuitable and unnecessary to American defence strategy. But the British Government simply refused to admit this. As Michael Howard remarked, 'Whitehall has been inexcusably naïve if it really expected the United States to develop at vast expense a weapon they no longer need, so that we could pursue a policy of which they disapprove. Loyalty to allies has its limits.'[7]

British Ministers still gave the impression that they were blissfully ignorant of the full meaning of this new-fangled term 'cost effectiveness', which was now the chief criterion in the American assessment of the value of every weapon. Terms like 'pre-emptive strike', 'second-strike capacity' and 'counter-city retaliation' meant little or nothing in London. Indeed, on more than one occasion, senior American officials felt compelled to reproach their British opposite numbers and remind them that defence really was a serious matter and not merely a political pawn. But the technical refinements about which the Americans were so concerned were largely irrelevant from the British point of view. Skybolt was for Britain a strategic weapon—the strategic weapon. The deterrent was a political instrument, and indeed at times the simplicity of defence thinking in London was akin to the Maginot-line mentality, which Kennedy had so forcefully attacked. What really matters, Ministers argued, is that we have the deterrent. Its effectiveness, or indeed its very credibility, were never seriously challenged.

American defence officials warned their colleagues not to put all their eggs in one basket, and this was sound advice within the framework in which the Americans were talking. It was even sounder advice in a different context, for when Skybolt was cancelled, as one British official remarked, 'there was no other egg and no other basket!'

But even as late as the spring of 1962 McNamara had taken no definite decision about Skybolt's future. Indeed, according to one of his colleagues, 'there was no thought in anybody's mind, certainly not in Mr McNamara's, that Skybolt wasn't going to work. It was an on-going programme and there was no reason to cast any doubts in Mr Watkinson's mind over the programme.' Watkinson certainly returned from his meeting with McNamara in May with no indication that Skybolt was in any kind of trouble. He was later to recall in the House that McNamara had asked him whether he could confirm the British order for Skybolt in terms of numbers. To Watkinson at least, that was hardly the way you speak to a customer when you're thinking of cancelling his order!

British Ministers have consistently argued that before November they were never told that Skybolt was in any kind of trouble and the American cancellation thus came as a bolt out of the sky! Principal American officials, however, are equally adamant that they kept their British colleagues as fully informed as possible about Skybolt's troubles. Certainly the problem of communication was made more difficult by the fact that different people were offering different progress reports according to their own points of view. Not surprisingly, the Douglas management tended to cloud over the difficulties Skybolt was experiencing. But the British Government, or at least the Defence Ministry, must have known about the troubles of the missile since they had two senior R.A.F. officers assigned to Douglas solely for the purpose of keeping the Government informed as to Skybolt's progress. The Government thus either did not understand, or alternatively refused to understand, the full significance of the warning signals they were receiving. Skybolt was so crucial to the validity of their policy that Ministers discounted the more alarmist reports they were getting, preferring instead to put their faith blindly in the optimism of the contractors and the American Air Force. The political implications looked so embarrassing that Ministers shied away from any debate perhaps in the hope that some sudden dramatic break-through would change the bleak outlook.

Hope, as Francis Bacon said, 'is a good breakfast, but it is a bad supper.' And, unfortunately for Macmillan, progress in this world is not made merely by optimism. Skybolt made precious little progress in the following months and, after spending a day and a half at the Douglas-Norfolk Plant in August, McNamara and Gilpatric came to the conclusion that Skybolt was in fact never going to work and ought to be abandoned. But again McNamara deferred a final decision on Skybolt's fate until October. Accordingly, he concluded that there was little point in casting any doubt about the project in the mind of the British Minister of Defence when he visited Washington in September 1962.

By this time, however, the Minister of Defence was Peter Thorneycroft, Watkinson having fallen victim in July to Macmillan's Night of the Long Knives. Thorneycroft was the complete opposite to Watkinson. Where the latter had few political pretensions, Thorneycroft was first and last a politician. A flamboyant, unpredictable personality, making a come-back to power and determined to make his mark, Thorneycroft represented a challenge of a different order for McNamara. Watkinson had always felt a bit out-gunned and out-smarted by the ruthless and efficient executive from General Motors, and it was widely believed that McNamara would similarly overpower Thorneycroft. But, though he never regarded the British Minister of Defence as his intellectual equal, McNamara was compelled to admit that Thorneycroft was a formidable character within his own frame of reference. Thorneycroft's own personality and ruthless ambition refused to allow him to be put on the defensive by McNamara. In their approach to defence it would in fact be difficult to find two more diverse characters. Where McNamara gave a primacy to quantitative analysis, Thorneycroft would give a primacy to instinctive political feel. Unfortunately, this was to bear quite considerably on the breakdown in communication over the Skybolt question. The two men quite simply were on different wave-lengths: McNamara looked at Skybolt from the American and NATO point of view, Thorneycroft viewed it primarily in the context of domestic politics.

When the two Defence Ministers met in September, McNamara refused to give more than guarded responses on Skybolt. He was wary of telling his opposite number that he was considering cancellation not least because he feared that through Thorneycroft the United States Air Force would get to hear and would then mobilise Congressional opinion for a last-ditch, and unpleasant, public battle. But, though Thorneycroft was later to insist that he had been given no indication that Skybolt was in any kind of trouble, the fact that there had already been four successive test failures of the missile must surely have been cause for anxious discussion in the smoke-rooms of Westminster.

McNamara had originally intended taking the final decision on Skybolt's future in October, but this had again to be deferred for two weeks when the Administration became preoccupied with its most severe test, the Cuban missile crisis. Skybolt, it seems, was the victim not only of its own shortcomings but also of time and circumstance. The exultation, bordering on euphoria, which followed in the wake of the Cuban crisis had its own place in the Skybolt story for when, on 7 November, the President, Rusk and McNamara met to discuss among other matters the future of Skybolt, they were much inclined to believe that they had been through the GREAT problem of their lives and that all problems thereafter were small. If there had not been a traumatic experience like the Cuban crisis, Skybolt would have seemed like a big problem. But it didn't. Golf was the order of the day, not (more) missiles.

Skybolt's fate had been brought to McNamara's attention at the end of October when he received a memorandum from the Budget Bureau Director, requesting his comments on Skybolt's place in the preparation of the forthcoming Budget. By 3 November, Thorneycroft had begun to smell a rat, and since John Rubel, the American Deputy Director of Defence Research and Engineering, happened to be in London, Thorneycroft decided it would be opportune to ask him about Skybolt's fate. But Rubel could not give Thorneycroft a definite answer; he did not know himself. The following day, as he was preparing to kill Skybolt, McNamara received an extraordinary telegram of congratulations from Thorneycroft. The British Minister gave the impression that he had understood Skybolt to have at last reached its production phase! In view of Rubel's uncertainty and the known difficulties of Skybolt, this explanation seems highly untenable, and Thorneycroft's telegram was probably less an expression of satisfaction than a subtle attempt to ferret out McNamara's true intentions.

The traditional intimacy and cordiality of Anglo-American relations was beginning to seem sadly absent.

McNamara's meeting with the President on 7 November reflects the almost complete failure of the Administration fully to appreciate the political consequences likely to result from their decision to cancel Skybolt. Indeed more attention was given to the developing crisis on the Indian-China border. The sense of relief after Cuba led McNamara to volunteer to see the Skybolt problem through, to which neither the President nor Rusk objected. This was, to say the least, a rather unusual way to conduct government business. Rusk merely warned that something ought to be done to ease the British position, which did not at the same time complicate relations with other NATO allies, and then deferred to McNamara an issue that should clearly have been the primary responsibility of the Secretary of State. Indeed Rusk's total lack of interest in Skybolt was such that he thought it more important to attend a diplomatic function in Washington than to go to the Nassau Conference: a decision that will mark him down in history as 'the man who went to dinner' when he should have been making the preservation of the Anglo-American alliance his total concern.

Rusk's acquiescence, however, was a reflection not merely of his lack of assertiveness as Secretary of State, but also of the general style of decision-taking under the Kennedy Administration. As one columnist remarked, 'President Kennedy left it to McNamara and Rusk didn't interfere—that's the way things were done in the Kennedy Administration.' Impatient with procedures, Kennedy preferred to rely on the individual brilliance of a few people. There tended to be immediate involvement at the top but little real study or appreciation of the detailed implications of decisions. At no time during the Skybolt story was there any real recognition of the fact that defence hardware decisions can and do carry major repercussions for foreign policy. It was, as a present government official put it, 'the most disorderly arrangement you've ever seen', the consequence of which was that the Administration at times spoke with more than one voice. Unfortunately for the British Government, this meant occasionally two contradictory voices. While McNamara was warning Thorneycroft to minimise the difficulties Skybolt was experiencing, his Secretary of the Air Force was confidently predicting the success of the venture. The British and North American (B.N.A.) desk inside the State Department almost alone assessed correctly the magnitude of the crisis for Macmillan but their memorandum never seems to have reached the President. No doubt a White House official concluded that they were biased anyway!

McNamara's willingness to see the Skybolt problem through was fully in keeping with his character. He was a man who believed in accepting responsibility for his own decisions. Skybolt, however, was now a political issue for which McNamara had neither training nor experience. Political acumen was never one of his cardinal virtues. Indeed he was a man with little political sensitivity or understanding of political communication. In consequence, in the ensuing weeks, he produced not arguments but figures, not gestures but a slide-rule. It was a reversion to his General Motors' approach, and as such was resented by the British Government.

McNamara saw Ormsby-Gore on 8 November and reviewed with the Ambassador the entire history of the Skybolt programme. While he emphasised that no definite decision had been taken, he clearly indicated that he was considering cancellation. The British Ambassador in turn told McNamara that any such decision would be absolute political dynamite in London, and he urged the Secretary to send a full memorandum to Thorneycroft. McNamara, however, had already decided that he would personally telephone Thorneycroft but that he would delay doing so to allow the Ambassador a chance to report back to his Government. Ormsby-Gore returned to his Embassy and dictated a long and sober telegram to London.

The following day, in his conversation with Thorneycroft, McNamara reiterated the points that he had made to the Ambassador. He also expressed a willingness to discuss possible solutions to the problem, though he took the view that any initiative must come from the British Government. Thorneycroft, like Ormsby-Gore, stressed the political repercussions for Anglo-American relations and insisted that any alternative weapon must carry the same degree of 'independence' that Skybolt would have had. Polaris certainly came up in the conversation but, if Thorneycroft was adamant later that he had asked for the submarine weapon, it was certainly not the kind of request that McNamara needed for his own bureaucratic purposes. Moreover, as one of Thorneycroft's colleagues recalled, 'he had certainly not written off Skybolt at that stage.'

The ensuing weeks witnessed a combination of uncertainty, distrust and complete confusion hitherto seen only during the Suez crisis. Washington, it seems, was waiting for London to make suggestions, London, it seems, was waiting for Washington to do the same. The Anglo-American alliance had reached a stange impasse! Members of the American Administration, however, have tended to 'pass the buck' to the British Government. As one official recalled, 'five weeks went by and they didn't say a word. That period could have been used.' It could indeed have been used. But, if the Macmillan Government had failed to realise until it was too late that Skybolt was only marginal in American terms, the Kennedy Administration had equally failed to comprehend the fact that the project was crucial in British terms. Ministers had warned their American colleagues of the political repercussions for Anglo-American relations: but not once had they really made clear that this was of secondary importance. It was the domestic and internal political consequences which most worried the British Government, and about which they had been silent.

1962 had been a disastrous year for Macmillan. His popularity had slumped badly. The 'Supermac' and 'Never Had It So Good' images were beginning to turn sour on him. His economic policy seemed in ruins, Selwyn Lloyd's infamous 'pay-pause' was unpopular, as was the British application to join the Common Market. One electoral humiliation followed another. The Tories lost Orpington to the Liberals in March and came an ignominious third in a bye-election at Leicester North-East in July. The following day the 'unflappable' Macmillan flapped! In a drastic measure to prevent the credibility of his Government waning further, he proceeded to axe a third of his Cabinet. But he was given little time to recover. The Cuban missile crisis provoked a heated debate as to the futility and impotence of British power in the world. Britain, it seemed, had been reduced to the position of an onlooker in a great international confrontation. What, the press asked, had the existence of the British deterrent done for the

Government over Cuba? For Macmillan there was no alternative but to defend his policy with renewed emphasis. In short, therefore, the political credibility of Macmillan's Government was waning at a time when it was relying more and more on the success of the Skybolt venture.

As a politician himself, Kennedy should have been more aware of the nature of Macmillan's problem. But he wasn't. Later he was to express astonishment that Macmillan had done nothing even though the life of his Government was at stake. But Kennedy's failure was itself important, especially since he alone had the authority to take the decision which the British Government most wanted. The President, however, felt that no-one had kept him properly informed of the developing crisis. 'Later Kennedy would wonder aloud why . . . Bruce . . . Ormsby-Gore, or Macmillan himself, or Rusk, or *someone*, had not warned both sides in advance of the storm?'[8] Bruce was aware of the political stakes involved but felt immobilised because he had received no instructions from the State Department. He had been informed about the proposed cancellation by Paul Nitze in an 'Eyes Only' telegram dated 12 November, which was the first such telegram he had ever received from any person other than the Secretary of State. He may even have concluded that at that stage the State Department itself was being kept in the dark.

Though he had almost unlimited access to the President, Ormsby-Gore, like Bruce, was blind as to what his own Government was thinking and, more important, doing. He sought clarification but none was forthcoming. One person close to the President has suggested that 'if Kennedy had really seen how serious this was, obviously different things would have happened.' Kennedy obviously thought, as another remarked, that 'if he had a good talk with Macmillan he could handle everything.' Clearly troubled by the lack of communication between the two governments, Macmillan himself wondered whether he should telephone Kennedy, but Ormsby-Gore advised against such action, erroneously assuming that the President was fully aware of the facts in the Skybolt story. Indeed, at no time during these intervening weeks was the Mac-Jack line used. If Macmillan was puzzled at what Kennedy was doing, Kennedy was equally to be surprised at Macmillan's apparent inaction. Both men seemed to think it unnecessary to remind each other of the stakes involved since both mistakenly assumed that this was already appreciated.

Ormsby-Gore was wrong in thinking that Kennedy was fully aware of the nature of the problem, but right in thinking that a telephone conversation between the two men would be of little value. The impasse in November was indeed due as much as anything else to the fact that neither government had at that stage made up its mind how it would play its hand and what it wanted or was prepared to offer. And while this uncertainty remained, charges of bad faith were inevitable.

In London Ministers went about their business as if nothing had happened. If the United States was going to cancel Skybolt, was it not up to the United States to make amends? Reluctant to be seen requesting an alternative, Ministers may have hoped that Kennedy would feel some moral obligation to compensate for Skybolt's cancellation. Their passive attitude seemed to reflect their (not unsound) conviction that any new deal was certain to be less advantageous to Britain than the Skybolt agreement which had cost Britain nothing. Ministers may also have hoped that by doing nothing, pressure would be put on Kennedy and McNamara to reverse their intentions. Perhaps they still mistakenly believed that the U.S.A.F. could force McNamara's hand. This of course was itself a reflection of the uncertainty surrounding Skybolt's viability. As one senior British defence official complained: 'If McNamara had said straight out, and proved, that Skybolt was a failure, that would have been the end of it. But he didn't.' Nor could he, for Skybolt was never convincingly proved a failure. It was cancelled not because it was technically impossible but because the Americans didn't want it. And, when this fact finally dawned in Britain, a hostile atmosphere had sprung up, since the American failure to propose a solution was interpreted in London as meaning that the Administration was making a determined effort to get Britain out of the nuclear business!

But London's failure to make proposals was, paradoxically, in part the Kennedy Administration's own fault. No full internal British debate was possible since, in both his meeting with Ormsby-Gore and in his conversation with Thorneycroft, McNamara had stressed that no final American decision had yet been taken. The American Joint Chiefs of Staff had still to make their recommendation, which they did on 20 November, and which, to no-one's surprise, was in favour of continuing Skybolt. McNamara had assured Thorneycroft that a definite decision would be taken between 23 November and 10 December, the latter being the last date beyond which McNamara considered leaks to the press unavoidable. He was obviously conscious of the need to prevent Skybolt developing prematurely into a major row. But, as so often happens in politics, he failed to heed his own advice. He had told Thorneycroft that he would come to London as soon as a government decision had been taken—which happened on 23 November at Kennedy's summer retreat in Hyannisport. Yet McNamara did not in fact come to London until 11 December, by which time the press had of course already learnt of the American intention to kill Skybolt. McNamara had committed a grave blunder—he had forgotten his own leak deadline! The atmosphere between London and Washington had become electric. Ministers began to suspect the worst. They even wondered whether Dean Acheson's ill-mannered public outburst in early December had been officially inspired. Such an atmosphere of tension was hardly conducive, at least from the American viewpoint, to sensible negotiation.

There was no doubt in McNamara's mind that Skybolt ought to be dropped and that something ought to be done to help Britain. But he was far from sure in early November, when he talked to Thorneycroft, that he was going to win the battle within the Administration either for getting Skybolt cancelled or, if that was accepted, for providing Britain with an alternative weapon. It may not have been very determined policy of the Kennedy Administration to end the 'nuclear special relationship' with Britain, but then neither was it very clear policy. The tragedy of the Skybolt story was that the internal battle within the Administration prevented any policy at all emerging until it was too late.

Though the State Department never really got into the act, a number of officials at the European desk and in the Policy Planning Group were sufficiently influential to obstruct the only meaningful solution to the problem, namely the offer of Polaris to Britain. McNamara knew Polaris alone would satisfy the British, and, in their heart of hearts, the Europeanists knew this too. But they refused to face the realities of the situation. Later to be somewhat irreverently referred to as 'theologians', these conceptualists, who included in their number George Ball, Walt Rostow, Bob Bowie and Henry Owen, all of whom approached foreign policy from a long-term theoretical perspective, saw in the Skybolt cancellation the opportunity to reassess American European policy. An essential prerequisite for the restoration of Franco-American relations, as they saw it, was the ending of the favouritism towards Britain. 'No wonder De Gaulle is annoyed with America', they argued 'when we continue the anomaly of a "nuclear special relationship" with Britain.' But, as usually happened with their arguments, the conceptualists failed to take account of the political landscape. It was a landscape which included a France which, irrespective of American gestures, was determined to be unilateral; a West Germany which was so politically dependent on the United States; and a Britain where it was known that, when Labour came to power, ideas of unilateral disarmament would be discreetly but promptly shelved. Nevertheless, deeply distressed at the possibility that Britain would be offered Polaris, the conceptualists met Henry Rowen of the Defence Department to plan their strategy, ironically on the same day that Kennedy and McNamara were meeting at Hyannisport to decide what to do for Britain. As a result of the meeting between the conceptualists and Rowen, which took place in the State Department, a letter was drafted which, with only minor alteration, Rusk signed on 24 November. It was in effect a letter of instruction to McNamara which clearly put limits on what he could offer Britain when he saw Thorneycroft in London. He could offer Hounddog. He could even propose compensation terms for the cancellation of Skybolt. But on no account was he to offer Polaris to Thorneycroft. Bowie was particularly insistent that the American Government must now be firm with Macmillan: 'If the Tory Government falls, let it fall!', he declared, convinced that if Kennedy stood firm, Macmillan would not be obstinate. Certainly McNamara gave no indication to Thorneycroft, when they met in London in December, why he was unable to offer Polaris.

McNamara's decision to cancel Skybolt was logical from the American standpoint, but it was a disaster for the British Government. The error in the American judgement lay not in its internal logic but in its external impact. No one in the Administration felt that this would develop into a major political crisis. No attempt was made to look at the matter from the British point of view. If such an attempt had been made perhaps the Administration would have realised that the British Government was hoping for a generous gesture from the Americans, which, more importantly, was seen to come from the Americans. But no such gesture was forthcoming.

The British Government was certainly reluctant to be seen asking for something from the Americans. But Macmillan and Thorneycroft also had good reasons for at least not appearing to be deeply involved in an internal debate. Aside from the possibility that the Government itself might fall on the issue, the personal positions of both the Prime Minister and the Minister of Defence were far from secure at this stage. Thorneycroft, in particular, never deceived himself as to the fact that his own political ambition depended upon the successful outcome of the Skybolt problem. He could ill afford to be seen an advocate for abandoning Skybolt especially since he had been warned, not told, of the imminent cancellation. He was clearly unwilling to take a stand which, in the light of his earlier position, made him appear as an ally of Zuckerman's, a long standing critic of the project. Furthermore he may well have foreseen the likelihood of inter-service rivalry in which he would eventually have the unpleasant task of arbitrating. Just as Thorneycroft was wrong in thinking McNamara had the power to put forward Polaris as an alternative to Skybolt, so McNamara was wrong in believing that, like himself, Thorneycroft could dominate his Chiefs of Staff. Perhaps the greatest blunder that Thorneycroft and McNamara committed, in a whole chain of blunders, was in allowing the two Air Forces to scheme together. Both the R.A.F. and the U.S.A.F. had vested interests in maintaining the Skybolt programme, and as a consequence they struck up an alliance whereby each helped the other to exert pressure on their respective governments. McNamara's and Thorneycroft's reluctance to keep open the channels of communication for fear of leaks merely, and tragically, sustained the already-held misconceptions about each government's intentions and actions. Men, said Richard Neustadt, 'reasoned [about each other] and thereupon perceived what they projected!'[9]

Meanwhile, miscalculations fed on each other. With no evidence of special concern from London, Washington concluded that Skybolt did not demand their exclusive attention. Only cursory, and somewhat frivolous, mention was made of it at a defence policy conference at the end of November. And, when the Nassau Conference was announced, Skybolt was not even on the agenda for discussion! It was to be just another of the informal Mac-Jack meetings to review world affairs. There was nothing newsworthy in that, or so it seemed.

A fifth successive test failure of Skybolt miraculously escaped the attention of the press but fearful that the issue would mushroom prematurely into a political crisis, McNamara on 29 November granted a further $20 million to Douglas Aircraft for the development of Skybolt. The project, the British Secretary of the Air, Hugh Fraser, told the House, was still proceeding as far as the British Government was concerned.

But McNamara's luck could not last and it didn't. Rumours began to spread about Skybolt's fate: one British correspondent claimed that he had been given a deliberate tip-off by the State Department; one American newspaper claimed that the leak had emanated from British official sources. In probability, it was neither. The press was just too good at its job for Skybolt to remain out of the public eye any longer. More astonishing is that the press didn't pick up the clues sooner. Charges and counter-charges were rife and the Thorneycroft-McNamara meeting thus assumed great importance. Unfortunately, their meeting on 11 December was, as Arthur Schlesinger put it, 'a Pinero drama of misunderstanding: Thorneycroft expecting McNamara to propose Polaris, McNamara expecting Thorneycroft to request it.'[10]

The atmosphere was disconcertingly cool. McNamara began with a detailed explanation of Skybolt's technical shortcomings, based on a short paper which he had presented to Thorneycroft before the meeting. 'It is clear', he said, 'that on balance to carry on with Skybolt would be an unsound use of American resources.' Thorneycroft, however, quickly dismissed the technical and budgetary arguments which McNamara was putting forward. 'One can find', he said, 'experts who can provide convincing arguments both for and against Skybolt.' He was much more interested in discussing the political implications of McNamara's decision.

Thorneycroft developed his theme with both eloquence and emotion. He recalled that, whether intentional or not, McNamara had given the impression, particularly in his speech at Ann Arbor, that he was critical of the British deterrent. 'It is American good faith that is in question,' Thorneycroft said. If McNamara did not seek to deprive Britain of her deterrent, would he be prepared not only to help Britain maintain it, but to say so publicly? It was indeed a blunt discourse from Thorneycroft, but not wholly unexpected. He did not mince words with diplomatic niceties. Unfortunately, it was what McNamara had neither expected nor hoped for. He had come to London to find a technical way of helping the British Government out of its political dilemma. He did not know how to handle a political negotiation. He thus sought hurriedly to steer the conversation back to the technical possibilities. 'If the British Government would like to continue Skybolt,' he said, 'I will be willing not only to hand over all the development work so far conducted, without any charge, but will also consider a contribution in the order of $30 million to counter any charge of American bad faith.' Made a month or so earlier this might have seemed a generous offer. But not now, not to Thorneycroft. But Hounddog was the only other weapon which McNamara was instructed to offer and Thorneycroft dismissed that with equal contempt. He was playing for high stakes. 'I think Polaris is the only conceivable weapon for Britain,' he said. The ball was well and truly in McNamara's court, but unfortunately he had no racket!

Clearly unwilling to tell Thorneycroft why he was in no position to offer Polaris, McNamara merely pointed out the technical and legal problems involved. What would be the political repercussions in Europe, he enquired, if Britain were to be given such an advanced weapons system? Cautiously, he asked whether the British Government, if offered Polaris, would be prepared to commit such a force to the multi-lateral concept. 'That', replied Thorneycroft, 'is for Britain to decide as an independent nation.' Since little else could be achieved, the meeting broke up with McNamara promising to provide the British Government with more information about the submarine missile.

The London evening papers produced that night sensational headlines depicting the proceedings of the Thorneycroft–McNamara confrontation. Thorneycroft was portrayed as the steadfast British lion bravely resisting Uncle Sam's shackles! Such stories, McNamara was later to believe, had been deliberately inspired by Thorneycroft, and he never forgave the British Minister for what he considered was a leak deliberately designed to provoke a crisis atmosphere. On the surface, however, there seemed no necessity for such a leak, since the clues were there for the press to pick up. Indeed McNamara had himself, on his arrival at London airport, somewhat imprudently drawn the attention of the press to the fact that there had been five successive test failures of the Skybolt missile. Thorneycroft, however, was much cleverer than McNamara ever really gave him credit for. He knew of the pressure inside the State Department for ending the nuclear special relationship, even though he probably only realised for the first time after his meeting with McNamara that the United States was not putting up any alternative to Skybolt that would satisfy the British Government. He may well thus have concluded that it was now necessary to provoke a crisis, both to obtain Polaris and also to ensure his own political position was not harmed. He was fully conscious of the fact that his political reputation would be in danger and that he would have 'to eat' his words in Parliament when the cancellation of Skybolt became general knowledge. If, however, in the end he appeared to have 'won' Polaris, or at least to have defeated the pressure within the American Administration not to help Britain, his political prestige would have suffered little and may indeed have been enhanced. That Thorneycroft deliberately provoked a crisis atmosphere is certainly the view of some officials in the State Department. As one of them put it 'the thing was whipped up into a crisis on purpose by Thorneycroft and Macmillan. Thorneycroft didn't want to have the issue discussed at lower levels.' In itself hardly surprising, given the degree of American opposition to any Polaris arrangement. A crisis atmosphere would, Thorneycroft surmised, necessitate the President's intervention, and was he not friendly with Macmillan? Moreover, the inevitable inference of bad faith would put pressure on Kennedy to help the British Government. Certainly surprise was used as a bargaining counter at Nassau.

The fact that Skybolt had now developed into a major political crisis may well in its own way have suited Macmillan. It is not inconceivable that, had they been asked, a majority of the Cabinet would not have been prepared to retain the 'independent' deterrent at the cost involved. For Macmillan this was not only a domestic political problem, nor merely a party political problem, but also an internal government problem. As it turned out, at Nassau Macmillan was able to present his Cabinet with what was in effect a *fait accompli*. As one of his Cabinet colleagues recalled, 'We were told "take it or leave it", we had to accept it.' Finally, like Thorneycroft, Macmillan probably concluded—and in this he was right—that he could gain more by crying on the shoulder of a brother politician. A crisis atmosphere meant that, although there were further discussions between McNamara and Thorneycroft in Paris, no final decision could be taken until Kennedy and Macmillan had their meeting in the Bahamas. The Nassau meeting was to be anything but an informal Mac-Jack get-together, and indeed was to be one of the great confrontations in the history of Anglo-American relations.

1. Henry Brandon, *The Sunday Times* (8 December 1963).
2. Hearings before a sub-committee of the Committee on Appropriations, The Department of Defence Appropriations for 1964 (7 February 1963).
3. *The Daily Express* (3 June 1960).
4. Ronald Steel, 'Britain and Europe: The Lesson of Skybolt', *Commonweal* (8 February 1963).
5. Arthur Schlesinger Jr., *A Thousand Days* (André Deutsch, 1965), pp.285-6.
6. See Note 2 above.
7. Michael Howard, *The Sunday Times* (23 December 1962).
8. Theodore Sorensen, *Kennedy* (Hodder & Stoughton, 1965), p.565.
9. Richard Neustadt, *Alliance Politics* (Columbia University Press, 1970), p.69.
10. Arthur Schlesinger Jr., *op. cit.* p.734.

I I

The Nassau Conference

It was pleasantly warm, serene and picturesque: in fact, Nassau was at its most attractive and appealing when Macmillan's Air Force plane landed on 18 December. Unfortunately, Macmillan was in no mood to enjoy the Caribbean sunshine. He was depressed and desperately tired. The weight of years was beginning to take its toll. He had spent much of the flight reading about the decline of the Roman Empire. Had the time now come, he perhaps wondered, when he should himself declare before history that his act was ended? Gone was the vigour and dynamism which had characterised the earlier years of his Premiership. He had already been Prime Minister for nearly six years, in itself no mean achievement for a man who had been convinced that his administration could not survive six weeks! His time was drawing to an end but it did not now seem possible that he could make a dignified exit, which is of course every politician's last wish. He had been so badly mauled by his critics. What had gone wrong? Like every politician, he had suffered setbacks but these he had been able to overcome. Yet, in December 1962, he seemed to be the unfortunate victim of the combined assault of events and their repercussions. How had Skybolt been allowed to develop into a major political crisis? Why hadn't Kennedy, his friend, intervened? Something had to be worked out at Nassau. Everything depended upon it—the future of the Anglo-American alliance, which he had cherished for so long, the future of the Conservative Administration, the future of Macmillan himself.

Macmillan's mind may have wandered back to a couple of

days before when he had met General De Gaulle in the drizzle at Rambouillet. The meeting had not gone well. Indeed it had been as chilly as the weather. The General's mood had changed since their last meeting at Champs in June. Macmillan now confronted a man with towering self-confidence. The Algerian war was behind him. The November elections had strengthened his hand, and the French people had welcomed the opportunity of establishing a direct relationship between themselves and their President. De Gaulle seemed almost to revel in his own triumph. He now had more freedom to pursue his true diplomatic objectives. Britain, he had told Macmillan, does not really belong to the Common Market: 'Would it not be better for you to apply for associate rather than full membership to the Community?' If this really was a hint of what was to come—and what else could it have been?—Macmillan never really took it. In fact he had been tempted to walk out on the General after the first day, but stayed only to try to impress upon De Gaulle that his one aim at the forthcoming Nassau Conference was to find a means to preserve the independent British deterrent. He did not mention the European deterrent but he indicated that once Britain was a member of the Community he would obviously consider the possibilities of political and military co-operation. It was typical of Macmillan's diplomacy: he dangled the carrot. Unfortunately for Macmillan, De Gaulle was to take exception to the Nassau Agreement not because Britain had succeeded in preserving her independence but because, in his view, she had lost it!

Macmillan had told De Gaulle that his aim was to preserve the independent British deterrent but he was far from optimistic that he could achieve this as he left for the Nassau Conference. There was a feeling of bitter indignation towards the Americans for allowing the crisis to develop. And there was little comfort for Macmillan when he arrived at Nassau, for, at the airport, he learnt for the first time of President Kennedy's scathing remarks about Skybolt on American television the previous evening. In answer to a question, Kennedy saw no point in spending two and a half billion dollars on Skybolt's development when 'we don't think we are going to get two and a half billion dollars' worth of national security.' Here was another case, said the President, where the British were simply going to reap the rewards of American labours.

Macmillan was both surprised and upset that the Americans had not considered it of sufficient importance to inform the British delegation officially of Kennedy's speech. He had already been somewhat annoyed at remarks made by MacGeorge Bundy, the President's National Security Adviser, on American television's 'Meet the Press'. In his inimitable way, Bundy had refused to disclose the American hand in advance of the Nassau Conference, merely stressing that, while Skybolt posed the necessity of deciding how Britain and the United States conduct their affairs with each other, any agreement reached must 'not entangle our relations with the great countries of the Continent.'

Macmillan's precarious political position at home, the complete uncertainty as to how the Nassau Conference might end, and the indignation provoked by the ill-timed comments of the President and Bundy combined to produce a resentment and suspicion of American intentions unique to Anglo-American meetings. The conference seemed destined to be more of a confrontation. The atmosphere was tense, as one principal recalled, 'because for the first time we were competing.' When Macmillan welcomed Kennedy on his arrival at the airport, their meeting seemed unusually cool, stiff and stylised. There appeared something absurdly significant in the fact that, as the President reviewed the guard of honour, the band played 'Early One Morning'. Its refrain 'Oh, don't deceive me/Oh, never leave me'—seemed almost to give expression to Macmillan's own private thoughts!

In striking contrast to Macmillan's almost pathological concern that a solution be found to the immediate problem, the American delegation gave the impression that they simply were not interested in either the Nassau Conference or its outcome. Indeed, at his first press briefing, Pierre Salinger, the President's Press Secretary, let it be known that Kennedy was much more interested in discussing the Katanga crisis than in solving the Skybolt question. As a professional politician, Kennedy of course knew that Skybolt was what really concerned Macmillan and, in his own little mischievous way, Salinger was making things beastly for the British! But there were other reasons for Kennedy's apparent lack of interest and his early reluctance to offer Polaris, a much more advanced system, to Britain. He had in fact already considered the possibility of relating such an offer to a British commitment to

integrate any Polaris force within NATO. But, if the conceptualists were unrealistic in their attitude, Kennedy could not totally
ignore their representations and, in the days leading up to the
Nassau Conference, the battle lines had been forming in Washington. Some of the conceptualists were chiefly concerned about the
M.L.F., others about the British application to join the Common
Market. But, since it now appeared that both were in danger, the
two groups joined forces in a last-ditch attempt to prevent a
Polaris offer to Britain. William Tyler, the head of the European
desk, and George Ball, the Under Secretary of State, presented
their case in a debate before the President, impressing upon him
the disastrous consequences, as they saw it, of any Polaris deal
with Macmillan. Walt Rostow, the highly articulate Chief of the
Policy Planning Group, made an impassioned plea that here was an
historic opportunity to close the door on the British deterrent.
Kennedy knew that he would eventually be compelled to arbitrate
between the irreconcilable positions of the conceptualists and those
in his Administration, including Bundy, whose judgement was
that not to help Britain would be even more damaging to the
President's European policy. This internal battle was of course
later to crystallise over the M.L.F. debate. But, in displaying at
Nassau a lack of interest in its outcome and a reluctance to make
an early offer of Polaris the President was at least recognising that
the conceptualists had a valid case.

The President had invited Sir David Ormsby-Gore to join him
in the presidential plane for the flight to Nassau, and the two
friends very quickly got down to a long discussion on the Skybolt
question. The Ambassador warned Kennedy of the likely wave of
anti-Americanism in Britain if he were suspected of wanting to
deprive Britain of her 'independent' deterrent. In less than half
an hour, the two men had worked out a proposal whereby the
Americans would abandon the missile for their own use but they
would split the future development costs of Skybolt evenly with
the British Government. It may have been that the failure to
exchange papers in advance of the conference meant that the
Ambassador was still under the impression that the British
Government wanted Skybolt after all. But it was more likely a
proposal worked out for reasons of internal American politics.
Though it was a generous offer, the cost involved in continuing

Skybolt solely for the British would still have been prohibitive. Besides, Kennedy's television remarks had destroyed any lingering interest Macmillan might have had in Skybolt. 'The lady has been violated in public,' he later told Kennedy. Very soon after their arrival at Nassau, Macmillan and his Private Secretary, Philip de Zulueta, let it be known that they were only interested in Polaris. And, when he visited Kennedy's bungalow that first night, Macmillan reiterated this point, insisting that Polaris must be given under conditions that would preserve the credibility of his Government's deterrent policy.

The formal talks opened the following morning in a tense atmosphere. Since the meeting had orginally been scheduled for a review of world problems, the two leaders discussed briefly, and essentially with agreement, the questions of Katanga, India and the test-ban treaty. But Skybolt very quickly became the central issue of the conference and, in retrospect, it proved to be one of Macmillan's finest hours. He was at his most eloquent and emotional and his skilful presentation of his case greatly impressed the American delegation. 'I never realised until Nassau', recalled one official, 'how sentimental Macmillan was.' Kennedy was moved by the articulation, phraseology, and historical perspective of the British Prime Minister. Indeed, one American principal believed that 'had Macmillan talked to the British people as he talked to us at Nassau he could have sold the Common Market to them.' Macmillan was no Churchill orator, but his was the rare ability to captivate his audience and impress upon them his sincerity, with seemingly mere changes in the inflection of his voice. When the situation demanded, Macmillan could be a master of the dramatic crescendo, and he used this with effect at Nassau, faced as he was with one of the severest challenges of his political career. He opened almost as a Mark Antony—admittedly, with muffled pathos—giving the funeral oration. As Henry Brandon remarked, 'even some of Antony's lines would have fitted'.[1] Macmillan had come to Nassau to bury Skybolt not to praise it!

Macmillan began by invoking all the past glories of the Anglo-American alliance. He looked back with pride on the days when Britain had truly been a world power, and how together with the United States, in two world wars, she had fought to make the world 'safe for democracy'. His memory, after all, stretched back further than anybody else's in the room, and his recollections of Paschendaele and of Casablanca gave him enormous authority. He had seen much of history in the making. He reminded the President of Britain's invaluable contribution to the development of the first atomic bomb and of how, in the spirit of complete friendship and trust, Churchill had willingly agreed to all the research being carried out in the United States. The passing of the MacMahon Act had understandably upset the British Government, he said, but had not he and his wartime friend and colleague, Eisenhower, restored the special relationship after the Suez débâcle? Reviewing the history of the Skybolt agreement, Macmillan recalled the understanding he had reached with Eisenhower over the American Polaris base at Holy Loch. 'That had been politically embarrassing for me,' he said, 'but I welcomed the American presence in Britain.' Macmillan, at least, was not one to welch on agreements.

Macmillan then proceeded to dismiss all the arguments put forward against a straight switch from Skybolt to Polaris. William Tyler had suggested that a joint study group be set up to look at the problem and report back to Kennedy and Macmillan by 20 January at the latest. This was a proposal which gained powerful support from George Ball, who was anxious that any decision at Nassau should not irritate the General. But it was a proposal which Macmillan rejected. A solution, he argued, must be found at this conference. Besides, he rejected the argument that a Polaris deal would complicate the British application to join the Common Market. Had he not seen the General only a few days before at Rambouillet and had not the General appeared sympathetic on the issue of the deterrent? 'No, agriculture is the stumbling block there,' he said, 'not the nuclear special relationship.' And as far as other European countries are concerned, Macmillan could not see any reason why they should be annoyed at preferential treatment being extended to Britain. 'They know of our unique contribution in the nuclear field and they will understand.' He then sought to impress upon the President that there was no contradiction between the concepts of national independence and multilateral interdependence; indeed, he said, a means must be found to provide for both. As to Polaris being a different missile system, the only difference from Skybolt, as Macmillan saw it, was that one was fired from the sea, the other from the air! It was a superb performance by Macmillan, a professional presentation of his case of which the late Foster Dulles would have been proud. Fighting for his own survival, and for the preservation of the Anglo-American alliance, Macmillan demonstrated another side of his character: this was not the languid, urbane, 'never had it so good' Macmillan. It was a testier amd more stubborn character than Kennedy had previously encountered. For Macmillan, the central issue of the Skybolt debate was the possible consequence for Anglo-American relations if the President were suspected of wanting to deprive Britain of her independent deterrent.

Kennedy, however, sought to fight off the political arguments. He was under pressure from within his own delegation not to allow himself to be swayed by Macmillan's eloquence. 'The decision to cancel Skybolt', he said, 'has been taken on technical grounds, and it is not my fault that there have been political repercussions in Britain.' Since he was convinced that Skybolt was a technical failure, the President refused to countenance a proposal put forward by Gilpatric to budget for Skybolt for a further six months. Besides, said the President, was he not offering favourable alternatives? He then brought up the proposal he had worked out with the British Ambassador on the plane down to Nassau. But it was too late, now, for his own remarks on television had signed the death warrant of Skybolt. The President then suggested that Hounddog might be a possible replacement. The fact that it was technically very difficult, if not impossible, to have adapted the V-bomber to take Hounddog was largely immaterial. It was never meant to be a very serious alternative. The President had at least exhausted all the possibilities before bringing up Polaris. And even when he discussed Polaris, Kennedy reminded Macmillan of his administration's commitment both to a policy of multilateralism and also to the prevention of the proliferation of nuclear weapons. This really brought the two leaders to the heart of the problem: the future of the independent British deterrent.

More eloquent than ever, Macmillan insisted that Britain was going to stay in the nuclear club. 'Britain', he said, 'has had a great history and is not about to give up now.' If the United States refuses to help Britain, then we must carry on our own programmes, 'whatever the cost'. Britain certainly had the technical capability to have developed her own deterrent programme but the high cost involved would have made more likely the possibility of Anglo-French nuclear co-operation. Perhaps one of the ironic quips of history is that, had Britain not been offered Polaris, she would, likely as not, have been allowed to enter the Common Market much earlier!

'We have gone a long way in this nuclear business,' Macmillan went on, 'but if we cannot agree, let us not patch up a compromise. Let us agree to part as friends.' Like Thorneycroft, he was playing for high stakes. He painted the future of Anglo-American relations in gloomy colours. For her part, Britain would not welch on any past agreements honourably made with the United States. The Polaris base at Holy Loch could remain. The missile early-warning system at Fylingdales could remain. The bomber bases could remain. But it seemed odd to Macmillan that Britain had been exposed to possible nuclear annihilation by the presence of these bases, yet now the President was proposing that Britain be allowed to continue to run these risks without being able to exercise any of the powers.

Macmillan warned of further consequences. 'It is possible', he said, 'that my Government will fall on this issue', and did the President really want to be held responsible for this? 'If the United States fails to help Britain,' he said, 'public opinion, fickle as it is, will inevitably become anti-American.' This would lead, he argued, to the assumption of power of a more neutralist group from within either of the two major political parties. Indeed Macmillan hinted that it was not inconceivable that his own party might accept an anti-American platform in order to retain power. It was 'not a threat: it was a lamentation.'[2]

Kennedy had been reluctant to consider an unconditional offer of Polaris. But the kind of break with London which Macmillan envisaged was something that he had neither contemplated nor was prepared to face on the issue of an 'irrevocable' commitment of British force to NATO. Friendship with Britain was valued highly in view of Kennedy's inability to establish a close rapport with his other major allies. As Dean Rusk later remarked, 'We can't break with Britain. We have to be able to discuss world problems with someone. We can't discuss them with De Gaulle. We and the British don't always agree. But we discuss.'[3] Macmillan's agony seemed also to be Kennedy's.

Though it was known that a Labour Government would not be fundamentally anti-American—indeed Kennedy had a genuine affection for Hugh Gaitskell—the President was clearly unwilling to be held accountable for the collapse of the Macmillan Government. Moreover, this was something that genuinely he did not want to see happen. He had developed a warm liking for Macmillan, a brother politician whom he sincerely wanted to help out of his unenviable predicament. With his shrewd political judgement, and with his attention now focused exclusively on the matter at hand, Kennedy soon realised that it was essential to find a solution which was acceptable and honourable to both governments. He accepted that, viewing the problem from the British point of view, the United States might be considered to be under a moral obligation to put forward a satisfactory alternative. After all, there had been precious little of 'the prior consultation' which had been stipulated under the original Skybolt agreement. Moreover, Kennedy was not unaware of the growing criticism at home of American treatment of Britain. *The Washington Post* had reprimanded his Administration for its failure to show greater concern for America's 'closest and best ally'; and *The New York Herald Tribune* had complained of the 'inexplicable show of discourtesy' in suggesting that if the British Government did not like the way things were done, then they ought to take charge themselves. The President knew that such criticism could dangerously snowball. He was becoming increasingly conscious that American good faith was being challenged, and he was well aware of the disturbing effect that an apparent disregard for the policy and interests of a close ally might have on America's other allies.

Kennedy thus came to the conclusion, at least by the end of the first day if not before, that Polaris alone would satisfy the British Government. He then sought to steer his delegation towards a formula based on Polaris. The question remaining was how to reconcile this with the claims of multi-lateralism and European Partnership. Fortunately, Macmillan now appreciated Kennedy's predicament. He had suggested earlier that he would be willing to commit a British Polaris force to NATO provided he retain the right to withdraw it in the event of a national emergency. This, it seemed, was enough to sustain the credibility of the Government's policy. A formula was thus found which would allow Macmillan to claim that he had saved the British deterrent but which did not openly contradict multi-lateralism.

But national independence, as De Gaulle claimed, was to a certain extent incompatible with multi-lateral interdependence. No doubt in recognition of this inherent contradiction, the Nassau Agreement itself was drafted in masterly ambiguity. It was certainly, as one American principal recalled, 'the worst drafted language anyone had ever seen!' Misunderstandings later arose both over the expected British contribution towards the research costs of Polaris and also on the degree of commitment made by Britain to the M.L.F. concept. Article 6 of the Statement on Nuclear Defence Systems contemplated the formation of a NATO multi-national force—that is, the pooling of national nuclear forces under a single NATO command. Article 7 pledged both governments to strive towards the creation of a multi-lateral force—that is, a mixed-manned force, indistinguishable in terms of national elements. And Article 8 agreed that a British Polaris force, supplied by the United States (though of course without warheads), might be included in either a multi-national or a multi-lateral force! The ambiguity in these clauses, compounded by the similarity of names, lead to bitter disagreement in 1963. It may be that in their haste to announce an agreement the two delegations did not give enough thought to the significance of the commitments they were making: the ambiguity may indeed have been deliberate. Certainly, with both Kennedy and Macmillan facing strong domestic opposition to the agreement, neither had any real incentive to clear up the ambiguities.

For Macmillan, the Nassau Agreement was the best solution to a difficult and embarrassing problem. If in fact such a compromise could only have been reached in the heat of a crisis, then the Nassau Agreement could almost have been considered a victory for Macmillan. But he was too badly wounded politically to have a success like Nassau judged fairly. Almost everybody in Britain had some objection to the agreement. Tory M.P.s bewailed what they depicted as an American thrust at Britain's great-power status. The Labour Opposition was equally critical of an arrangement that would still tend to keep Britain in the nuclear business— a criticism which had more electoral than factual foundation. Macmillan was mauled by the Press. One paper called the agreement a 'sell-out', another referred to the emergency escape clause as 'a paper-concession'. Polaris, it seemed, was to be the Non-British Dependent Nuclear Non-Deterrent! Millions of pounds were being spent, or so it was argued, to allow Conservative Members to 'pretend' that Britain was more independent than she actually was. After all his efforts, which had exhausted him both physically and mentally, Macmillan may have been justified in believing that politics can be a cruel experience!

For Kennedy, the Nassau Agreement was a reasonable adjustment to an awkward problem, a solution which he hoped would still allow enough freedom for him to pursue his European policy in a number of directions. But it was a bitter defeat for the conceptualists within his Administration, who sought thereafter to fight for the M.L.F. with renewed determination. George Ball even tried at one stage to buy back the Polaris missiles from Britain! Ironically, the conceptualist approach was unrealistic in all but one respect: the Nassau Agreement did infuriate De Gaulle. Conscious of a possible adverse reaction from the French President, Kennedy had insisted that Polaris be offered to France on the same terms as to Britain, a proposal with which Macmillan apparently acquiesced. Kennedy and Macmillan even briefly considered going to see De Gaulle about such an offer but they quickly dismissed the idea. It would anyway have made no difference. The General was much upset. Three weeks later, the Elysée Palace shook with his three-pronged reply to Kennedy's offer: it was NON to Polaris, NON to British entry into the Common Market, and, above all, NON to the Grand Design.

1. Henry Brandon, *The Sunday Times* (8 December 1963).
2. Arthur Schlesinger Jr., *A Thousand Days* (André Deutsch, 1965), p.737.
3. Quoted in Robert Kleiman, *Atlantic Crisis* (Norton, 1964), p.55.

12
Kennedy and the British Application to Join the Common Market

On 14 January 1963, in his State of The Union Address, President Kennedy told Congress, 'Free Europe is entering into a new phase of its long and brilliant history . . . moving towards a unity of purpose and power and policy in every sphere of activity.' Yet on that very same day thousands of miles away, in Paris, General De Gaulle expounded his own philosophy of exactly what the new phase in unity entailed. In one of his twice yearly News Conferences, he spoke disparagingly of the British application to join the European Economic Community. Britain had, he said, 'requested membership but on its own conditions.' With British entry into the Common Market therefore, he went on, it was entirely foreseeable that its cohesion 'would not hold for long and that in the end there would appear a colossal Atlantic Community under American dependence and leadership which would soon completely swallow up the European Community.' At one stroke, the General had effectively vetoed the British application: at one stroke, Britain's bid had been wrecked by the blind obstinacy of one man and his arrogant ambition to see France dominate Europe. The high hopes of many, and none more than Kennedy and Macmillan, had been thwarted by the political designs and machinations of the French President. It was a unilateral action which Macmillan described as 'bad for us, bad for Europe and bad for the whole free world'. As he said on British television, 'A great opportunity has been missed and it's no good trying to minimise or disguise that fact. What's happened in the last few weeks has revealed really a fundamental division of purpose.

I hate saying it but France, or any rate France's government, is looking backwards. They seem to think that one nation can dominate Europe or perhaps even one man—that's all wrong.'

Coming as it did within three weeks of the conclusion of the Nassau Agreement led many commentators, and especially the French themselves, to suggest a direct, if not natural, relationship between the two momentous events. Frenchmen certainly made much of the fact that Britain had been unable to reach agreement with the Common Market after sixteen months of negotiation: yet she could conclude a major defence pact with the Americans in less than three days! De Gaulle was himself careful in his Press Conference not to link the veto with the Nassau Agreement; yet, in informal remarks at a reception for National Assembly deputies, he suggested that 'England has turned over to the Americans what meagre atomic forces she had. She could have turned them over to Europe. Well, she has made her choice.' Politely, but nonetheless firmly, Macmillan had, at both Champs in June and at Rambouillet in December, turned down any suggestion of a European or Anglo-French nuclear deal. And how could Britain, De Gaulle argued, enter a political union with Europe now but keep out her nuclear deterrent until 1980 at the earliest? A forceful argument, but if it was in part justified, and if the nuclear issue did play a critical role in the British application, it did not do so in the way that the General was to intimate!

The very brutality and timing of the French veto left the impression that De Gaulle's decision had been perhaps a momentary flight of anger, an act of impulse. The reasons put forward for such a decision were numerous: Kennedy's offer of Polaris, the Nassau Agreement itself, some even deriving from the treatment accorded the General by 'Les Anglo-Saxons' during the War. Certainly both the Polaris offer and the Nassau Agreement infuriated De Gaulle. Nassau seems to have dispelled any lingering doubts he might by that time still have held as to Britain's unfitness to be associated with his own design for Europe. Even if it did so reflect signs of hasty improvisation and high-level imprecision, the Nassau Agreement nevertheless meant that Britain had concluded a major treaty with America without having undertaken more than cursory consultation with France. Had Britain treated France with greater courtesy, it would at least have placed the subsequent debate in a better context, from the British point of view. But it would not have deterred the General from his veto: it was simply not on for Britain and the United States to perpetuate their nuclear 'special relationship' without arousing French resentment.

If Kennedy himself was conscious of this, as his offer of Polaris to France would seem to suggest, the manner in which it was made was hardly likely to placate the General, though he was made fully aware that his acceptance would in probability open up other possibilities of co-operation in the nuclear field. As it was, Frenchmen took the not wholly unjustified view that, as one American official put it, '[at Nassau] we had done something offensive to them and now we were insulting their intelligence.' 'As it was conceived,' declared De Gaulle, in declining Kennedy's offer, 'undoubtedly no one will be surprised that we cannot subscribe to it. It truly would not be useful for us to buy Polaris missiles when we have neither the submarines to launch them nor the thermonuclear warheads to arm them.' Controlled as this rebuff may have been, it did nothing to conceal the General's bitterness: yet he was essentially a man who used anger very much as an instrument for his authority. His veto was no passing annoyance or impulse. If he was to show no passion for Nassau, nor was he to show any real acrimony against it either. The roots of his action went much deeper: they lay embedded in his view of Europe and more, in his assessment of France's role in Europe. As one official concluded of his rejection of Kennedy's Polaris offer, 'nothing would woo him back . . . De Gaulle was playing his own game for his own reason.'

In so far as it perpetuated the element of distinction between the nuclear and non-nuclear powers within the alliance, the Nassau pact understandably annoyed both West Germany and Italy. Yet Adenauer was almost alone in considering the veto a natural response to the Anglo-American arrangement. For nearly all the other principals involved, Nassau was the heaven-sent opportunity for the General. As Macmillan himself replied, when asked whether the Brussels talks might not be affected by the Nassau Agreement, 'They have nothing to do with it!'

Any explanation of Nassau other than a convenient pretext conceals the essential truth that in virtually no circumstances was

De Gaulle either prepared or indeed willing to allow Britain into the European Community. 'No power on earth can keep Britain out,' Couve de Murville had stated in January 1963: but this did not apparently constrain or perhaps even apply to De Gaulle!! The negotiations broke down not because they were on the point of failure, but because, on the contrary, they were on the point of succeeding! 'The General was getting more and more concerned that the negotiations might reach a solution which the French would have to accept,' recalled one British Minister, 'when he was in fact quite determined to keep us out.' And he was so determined to keep Britain out, as another Minister concluded, 'because Britain entering the Common Market would have upset France's intention to run it as France desired: a simple reasoning of the General.'

If Europe and Britain are like a married couple who somehow cannot live apart, nor it seems can they really live happily together. In fact after the War Britain and Europe to a great extent went their separate ways. Only on occasion did they converge and then they usually conflicted. Churchill in 1946 had spoken eloquently of the goal of a 'kind of United States of Europe', but Britain had done very little to further it. She refused to join the Coal and Steel Community in 1950, and in 1951 rejected any association with the supranational European Defence Community, itself eventually vetoed by the French National Assembly. 'We continuously encouraged close co-operation and unity between the continental powers,' recalled Lord Avon (formerly Sir Anthony Eden) in an apologia for British negativism, 'but we did so from the reserve position that we would not accept a sovereign European authority . . . . Others found this outlook patronising and irritating . . . [but] we have a different and distinct outlook. . . . It is because, as a people, we like to proceed by trial and error. We prefer to see how a principle works in practice before we enshrine it, if we ever do so.'[1]

Yet, in the wake of Suez, Britain and Europe seemingly moved even further apart: Britain drew closer still to the United States, while Europe became more interested in its supranational organisation. And, far from merely waiting to see how the principle worked in practice, British abstention from European experiments was from 1956 supplanted by proposals deliberately competing with, and contrived to undercut, those of the Six! Thus, within a week of refusing to participate in the six-nation Euratom, Britain encouraged the Organisation for European Economic Co-operation (O.E.E.C.) to push ahead for a seventeen-nation Nuclear Energy Agency without any supranational features. And, not content with declining the invitation to join in the drafting of the Treaty of Rome, Macmillan (at least if we are to believe the General) in June 1958 actually 'begged' him to give up the idea of a Common Market. Certainly until 1958 Britain pressed for a seventeen-nation Free Trade Area which would have destroyed the effectiveness of the European Economic Community external tariff wall. And, when that was finally defeated in November, Britain set out to establish the seven-nation E.F.T.A. and pressed hard for a preferential tariff deal—the old Free Trade Area under a new guise—between the Six and the Seven.

In April 1960, when asked by De Gaulle why Britain did not join the Common Market, Macmillan remarked 'that would be unthinkable!' Yet within two years his Government, as one Minister confirmed, 'was certainly discussing the necessity of recalling Parliament in September (1962) in order to finalise the final acceptance.' Sometime in 1960 Macmillan had radically changed his mind as to the desirability of British entry into the European Community. With their instinctive ability to recognise a success when they saw one, the British gradually adjusted to the European *fait accompli*. The E.E.C. had not only become a reality: it had exceeded its framers' wildest expectations! In May 1960, indeed, the Community decided to aim for a full customs union in eight years instead of the originally planned twelve to fifteen years.

Macmillan himself was a dedicated European of long-standing. During his years in Opposition in the post-War Parliament, he had shared with Churchill a leading and distinguished role in the European movement. He had helped to set up the Council of Europe and had been an enthusiastic supporter of the Schuman Plan. Yet his enthusiasm was not always complete. Like many Englishmen, he agreed intellectually that Britain's future was in Europe but his emotional ties were too often elsewhere. He had nevertheless to face the realities of 1960, of Britain's declining political influence and recurrent economic crises. He recognised the economic advantages that British membership of the Community would be likely to bring and similarly witnessed the development of greater cohesion between the Common Market countries themselves: in December 1960, they took the final decisions on a common agricultural policy and, in February 1961, a Summit of the Six was held to discuss the possibilities of increased political co-operation within the Community. Macmillan was to be much moved in his decision by the historic British fear of the European continent being organised by someone else.

But, whatever his motivations, Macmillan approached a possible British application with characteristic caution. He edged his party and the nation into Europe in much the same way that he brought them out of Africa—slowly, (he hoped) painlessly, and with many diversions. He first reconstructed his Administration in July 1960 to fit into his Cabinet dedicated Europeans like Christopher Soames and Duncan Sandys, both of whom were assigned offices, (Agriculture and Commonwealth Relations respectively), of the utmost importance to the European policy which Macmillan was at the time contemplating. Then, during the summer and autumn of 1960 and in the spring of 1961, a succession of visits and exchanges took place between British Ministers and member-Governments of the Community by way of taking soundings on the likely European reactions to a British application. Macmillan himself saw Adenauer, De Gaulle and Fanfani to, 'test the temperature of the water', as *The Times* (1 March 1961) put it.

This very caution on the part of Macmillan, however, prevented him from presenting British entry as a national crusade, and as such increased European doubts as to British sincerity for Europe. It was nevertheless an approach which Macmillan justified in April 1961: 'What would be, I think, a great disaster,' he said on television, 'would be a formal negotiation which broke down. And so I think our present method, informal discussions and gradually getting forward bit by bit, is safer. Because a full-blown formal negotiation which failed would be really a great tragedy. Probably impossible to go back on for five or six or perhaps ten years.'

Gradually, so gradually, Macmillan's Government steered Britain in the direction of a Common Market application. The great potential of an enlarged Community was continually stressed, as were the existing advantages enjoyed by the Common Market: a grouping with a population of 170 million as against only 50 million of the United Kingdom, with a gross national product two and a half times that of the United Kingdom, with a much higher rate of industrial growth and attracting an ever increasing percentage of American foreign investment. The Common Market, as Edward Heath, then Lord Privy Seal, told the Commons in May 1961, has 'established itself and it is showing every sign of future success.'

By the summer of 1961 Macmillan was ready to commit himself. But even then, he had still to reconcile a British application with the fact that Britain was not simply a European power. Britain's real problem was not a lack of identity: it was rather that her sense of identity, as defined by successive governments, was incompatible with an unreserved entry into Europe. The Six had come together in their hour of defeat when the system governing relations between each other had been found wanting. Britain in contrast opted to join this new grouping precisely because it had already proved itself a success, because it had become an economic and political force to be reckoned with, and because it seemed a means to preserve, and possibly increase, Britain's prestige and prosperity. British attitudes to the application were essentially egotistical. The E.E.C. was not an alternative to either the Commonwealth, or E.F.T.A., or even the 'special relationship': it was rather an additional element, or ingredient, in British foreign policy. And it was because of this that Macmillan's qualification of support for British entry was later interpreted as a postponement of the real choice before Britain. Yet Britain's obligations and feelings towards the Commonwealth, her sense of loyalty to E.F.T.A., and her closely-felt ties with the United States meant that a decision on the Common Market could not merely be an acceptance of a principle. It inevitably hinged on the outcome of the negotiations. Heath told the Council of Ministers, in his opening statement of 10 October 1961, that Britain had really already made her decision: it was turning that decision into actuality which would have to depend upon the negotiations themselves. And it is very difficult to see, when all the details were impregnated with politics, how he could have said otherwise. Macmillan himself told the Commons on 31 July, when he announced the British decision 'to establish the conditions on which we might join': 'If a closer relationship between the United Kingdom and the countries of the European Economic Community were to disrupt the long-standing and historic ties between the United Kingdom and the other nations of the Commonwealth, the loss would be greater than the gain.'

The Government's obvious apprehension regarding Common-wealth reactions was reflected in its initial refusal to show Commonwealth governments more than a summary of Heath's important statement of October 1961. Such reticence, however, served only to confirm the worst fears that Britain was prepared to join the Community at the expense, if necessary, of certain Commonwealth interests when, as the text, which was eventually released, makes absolutely clear, what Heath meant was that the British Government believed that Britain could join the Common Market without damaging essential Commonwealth interests. The inexplicable nervousness displayed by the Government clearly did nothing to ease Commonwealth fears of a 'sell-out'. But no one, not even Macmillan, could have expected the inten-sity of Commonwealth opposition, particularly from New Zealand, in the summer of 1962.

Macmillan's initial caution reflected also his recognition of the domestic political problems posed by a decision which, as Hugh Gaitskell observed, represented a reversal of a thousand years of British history. Britain approached the issue somewhat as a confirmed bachelor approaches marriage: He will go through with it if 'suitable arrangements' can be made but there is no love in the old boy's heart! Macmillan had to work hard to con-vince his Cabinet, his party and the nation of the benefits which British membership would bring. If his decision was generally welcomed (and it was warmly supported by many newspapers, including *The Guardian* and *The Daily Mirror*), it was at least in part a sense of relief that the period of painful indecision was over, that the chief obstacle of Britain's own diffidence had at last been removed. Yet even then the issue brought together in opposition strange bedfellows, including Clive Jenkins, Anthony Fell and *The Daily Express*. 'The people have been deceived,' declared *The Daily Express* on 1 August 1961: 'Ten years ago the Tories regained power with the slogan: "Britain strong and free". Today the slogan is forgotten, along with the faith that inspired it.'

Despite a healthy House of Commons majority of 308 in favour of the decision to apply, the plunge was taken by a shivering Government. Macmillan's announcement was hedged with doubts and reservations and his television talk of 4 August did the Community a little less than justice when he suggested that Britain needed to join in order to succeed in the Cold War. Macmillan's hesitations were not, however, altogether unjustified in view of the then climate of British public opinion. A poll in July had shown a large majority in favour of a union with the United States rather than with Europe. And a Gallup Poll, produced in *The Daily Telegraph* of 1 August 1961, found that only thirty-eight per cent of a British sample were prepared to join the Common Market, with twenty-three per cent disapproving and a staggering thirty-nine per cent of don't knows. Unfortunately for Macmillan, enthusiasm for Europe, far from gaining ground, waned even more as time went on.

With the Commonwealth hostile, public opinion sceptical or just plain ignorant, and his own Government split—Maudling, Butler and Hailsham were all doubtful or opposed—Macmillan naturally looked with keen interest to the attitude adopted by President Kennedy, especially since his predecessor had been decidedly cool to British ideas for Europe, particularly those concerned with a possible merger of the Six and the Seven. Eisenhower found the idea of a thirteen-nation preferential zone as unacceptable as the earlier proposal for a seventeen-nation preferential zone, both of which would have discriminated against American exports without in any way advancing European political integration. To Macmillan's relief, Kennedy proved in contrast to be surprisingly enthusiastic for British entry into the Common Market; indeed, he was to take many opportunities to publicly endorse the British policy though in the end this may well have been a distinct liability to Macmillan!

The first soundings of the new Administration's attitude to a possible British entry were made by Heath when he saw Under Secretary of State, George Ball, in London on 30 March 1961. Though Ball had to confess that he had as yet not discussed the specific question with President Kennedy, he nevertheless gave, as he was himself to recall in his *Discipline of Power*, an unambiguous answer which he was confident that Kennedy would support: ' "If," I concluded, "Britain is now prepared to recognise that the Rome treaty is not a static document but a process that could eventually lead to an evolving European community—something in the nature of a European federation—and if Britain can make the great national decision to join Europe on those terms, I am confident that my government will regard this as a major contribution to Western solidarity and the stability of the free world. So long as Britain remains outside the European Community, she is a force for division rather than cohesion, since she is like a giant lodestone drawing with unequal degrees of force on each member state. But if Great Britain now decides to participate in the formidable efforts to unite Europe, she can, and I am sure will, apply her unique political genius—in which we have great confidence—towards the creation of a unity that can transform the Western world." '[2]

Finding the British Government now willing to embrace the idea of a common external tariff, and now prepared to admit that joining Europe included accepting the Community's political institutions as a full member (on both of which it had until then been undecided), Ball left his meeting with Heath 'with a sense that something historic might have happened'. His enthusiasm was not wholly shared by some of his colleagues who considered that too much encouragement of British entry would undermine the position consistently taken by the Americans in regard to a merger between the Six and the Seven. But President Kennedy had no such hesitation. When he saw Macmillan in Washington in April 1961 he enthusiastically endorsed Ball's position. And this made the Prime Minister even more determined to sign the Rome Treaty. Ball recalled that Macmillan drew him aside twice during the second evening of the Washington meeting, declaring: 'We are going to need some help from you in getting in, but we are going in. Yesterday was one of the greatest days of my life.'[3]

'I don't want to criticise the last Administration,' remarked Macmillan on his return from Washington, 'but we've always had a feeling that the Americans were rather anxious that we shouldn't [join the Common Market] on economic grounds. I think the new Administration would accept the degree of discrimination that would result on a wider field against American goods . . . because they would feel that the political advantages are on a more solid basis. . . . That is a reversal or change of mood.'

Kennedy's view of Europe in fact fitted well with Macmillan, who saw British entry as a way of coming even closer to the Americans. Kennedy was fully aware of the economic difficulties which America would experience as a result of Britain's entry, but these were in his mind overborne by its political benefits. He thought it would be good politically and economically for Britain, in that it would give her a future political role and greater financial stability. It was perhaps no coincidence that, at the time that Britain announced her decision to apply, she was asking the United States and the International Monetary Fund for a loan of £714 million. Kennedy thought British entry would similarly be good for Europe and for the Alliance. With Britain inside the Community, London would be able to counterbalance the eccentricities of policy in Paris and Bonn, and also help to prevent Gaullism seeping into Germany. Such advantages could not, of course, be stated in public. But Kennedy further hoped that, with her worldwide commitments, Britain would prevent the Common Market from becoming an inward-looking and purely commercial organisation. With British membership he looked to an enlarged Community as a step towards his ultimate hope of a transatlantic partnership between a politically-federated Europe and the United States. So much in favour of British entry was Kennedy that in early 1962 he mobilised half of his Cabinet in a vain attempt to convince Hugh Gaitskell of its advantages.

So enthusiastic was his Administration for British membership that it rejected the amendment introduced by Henry Reuss of Wisconsin and Paul Douglas of Illinois, which would have permitted the implementation of the Administration's Trade Expansion Act, with or without British entry. In an attempt to ensure that the Atlantic Community did not become composed of two fiercely competitive trading blocs, Kennedy in 1962, rather than seek amendments to the existing trade bill, had requested from Congress sweeping powers to engage in tariff cuts with an enlarged Community. But he did so in a manner which made such bargaining dependent upon British entry. The purists within the Administration strongly resisted the Reuss-Douglas amendment because, as George Ball himself put it during the hearings on the Act before the Senate Committee on Finance: 'Opponents of the entry of Britain into the Common Market could say that there was an alternative presented to Britain which had not been available before.' Ball was so concerned that Britain might lose interest in the Common Market, that the amendment would only encourage the anti-Marketeers, that its rejection meant in effect, as Reuss put it, the T.E.A. was 'tailored to force Britain in'.

Under the Trade Expansion Act, which passed Congress virtually intact, President Kennedy was given a five-year authority to cut all tariffs by as much as fifty per cent and to cut tariffs down to zero on certain commodities traded predominantly by the United States and the Common Market. But this portion of the Act, which after all was primarily an instrument to mitigate the trade discrimination against the United States, aroused European suspicions as to American intentions. It was feared that this was just an American attempt to get an Atlantic Free Trade Area, which obviously would have undercut the effectiveness of the Common Market's external tariff wall. Ball recognised that the zero-tariff proposal was likely to complicate the British application, but he had been overruled. As it was, Europeans suspected a British hand and concluded that the Americans were interested in protecting their own trade but not in sharing real power in Europe.

'It was a gallant and indefatigable effort,' wrote Ball of the British handling of the Common Market negotiations, 'but inevitably marred in technicalities. During the ensuing debate the British purpose became obscure; the political momentum was lost in niggling bargaining.'[4] The seriousness with which Britain approached the negotiations failed to carry its desired conviction. This was not in itself surprising when, in the ten months which followed the British application, Macmillan maintained the fiction that Britain had not really applied at all. His attempt to get into the Market under the guise that it was little more than a commercial arrangement greatly hampered Britain's efforts, as did the fact that Heath was not merely negotiating with the Six but also with the individual capitals and with his own Cabinet, Party and electorate. There was in fact universal praise for the skill displayed by Heath and his team of negotiators, but this did little to accelerate the progress of the negotiations. The talks had opened in October 1961 but it was not until May 1962 that the Italian Chairman of the Commission announced that a landmark had been reached from which they could 'begin the actual negotiations on British accession.'

When there was a mutual willingness to enter into serious negotiation, progress was rapid, as between May and August, 1962. But, to the consternation of many, Britain in October raised a fundamental objection to the period of transition of British agriculture to the Market's system, an issue that was seemingly intractable for three months. By December, not only was De Gaulle opposed to British entry, but the enthusiasm of the other members of the Commission had given way to considerable disenchantment. In the end the concessions which Britain was to make were too little and, worse, came too late.

Inclined to believe that Britain underestimated the political significance of an enlarged Community, the Kennedy Administration argued that many of the problems involved with British entry could have been resolved once Britain was a member of the Common Market. The Commonwealth and E.F.T.A. were seen as 'hostages' of Britain's own making and agriculture an excuse. Yet, if De Gaulle's opposition to Britain's entry developed and hardened during the negotiations themselves, how much more quickly would it have become apparent, had Britain been prepared to sign the Rome Treaty without reservations? And if such an act of faith had meant Britain conceding everything in the economic negotiations, even assuming that this would have satisfied the General and then been acceptable to British public opinion, Britain would have entered Europe so weak as to have been unable to contribute much to European federalism. A fundamental mistake in the British attitude was that we would somehow be able to negotiate a completely new treaty, that Britain could in the negotiations help to shape (and by that change) the Community structure. 'We started with far too optimistic and ambitious ideas of the terms we could obtain,' admitted one British negotiator. Ultimately what was Britain's major undoing was that she was unable to play in the negotiations the kind of role in shaping the Community that the nature of her ambitions for herself and the Community required.

But if the British were optimistic about membership the

Americans were even more so. When Macmillan first told Kennedy that he was thinking of applying, the Administration all but assumed that this was synonymous with British entry. They greatly under-estimated the problems requiring resolution. It was no good saying that agreements on kangaroo meat or Indian tea were merely trifles: they were not trifles at all. Combined, they were the answers to the various propositions about British entry.

While a supporter of British entry for the political opportunities it opened, Kennedy in the meantime took all possible precautions to protect American economic interests. When Macmillan went to Washington in April 1962, the President emphasised that Britain must not expect to take care of everyone in her economic wake—be it the Commonwealth or E.F.T.A.—at America's expense. He was particularly concerned with the implications of continuing the Commonwealth preference system. He recognised the need for certain transitional arrangements but was unwilling to accept a system which would have given Commonwealth farm products a permanent position in the Common Market better than that enjoyed by competing American products. His Administration thus urged that, with Britain in the Community, the Commonwealth preference system must be eventually abolished. Moreover, and as a condition of accepting certain trade disadvantages, the Kennedy Administration sought to emphasise the political potential of an enlarged Community, by opposing the simultaneous applications of the three 'neutral' states, Austria, Sweden, and Switzerland, to become associate members of the Community: applications which Britain considered desirable.

For Britain, the American stand complicated an already complex round of negotiations. More than this, it put both Britain and the Common Market countries in an unnecessarily ambiguous position. For neither Britain nor the Commission members could ever be sure whether American remarks were the result of *a priori* thoughts on the part of the United States or whether they were the result of confidential information acquired by the Americans from the other side.

Yet, and despite their protestations of the political opportunities of an enlarged European Community, the Kennedy Administration itself was to underestimate the Common Market's political importance. The sheer disparity in size between Europe and

America (which the Administration had seen as a compelling reason for Europe to organise itself) inevitably meant that individual European Governments were inclined to define their national interest, and hence national involvement, in terms different from the Americans. It was this that produced the paradox that, in the negotiations over British entry, the position taken by the Market Commission should have been surprisingly similar to that of France, even if their differences over the political organisation of Europe were profound. The economic interests of the Common Market have in fact frequently coincided with the political goal of France to assert a more independent role for Europe.

De Gaulle looked to Europe not to submerge national identity. No more than Britain was he prepared to forgo national sovereignty. He looked to European confederation as a way, above all, of ending American domination. It was axiomatic in his view that such domination was incompatible with European independence. The American handling of the Cuban crisis thus served only to confirm his fear of the dangers of reliance on American nuclear protection. De Gaulle did not attack American policy because it had been related primarily in terms of definitions of national interest. Indeed he insisted that such a relationship must similarly apply to the foreign policy decisions of all proud nations. The French possession of nuclear weapons thus necessitated, in his view, important modifications to the terms and conditions of the alliance, because its basis of integration, so he argued, had been proved invalid. Only in such a context can the relationship between Nassau and the veto be fully explained and understood. De Gaulle took exception to Nassau not, as Macmillan argued, because Britain had succeeded in preserving her independence, but because, in France's view, she had lost it!

Yet, when all is said and done, De Gaulle in January 1963 took much greater exception to American predominance than to British subservience. '[We wanted] to prevent,' he had declared when the Common Market was first established, 'certain others, in particular Great Britain, from dragging the West into an Atlantic system, which would be totally incompatible with a European Europe.'[5]

Britain was in many ways the unfortunate victim of De Gaulle's primary target: American domination. American support for British entry into the Common Market was in fact just another reason for De Gaulle keeping Britain out! 'If Kennedy had lied and declared his opposition to British entry,' as one Minister bitterly recalled, 'it is just conceivable that General De Gaulle might have thought there was some advantage to getting Britain in!'

But the collapse of Kennedy's European policy was at least as much due to its own failings as to the machinations of the French President. Kennedy had campaigned to reassert American (not joint American-European) leadership of the Western world. But, as his instrument to reassert America's dominant role in the alliance, Kennedy elected to rely upon a hastily and ill-conceived scheme, unhappily compounded of urgency, anxiety and ambition, coupled with an apparent unwillingness to abandon what was essentially an egotistical perspective: a scheme which acquired the grandiose, but ill-fated, title of the Grand Design.

1. Lord Avon, *Full Circle* (Cassell, 1960), p.29.
2. George Ball, *The Discipline of Power* (Bodley Head, 1968), p.79
3. *Ibid.*, p.79.
4. *Ibid.*, p.81.
5. Charles De Gaulle, *Memoirs of Hope* (Weidenfeld & Nicolson, 1971), pp.171-2.

13
Dependence, Independence or Interdependence?

'From a strictly economic viewpoint,' Kennedy somewhat sardonically observed a few days after De Gaulle's veto, 'we have known all along that British membership in the Common Market would be bad for us; so we are now better off. On the political side, our chief object was to tie Germany more firmly into the structure of Western Europe. Now De Gaulle is doing that in his own way.'[1] Realistic as these observations of the changed circumstances in the alliance may have been, they nonetheless barely concealed Kennedy's bitter indignation with De Gaulle's assault on his European policy. For the veto of 1963 not only effectively debarred Britain from entering the Common Market. Much more than this, the General had in the most brutal manner demonstrated to the world that he alone had been responsible for the collapse of Kennedy's Grand Design for Europe. Coined in a little book by Joseph Kraft, the phrase 'Grand Design' was never to be used by the President himself, and indeed, at least before January 1963, it was more of a general direction than a specific policy, more a hope for the future than a concrete programme to be implemented. Unfortunately, this very lack of detail was to prove one of the great weaknesses of Kennedy's European policy, which De Gaulle was able so fruitfully to exploit. For Kennedy's was a policy rather than a programme, however sound and desirable were its aims.

There were two essential, interrelated but nevertheless distinctive elements in Kennedy's Grand Design for Europe. The first element was the politico-economic goal, inspired by Jean

Monnet among others, which held to the concept of a united Europe, including Britain, as a part of a freely-trading Atlantic Community. The United States looked forward to a partnership with such a federated Europe on the basis of true equality of status. The second feature of the Grand Design was the military-strategic programme, the already noted brainchild of McNamara, which prescribed a united military posture, emphasising the interdependence of allies. But in essence this meant (at least for McNamara) a continuing reliance on the American nuclear deterrent. Ultimately to reject both elements, De Gaulle perceived much more clearly than did the Kennedy Administration itself a fatal contradiction within the Grand Design between these two concepts of partnership and interdependence. The Skybolt crisis was to highlight the contradiction and, further, in so far as it also involved the special privileges extended to Britain, was a problem explained by neither partnership nor interdependence, and are not fully compatible with either! For, as merely further confirmation of the continuing existence of a nuclear special relationship between Britain and the United States, Nassau cut directly across the more basic American objective of fostering a united Europe, the essential precondition to achieving Kennedy's ultimate goal of Atlantic Partnership.

'As an objective, the duality of European unity and Atlantic Partnership', wrote Ball, 'seems to me beyond cavil. Yet it is possible that the habitual linking of these two concepts in American official statements has not been altogether wise. It may have tended to create false conceptions both at home and abroad.'[2] Such false conceptions have carried consequences of a far-reaching nature particularly for American planners, since their repeated determination to strive for Atlantic Partnership too often confused the essential reality that it was first necessary to achieve the unity of Europe. It was as an attempt to focus on this problem and also clarify the purposes of his foreign policy, that, in his Independence Day speech at Philadelphia in July 1962, President Kennedy boldly outlined his goal of Atlantic Partnership. 'The first order of business,' he explained, 'is for Europe to go forward in forming the more perfect union which will someday make this partnership possible. . . . We see in such a Europe a partner with whom we could deal on a basis of full equality. . . . I will say here and now on this day of "independence" that the United States will be ready for a "Declaration of Interdependence." '

It is difficult for non-Americans, unfamiliar with the holy writ of Americanism, to understand how (almost) blasphemously far President Kennedy went in this speech. He talked not about American independence and the great American union but about interdependence and union between America and foreigners. He all but refuted George Washington's original dictum that American prosperity and peace should not be jeopardised by entanglement in the toils of European ambition, rivalry, interest and caprice. At least since 1940, if not before, to think of the United States as other than a major European power would be, as one Kennedy aide put it, 'to make a very great mistake', carrying the gravest of repercussions.

Kennedy's Declaration of Interdependence, like Marshall's speech fifteen years before, was imaginative, inspiring, courageous, even historic. But unlike Marshall's speech, which led to the most rapid reconstruction of Europe, there was neither immediate nor enthusiastic response in Europe to Kennedy's Declaration. And in fact only then did the realisation dawn within the Administration itself that its purpose was, to say the least, at some distance from its means. Sovereign nations, like Great Britain, Germany, and France, as MacGeorge Bundy admitted, 'will not be melted into a new nation of Europe by a wave of any American wand.'[3] If the movement for the political union of Europe was to be conspicuous for its lack of progress, it is clearly the Europeans themselves who were to bear the principal responsibility through their reluctance to surrender more of their national sovereignty. Yet, by its actions, the United States itself did very little that was likely to encourage that greater union and thereby advance transatlantic Partnership. Indeed, except in one important field, the Kennedy Administration held back from genuine partnership, the kind of relationship with others which involves actual participation and responsibility in the power of decision. The single exception occurred in the field of monetary relations and unfortunately served to confirm European suspicions that only when it suited them were Americans prepared to exert themselves to make partnership work.

Far from being dependent upon the United States, Europe by

1961 had achieved a high degree of monetary stability relative to the recurrent crises affecting both the British and American currencies. With American gold losses running at an annual rate of $6 billion, the series of currency swap arrangements between Britain and America, even if they helped to increase each others' gold and foreign exchange reserves, hardly scratched the surface of the international liquidity problem. Douglas Dillon, Kennedy's Secretary of the Treasury, accordingly concluded that existing funds were totally inadequate to meet America's needs and that a completely new credit arrangement was urgently required. It was thus that between 1961 and 1963, America asked continental Europe for $3 billion in stand-by credit and a further $1.9 billion in treasury bond purchases and swap arrangements.

In January 1961, Jean Monnet called for permanent machinery that would enable America and Europe 'to co-operate in this field on a continuous, rather than a crisis, basis.' But it was to the sixty-seven-nation (Anglo-American-dominated) International Monetary Fund, rather than the nine-nation O.E.C.D. monetary committee, that the United States looked for the stand-by credit arrangements it required. Plans were accordingly developed to expand the Fund's capacity to provide assistance by means of a special $6 billion arrangement between the ten most advanced Western countries. Disagreement arose, however, especially at the Fund's Vienna Conference in September 1961, over the exact procedure for borrowing, whether the I.M.F. or the lending countries themselves should decide upon the use of the new reserves. As the prospective chief borrower, the United States demanded close to automatic withdrawal rights. For their part, not wielding much influence within the I.M.F., the six Common Market Countries insisted upon safeguards including consultation before their currencies were drawn out. France went as far as to demand a veto for each country on the use of its own currency. In the end a compromise was reached, somewhat on the lines that Monnet had proposed, with France yielding on a veto, and the United States yielding on automaticity. The decision on the drawing of funds was made the joint responsibility of the ten nations contributing to the new reserves, on the basis of qualified majority voting. Here, then, was a remarkable and concrete achievement towards greater interdependence: with an ad hoc institution created with decision-making machinery, sovereignty had been pooled in a way entirely novel to the alliance. 'In effect,' as Robert Kleiman observed, 'the agreement was a step toward a limited kind of Atlantic reserve fund. . . . This beginning in true Atlantic partnership could have set a precedent for action on other critical economic problems as well as more permanent monetary reform. . . . But the precedent . . . was not followed up in any field, not even in the field of stopgap monetary measures.'⁴

With the American balance of payments problem at least temporarily brought under control in 1963, the Kennedy Administration did begin to take a more sympathetic view to proposals, which Macmillan among others had put forward, for a general overhaul of the international monetary system to meet the needs of expanding world trade: proposals which in 1961 had seemed to the American Treasury both unrealistic and irrelevant. Now, in the autumn of 1963, the U.S. supported the establishment of the Group of Ten, latterly to play a major role in the 1971 dollar crisis. But, with the United States still opposed to machinery to deal on a permanent basis with the long-term liquidity problem, and with the major thrust of American policy in the Atlantic economic field from October 1961 being the Trade Expansion Act (which only aroused suspicions of America's aims), it must be said that there was little progress towards meaningful interdependence. And, indeed, in the defence field the concept almost completely broke down.

Defence interdependence represented the recognition of the advantages of sharing among allies the production of their defence hardware requirements, so as to avoid costly duplication and also, and more importantly, to encourage a more integrated Western defence posture. As such, interdependence was a fine concept: unfortunately, it proved extremely difficult to implement and in fact American support for European integration was only to be strained and compounded by the bitter competition between the United States and its allies for arms contracts within NATO. In common with other European countries, Britain, inclined to suspect that a large section of NATO headquarters was nothing more than an American sales organisation, greatly resented American pressure and superior salesmanship techniques. 'The

United States didn't want a partner,' charged one embittered British Minister, 'they wanted a satellite!'

The British Government was especially incensed by the American failure, as they saw it, to live up to an agreement reached between the two countries in 1961, and initialled by both McNamara and Watkinson, on the sharing of the production of their defence requirements. As one British Minister recalled, 'the agreement, which might have been fruitful, and which incidentally would probably have meant that the Americans could have got the T.S.R.-2 almost free, just withered and died.' Case after case reinforced British suspicions that McNamara cared little for making the concept of interdependence meaningful. In 1962, for example, Thorneycroft felt compelled to cancel the order for the tactical nuclear missile, Blue Water, because the Americans withdrew their backing of it: an outstanding British weapon was thus thrown on the scrapheap because of the American reluctance to admit its superiority over their own Sergeant missile. The British anti-aircraft Thunderbird was similarly pushed out of Europe by American pressures for the Raytheon Hawk missile. With such cases so numerous, the British Government was understandably resentful that, as *The Sunday Telegraph* (2 September 1962) observed, 'in theory Washington preached interdependence in NATO; in practice little happened.'

That the concept broke down was not for want of trying to make it work: indeed, in 1961 in particular, McNamara tried hard to see whether the United States could not support the arms base of its allies, and he did achieve limited successes, like the American contribution of £12½ million in 1962 to the development of the Hawker P1127 vertical take-off close-support fighter. McNamara's efforts were, however, too often frustrated by the pressures exerted upon him, especially from Congress and more from the 'military-industrial complex'.

The philanthropy of American arms manufacturers did not extend to placing their markets at the disposal of British or European competitors, even in the great cause of interdependence. They were unimpressed by the claims for the vertical take-off aircraft, evidently confident of their ability to produce a similar aircraft, and one with the great advantage of being American. But it was more than a matter of intensely nationalistic sentiments.

The Pentagon was frankly uncertain of the ability of America's allies to produce really important defence material. Thus, of the advantages of T.S.R.-2 over the rival F.111, one Pentagon official admitted, 'we were sceptical that the T.S.R.-2 was anything near as good as the design specifications of the F.111. We just did not think Britain was a reliable, solid, Grade A producer of this kind of critically important piece of defence hardware.'

Herein lies the fundamental cause of the breakdown of defence interdependence: the great disparity between American and European capabilities, especially in terms of advancement of knowledge and scale of activity. For McNamara, this disparity made the need even more urgent for Europeans to organise themselves. For Europeans, however, in accentuating the differences between Americans and themselves, and thus adding to the fierceness of competition between them, it made only less likely and less desirable the kind of partnership which President Kennedy sought!

The American interpretation of 'interdependence' certainly represented a lurking vulnerability within Kennedy's Grand Design. But on no issue was the contradiction between partnership and interdependence more evident than on the nature of European participation in the operation of the nuclear arsenal of the alliance. The slogan of the era was 'interdependence', but it was a word which meant different things to different people at different times. Unfortunately for Kennedy's European policy, at no time did interdependence really involve for Americans a substantial abrogation of national sovereignty. And without such an involvement, especially as concerned the nuclear field, any American attempt to secure greater European participation was seen, and not altogether without reason, as a further assertion of hegemony, concealing dubious political motives. This became a matter of acute importance in 1963 when the Nassau compact and the veto led almost immediately to the enunciation of a defence strategy which devalued the policy of America's nuclear allies. Its consequences were greater when it appeared that the Administration neither understood nor regretted what it was doing.

To an extent rarely understood by Americans (for many years, at a comfortable distance from any likely nuclear holocaust), Europeans have been obsessed with the question of getting access to nuclear weapons. To be true, the issue of European participation had long been debated within the United States, but there had been, especially by McNamara, a considerable amount of dictation and a minimum of genuine consultation. The problem for the United States was to find a vehicle for meaningful participation which would nevertheless remain compatible with its responsibilities for the Pax Americana in the nuclear age. But not until 1963 did the Kennedy Administration recognise that it was insufficient to stress that Europe's contribution be limited to a conventional role: and by then it was unfortunately too late to impress upon Europeans America's sincerity for sharing the odium of responsibility. It was now recognised that a more meaningful sense of common purpose was required: but for Americans its urgency was dictated by the effort to prevent Gaullism filling the vacuum created by the rebuff of Kennedy's European policy in January 1963.

Kennedy's Ambassador in London, David Bruce, was recalled to Washington in February 1963 to conduct a reappraisal of America's European policy. Associating himself with Ball and the other conceptualists, Bruce concluded that the multi-lateral nuclear force (hereafter called the M.L.F.) was the best available means to reconcile the primary American objectives of interdependence—in the context of the indivisibility of the deterrent—with partnership and the build-up of a united Europe.

The indispensability of nuclear centralisation called, in Kennedy's view, for a NATO solution which, he hoped, would discourage national nuclear aspirations, and which would at the same time, as McNamara put it, emphasise the 'interdependence' of national security interests on both sides of the Atlantic. But what in fact McNamara meant was the dependence of Western security on the nuclear deterrent continuing under American control. And what participation would be possible, let alone real, as long as the United States insisted (as it always did) on a veto on the operation of such a deterrent? The firing of missiles by any agreed joint force would then inevitably seem indistinguishable from the firing of missiles under American control. 'It wasn't so much that we didn't take seriously enough the European desire for participation,' recalled one Kennedy confidant; 'it was that we hadn't found a vehicle by which such participation could take place.' There could be no solution found on the basis of a partnership with a hitherto non-existent and unequal Europe. Thus of necessity the vehicle had to be sought through the NATO framework, and it was thus that M.L.F. was conceived.

Prior to 1963, the Kennedy Administration had been decidedly cool towards the proposal for a NATO nuclear force advanced by Christian Herter in December 1960. At Ottawa in May 1961, Kennedy had talked vaguely of an eventual NATO seaborne force, which would be 'truly multi-lateral in ownership and control if this should be desired and found feasible by our allies, once NATO'S non-nuclear goals have been achieved.' In this way, Kennedy deliberately left the initiative to his allies who before anything else had to fulfil their conventional force-level requirements: and frankly he doubted whether either was likely. He was prepared merely to let the matter rest until European unity had been advanced, presumably by British membership of the Community. Nassau and the veto, however, forced his hand and necessitated quick action to reassert American leadership within the alliance. Unfortunately for Kennedy, in the M.L.F., his policy planners, as Andrew Kopkind was to observe, 'settled on the most unwieldly, unworkable, over-complicated and altogether absurd diplomatic contraption to secure its dominant role in Europe once more.'[5]

From a military standpoint, M.L.F. was a complete nonsense from the outset: it had no military value, there was no military need for it, and it carried almost insuperable technical complications. It was soon found, for example, that it was utterly impossible for a submarine fleet to be used as the platform for such a force. Nevertheless the multi-lateral concept did seem to combine desirable political goals. It appealed to those who advocated strategic interdependence as a means of preserving the unity of the deterrent while giving NATO allies a sense of nuclear participation. Moreover, while providing for a greater sense of common purpose, this new concept in participation also appealed to those in the Administration who were committed to the policy of the non-proliferation of nuclear weapons. M.L.F. seemed to them to be a useful receptacle for the eventual pooling of the atomic capabilities of the alliance, thereby integrating the British and French nuclear programmes and also reducing, if not halting, the aspirations for nuclear weapons which a future German Government might hold. At the same time, M.L.F. attracted advocates of economic partnership because it renewed the pressures exerted upon Europe to organise itself, since the only body to which the United States would even conceivably agree to yield a veto (if at all) was the authority of a politically united Europe. But, if M.L.F. was to attract support from many different quarters, it was also to unite in opposition equally strange bedfellows.

M.L.F. attracted very little support in Europe, which was not in itself surprising since it tended to be advanced in a way not altogether compatible with Atlantic Partnership. A multi-lateral force, conditional on the achievement of NATO's non-nuclear goals, was unlikely to carry any great appeal, even if the force itself did imply entry into the nuclear club. Largely for the acceptability it afforded, the West Germans (and only some of them) welcomed the M.L.F. But they were almost alone: France totally rejected it, Britain was sceptical and refused to support it, the Greeks and the Turks could not afford it, the Benelux countries were not frightfully interested in it, and the Italians, in their elections, effectively avoided it!

France, and to a lesser extent Britain, may be forgiven for seeing the M.L.F. as yet another American attempt to contain and control their nuclear aspirations. The integration of France's nuclear force within NATO was for De Gaulle something quite 'unimaginable' and contrary to all his principles for French defence and policy. If the arguments which Britain levelled against it were practical, the French objections were fundamental and deeply entrenched in De Gaulle's view of France.

It is difficult now to resist the conclusion that the mistakes of his old age went a long way towards balancing out the General's greatest deeds which had gone before. But certainly the key to both his successes and his failures was that De Gaulle regarded himself quite simply as the embodiment of his country. 'He is by nature an aristocrat,' Macmillan had written in his diary in June 1943. 'Just like Louis XIV and Napoleon, he thinks in his heart that he should command and all others should follow him. It is not exactly "fascist", (an overworked word), it is authoritarian.'[6] Given this authoritarianism, everything conspired, in De Gaulle's view, to make France the champion of peace in the nuclear age. But to assume this role, France had first to be free to act: she had to assert herself, especially when the Anglo-Saxons rejected any compromise on his proposal for a triumvirate leadership within NATO. Thus, having adopted such an independent line, De Gaulle had of necessity to reject any moves towards greater interdependence: though he only became actively hostile towards the M.L.F. when he saw the very real prospect of America and Germany getting together to create it.

Where France had opted for independence, Britain settled for a peculiar form of semi-independence. For her nuclear strength, Britain sought to be independent in policy and use but dependent upon the United States for the production and supply, positions which, at least until the weapons in question were actually delivered, were basically irreconcilable. Nassau and the dispute over the British contribution towards the Polaris support costs were to stir all the prejudices and incline the British towards a more sympathetic attitude to the French *force de frappe*. It may not have been a sensible or even ultimately a successful policy: it was at least coherent. It may have been nothing more than a dangerous, ineffective, strategic nuisance: but it was at least hers. It may have been home-made and as such an appalling burden on Frenchmen: but the only finger-on-the-trigger was French! Yet if France and Britain held contrasting postures towards reliance on the United States, at least they were at one in their opposition to M.L.F. For both saw one of America's primary aims, as one British official recalled, as 'to engage us in sufficiently heavy expenditure on the M.L.F. as not to be able to afford our own deterrent.'

In fact the British Government viewed M.L.F., as one Minister put it, as 'one of the biggest pieces of nonsense that anybody had ever dreamt up and rather a dangerous one as well'. Both Macmillan at Birch Grove in June 1963 and Home in Washington in October warned Kennedy that from the British point of view M.L.F. was likely to be a non-starter. They saw no need for it, no value in it and, worse, feared that it was likely to be divisive of the alliance, that the distinction between the participants and non-participants would cause more irritation within NATO than the more clear-cut distinction between the nuclear and non-nuclear powers. Above all, the British Government was fearful of the political implications of M.L.F., that such a method of associating the Germans with NATO's strategic power, even if it did prevent Gaullism from sweeping into Germany, was bound to do great harm to the developing détente with the Soviet Union, to which the British attached greater importance.

London was always obdurately opposed to the total integration of the British deterrent within either an American or a European context: a NATO force, fully integrated, and indistinguishable in terms of national elements, was thus hardly likely to carry any more appeal. As an alternative, Britain put forward her proposal for a multi-national nuclear force, comprised of existing national elements, including the V-bomber force and the American Polaris fleet. Such a force conformed at least with Macmillan's understanding of Britain's obligation as defined under the Nassau compact, and indeed it was this rather than the M.L.F. which NATO agreed to establish in May 1963. Macmillan even proposed a NATO trusteeship committee of ten nations to supervise the multi-national force, a proposal to which the Americans objected as unwieldy, usurping the fifteen-nation NATO Council and allowing the non-nuclear members to have an important voice in allied strategy 'on the cheap'. Yet the American opposition to M.N.F. proved to be nothing like as decisive as the British withdrawal of support for the M.L.F. For, had Britain gone into the M.L.F., other European governments would probably have co-operated in the venture. As it was, the British purpose for M.L.F. became demonstrably clear: 'We attacked it at every opportunity we could,' recalled one delighted British Minister, 'and I am happy to say it was eventually sunk.'

M.L.F. proved to be a complete dead duck but British opposition to it was not in itself sufficient to kill the project. Its demise owed just as much to its own shortcomings and, more, to the divisions within the American Administration. As the crystallisation of the conflict of approach between the conceptualists and the realists, M.L.F. became quite simply internally impossible. For the realists, there was every incentive abroad to portray M.L.F. as an American pressure: for the conceptualists, there was every incentive at home to present it as a response to European wishes. The latter group were again to be defeated precisely because they never could convincingly present the M.L.F. as a European-inspired project. And without such a presentation, neither President Kennedy nor later President Johnson were prepared openly to commit their Administrations to the M.L.F.

While he recognised that European aspirations for a nuclear say were genuine enough, Kennedy believed that for the United States to say how a NATO nuclear force should be manned, financed and operated would be out of keeping with the spirit of Atlantic Partnership. Yet, in arguing that M.L.F. was militarily unnecessary and of dubious value, the Administration only further discouraged its allies from supporting the project. More important, Nassau forced Kennedy's hand and led to hasty and ill-conceived improvisation. In 1963 the original posture of responding to European wishes was abandoned as also were the other conditions of a non-nuclear build-up and prior agreement on the control plan. That very abandonment, however, made the M.L.F. debate increasingly unrealistic, for the ensuing discussions sidestepped the basic political problems which had to be solved. With the conditions under which the force would be operated and controlled never agreed, M.L.F. became an attempt to overcome a basic political dilemma with technical tricks that were almost totally meaningless in either military or political terms.

With so many obvious flaws in the project, it is hard to escape from the impression that the M.L.F. debate was entered into by the United States, at least in part, as an educational exercise for the benefit of her Atlantic allies, to highlight the dangers and complexities of the nuclear age. One senior Kennedy official all but confirmed this impression when he recalled that 'the greatest thing the U.S. did was to call the European bluff. . . . These issues were much more complex than they thought: the lesson of which is that you should not prevent the Western Europeans from participation. You should demand it, require it, absolutely insist upon it, and insist they get themselves organised!'

Unfortunately this assessment belies the basic American position, best summarised in that parody of the Declaration of Independence, which holds these truths to be self-evident: that peace in the thermonuclear age can only be secured by an American monopoly of thermonuclear weapons; that although all nations are endowed with certain inalienable rights these do not necessarily include the pursuit of thermonuclear happiness! Where

M.L.F. fell down was that such a definition of Pax Americana was, first, incompatible with true partnership and, second, neither readily nor happily understood or accepted by Europe. Thus a proposal, destined to appear as an alternative to national nuclear forces, tended only to magnify the motives which gave rise to such forces in the first place. A proposal, which it was hoped would restore allied cohesion, became instead an additional element of friction and discord.

In retrospect it must be admitted that Kennedy's European policy in fact achieved very little: with De Gaulle's veto of British membership of the European Community, with the breakdown of interdependence, and the comparative failure of partnership; with the abandonment of the M.L.F., with France's continuing *force de frappe* and later her withdrawal from the NATO military command structure and running battle against the dollar: with all these elements, the strategy of the Grand Design became increasingly untenable. By the time of his death in November 1963 even President Kennedy himself was beginning to find European union getting in the way of East/West détente to which, like Macmillan, he attached a higher priority.

1. Quoted in Arthur Schlesinger Jr., *A Thousand Days* (André Deutsch, 1965), p.744.
2. George Ball, *The Discipline of Power* (Bodley Head, 1968), p.61.
3. MacGeorge Bundy, 'Policy for the Western Alliance—Berlin and After'. *Department of State Bulletin*, No. 1185, p.422.
4. Robert Kleiman, *Atlantic Crisis* (Norton, 1964), p. 120.
5. Andrew Kopkind, 'The Special Relationship'. *The New Left Review*, No. 51 (October 1968), p.5.
6. Harold Macmillan, *The Blast of War* 1939-1945 (Macmillan, 1967), pp.345-6.

14

Kennedy and Colonialism

Africa, Macmillan once remarked, is 'like a sleeping hippo: suddenly it gets a prod from the white man and wakes up: and it won't go to sleep again.' For centuries, a dark and mysterious continent, Africa has since the end of the Second World War been subject to the most significant upheaval. Yet, if the consequences of this rude awakening were to be painful for the white man, he was at least in part responsible for it. For, at the end of the last century, the rich nations of Europe had all scrambled furiously to acquire colonies over eleven and a half million square miles of the continent. In the cause of empires, new states with new territorial identities came into being almost overnight: some, like the British colonies, to be ruled indirectly from the mother-country, others, like the French and Portuguese colonies, to be directly governed as integral parts of developing Communities. In 1945 but four nations of the vast continent were independent. A decade later, despite the Atlantic Charter of Roosevelt and Churchill, four-fifths of Africa's population were still under European rule. Within a further ten years, however, Africa had suddenly surged towards nationhood. Two hundred million Africans became in this period the masters of their own homelands and no single year was more significant to this transition than 1960 which has aptly been termed Freedom Year.

1960 began peacefully enough with Macmillan's now historic address before the South African Parliament in February. 'The wind of change', the Prime Minister told his audience,' is blowing through the continent. Whether we like it or not, this growth of national consciousness is a political fact. We must all accept it as a fact. Our national policies must take account of it.' Delicately but masterfully, Macmillan explained how British policy had taken account of it. He dissociated Britain henceforth from automatic support of the apartheid regime in South Africa. He held that Britain bore a heavy responsibility in a world divided between the West, the communist bloc and the uncommitted nations: that Britain's task was thus not just to raise the living standards of the peoples of her colonies. It was also to create societies where men could grow to full stature, including an increasing share of political power and responsibility. With superb deftness, Macmillan told his South African friends that to support certain aspects of their policy, especially the denial of individual merit as the sole criterion for advancement, would be for Britain to be false to her own convictions.

Macmillan's speech did more, however, than merely define the future contours of relations with South Africa which but a year later was to withdraw from the Commonwealth. It did more than unleash a famous cliché. The wind of change was to stir nationalists everywhere. Few would deny that its effects were felt beyond the British colonies. In 1960 twelve of the former French territories secured their independence, as did the two French-administered trust territories of the Cameroun and Togo. The single Belgian possession of the Congo also became independent in the summer of 1960. Nigeria, alone of the British possessions, gained its independence in that year but Sierra Leone, Kenya, Uganda and Tanganyika were all soon to follow and major changes, including the possibility of secession, were recommended for the Central African Federation of Rhodesia and Nyasaland. So rapid was the progress towards independence in Africa that Macmillan, for whom the transition without due preparation was unacceptable, became genuinely alarmed about the forces to which he had given both expression and hope. The wind of change, he declared in March 1960 was 'not the same thing as a howling tempest which would blow away the whole of the new developing civilisation. We must, at all costs, avoid that.' He had accepted in principle the granting of full independence to the colonies: but it had to be a peaceful and orderly transition. Unfortunately he had unleashed a train of events which was now beyond his control, and his efforts to slow the process down came at precisely the time that the new American Administration of President Kennedy, determined to resolve the ambiguity of past policy, gave backing to the nationalist movements with an altogether more aggressive positivism.

Ever since Franklin Roosevelt, American Administrations have been nominally committed to an anti-colonial policy and in favour of the freedom and self-determination for all peoples. The United States would have rejected its own heritage had it not felt a sense of common identity with the struggles of others against colonialism. 'My nation was once a colony,' President Kennedy reminded the U.N. in 1961, 'and we know what colonialism means.' Yet its role as world leader often involved the United States, much to its embarrassment, in disputes between friends and allies: and on no issue was this a greater dilemma for American policy than over colonialism, a dilemma compounded by the fact that America's major allies have traditionally been also the major colonial powers. Yet in seeking to balance the demands of the new nationalists with the claims of its principal allies, the United States in the past too often lacked the forthrightness to state clearly enough its divided loyalties and to define its responsibilities, as it saw them, which determined the selection of one course of action over another. The consequence for American policy of such conflicting loyalties was, as Rupert Emerson suggested, 'to introduce a note of uncertainty and ambiguity. We can neither wholly deny the claims of friends and allies, nor turn our backs upon the Africans at the bidding of the present or former colonial powers.'[1]

Almost inevitably American policy towards Africa had been somewhat perfunctory. Africa was viewed as primarily a West European responsibility and, in the interests of NATO solidarity, it seemed best to defer to them on African matters. Its nominal sympathy with anti-colonialism led on occasion to American exhortations about the value of orderly transition to self-government but, whenever this conflicted with other interests, NATO came first. Suez was perhaps the single exception where Dulles discovered that he could in fact support the requirements of defence and be anti-colonialist at one and the same time: a discovery, the consequence of which was to cause the most profound misgivings in Europe. But Suez excepted, priority was always attached to the Atlantic alliance. Even Portugal, by far the most impervious to change of all the colonial powers, was during the 1950s able to exploit her membership of NATO to restrain world-wide criticism of her colonialism. Salazar assiduously presented African nationalism as a communist menace against which the Portuguese colonies were represented as the last bastions of West European civilisation. But by 1960, with nationalism a burning political fact, world opinion began to harden against Portugal, which henceforth could no longer count on the United States and its allies for support. For the United States, increasingly concerned with Africa's importance in the Cold War, the alliance with Portugal, and to a lesser extent the other colonial powers, constituted an acute moral embarrassment. How could the American desire to see African independence carry conviction in the face of a very real association with an obscurantist colonial power? It was evidently as an attempt to resolve this paradox that President Kennedy boldly changed American policy towards colonialism, an assertion of a new direction which not surprisingly upset his European allies, and of course none more than Portugal.

Kennedy's efforts to give American policy a complete face-lift, as he put it, to 'ally ourselves with the rising tide of nationalism,' earned him a special regard among African leaders. He was to talk to them not as a partner of any colonial power but as an American deeply interested in the affairs and problems of their countries. To underline the importance he attached to African affairs, Kennedy appointed some of his most able diplomats to the challenging ambassadorial posts in this continent—men like Edmund Gullion (Congo), William Attwood (Guinea) and Edward Korry (Ethiopia). His very first State Department appointment was that of former Governor of Michigan, G. Mennen Williams, as Assistant Secretary of State for African Affairs, a position of responsibility, which Kennedy said, was 'second to none in the new Administration'.

Kennedy took office with a record and interest in African affairs unique for a President. For the first time, Africa had figured prominently in a Presidential election. 'We have lost ground in Africa,' Kennedy, the Candidate, had charged, 'because we have neglected and ignored the needs and aspirations of the African people.' As chairman of the African sub-committee of the Senate Foreign Relations Committee, Kennedy had been highly critical of the Eisenhower Administration's non-policy. In the Senate in July 1957, for example, he had attacked France and America (in a speech which caused outrage in official Paris and Washington) for not coming to terms with the reality of nationalism in Algeria: 'No amount of mutual politeness, wishful thinking, nostalgia or regret should blind either France or the United States to the fact that, if France and the West at large are to have a continuing influence in North Africa . . . the essential first step is the independence of Algeria.' And what went for Algeria, in Kennedy's view, equally applied to the rest of Africa.

Kennedy believed that the United States, bound by neither established positions nor traditions, by neither fixed agreements nor vested interests, was in a unique position to create new policies to meet the challenges of the Third World, which he saw as the critical battleground between democracy and communism. He was convinced that the United States should increase its efforts to persuade the emergent nations that they did not have to turn to Moscow for the guidance and friendship they so desperately needed, and to help them achieve the economic progress on which the welfare of their people and their ability to resist communist subversion depended. 'We can no longer afford policies', he wrote in 1960, 'which refuse to accept the inevitable triumph of nationalism in Africa—the inevitable end of colonialism—or the unyielding determination of the new African states to lift their people from their age-old poverty and hunger and ignorance. We must answer the critical African need for educated men to build factories, run the schools and staff the governments by sending a growing stream of technical experts and educators to Africa. . . . We must establish . . . a full working partnership between the nations of the West and the nations of Africa.'[2]

In making the critical issue one of national independence, Kennedy invited the new states to find a common interest with America in resisting communist expansion. The Soviets had long wooed the neutrals and Kennedy had no wish to withdraw from the competition. 'We shall not always expect to find them supporting our view,' he proclaimed in his Inaugural Address, 'but we shall always hope to find them strongly supporting their own freedom.' He wanted to help the developing countries not merely in the hope that this would be politically beneficial, but more, because it was right. He rejected the Dulles practice of marking all nations as either communist or anti-communist. In Kennedy's view, neutralism for many nations was inevitable rather than immoral. He did not refuse to help non-aligned countries merely because they were non-aligned. Indeed, jointly with Macmillan, he was in 1962 to respond positively with military aid to meet the Chinese threat on the Indian border. But he did not blindly court the neutrals at any cost: in January 1962, for instance, he authorised American participation in Ghana's Volta Dam Project (again after consultation with Macmillan) only after attaching strict economic conditions. Even if the conditions were not to allow for the vagaries of Nkrumah—and later Kennedy stopped further long-term credits—the President at least felt that the people rather than the Government were to be the ultimate beneficiaries of the Volta Dam.

Essentially Kennedy sought to recast American thinking towards the developing nations, to a world where the Cold War was not the only reality, where it was worth encouraging national dignity for itself. But, in so doing, he ran head-on against deeply-entrenched and inherited policies on colonialism and neutralism. The State Department was still dominated by men who attached a higher priority to NATO and who flinched from anything likely to bruise the sensibilities of America's European allies. The lobbying by the interested desks, some of which were more concerned with the need to defend American investment, had in the past created tensions which, in the absence of clear Presidential direction, had prevented the emergence of a coherent policy.

In December 1960 the Afro-Asian bloc within the United Nations, having rapidly acquired an almost frightening unity of purpose, introduced a bold resolution which declared that 'all people have the right of self-determination', that 'inadequacy of political, economic, social or educational preparedness should never serve as a pretext for delaying independence', and that 'immediate steps' should be taken in all non self-governing territories 'to transfer all powers to the peoples of these territories, without any conditions or reservations, in accordance with their freely expressed will.' If it was to be less a plea for action than an affirmation of purpose, its language was at the time nevertheless sweeping: too sweeping apparently for Macmillan, who personally persuaded Eisenhower to order his delegation to abstain on the resolution. Ironically, the American delegation had actually helped to draft the resolution, and one delegate, Senator Wayne Morse, was in consequence publicly to condemn the Administration's indecision: 'on every major issue of colonialism at the Fifteenth General Assembly our voting record shows that we rejected our own history and allowed the communist block to champion the cause of those millions of people who are trying to gain independence.'

Even if it meant incurring the wrath of his European allies, President Kennedy was determined to end the ambiguity in American policy. And he saw an early opportunity to do so in March through supporting a U.N. resolution (on which France and Britain dissented) which called upon Portugal to comply with the December resolution. Again in April, when by a vote of 73-2 the General Assembly appointed a sub-committee to investigate the crisis in Angola, the U.S. voted for the resolution, Britain and France abstaining. The new Administration thus quickly shook off automatic identification with colonialism. Indeed, in June, it joined with Russia—Britain and France again abstaining—in calling upon Portugal to desist from its repressive measures in Angola. By the end of 1961, Portugal could count upon the support of only Spain and South Africa in the United Nations.

Not surprisingly, Portugal became increasingly distrustful of, and angry with, her ally and at one stage privately threatened to leave NATO. Equally unsurprising was Britain's position on the resolutions. It was hardly to be expected that she would vote for resolutions which, without too much imagination, could eventually be used against her in some awkward African relationships of her own. Yet if the anger of his European allies was not wholly unexpected by President Kennedy, it was too often aroused less by what American policy did than by what it said. Not all of his Administration were endowed with courtesy and tact. In 1961, for example, the British Government was reported as becoming increasingly annoyed with 'the Administration's penchant for making sweeping statements encouraging nationalistic aspirations in Africa'.[3] The worst culprit for such statements was none other than Mennen Williams himself who, within weeks of Kennedy taking office, embarked upon a moral crusade in Africa, which nearly had him thrown out of Nigeria, mobbed in Ethiopia and all but lynched in Kenya! Later to cause the President mild amusement[4], Williams' slogan of 'Africa for the Africans' sparked off a furore in Africa and the colonial capitals. In Addis Ababa on 18 February he imprudently suggested that 'The old colonial era is dead and with it the old power relationships that formerly shaped the world.' Realistic it may have been, it was undeniably discourteous alliance politics. Worse occurred in Nairobi where his enthusiasm for fraternising with the local African leaders led Williams ostentatiously to ignore white guests, including several Ministers, at a formal reception. If the British and settler reaction was unduly sensitive, it at least reflected the delicate nature of the problems involved and Williams' inability to solve them. It was not only British M.P.s who bewailed his outrageous breach of courtesy. His critics in Congress were no less vociferous, one charging that he was still campaigning in Michigan. 'Mr Williams has made great progress,' observed Representative Meader (R. Michigan). 'It took him twelve years to wreck Michigan. It only took him one month to wreck our African relations.' Another Congressman, William Miller, went as far as to urge Kennedy to recall Williams 'before he spreads hoof-in-mouth disease all over Africa': 'To send a bumptious, tactless, unskilled representative such as Williams to attend to the delicate affairs of Africa is an insult to the intelligence of the people of that area.'

Determined not to give ground to his critics, Kennedy, when asked to comment on Williams' 'Africa for the Africans' slogan, dryly observed: 'I don't know who else Africa should be for!' Like his Assistant Secretary, the President felt that the American mission would have been foredoomed had American remarks been tailored to the sensitivities of the colonial powers. Yet, in later trips to Africa, Williams was to moderate his remarks and, in place of the rather impulsive American politician, with the American political habit of speaking off the cuff with little regard for the consequences, he spoke diplomatically, refusing to be trapped by eager reporters. But his subsequent moderation was unable to undo the damage done by his first visit, which had also left some of his colleagues in the State Department aghast. Issues of colonialism were always to split the Department and in fact ultimately, despite his political background, Williams turned out to be none too proficient in this intramural warfare.

A certain measure of European resentment was unavoidable when the United States intruded itself on what they considered their private preserves. Europeans suspected—as, for example, did the Dutch over West New Guinea—that one of the primary American purposes was to squeeze them out so as to leave the field clear for American enterprise and political supremacy. They were concerned with the apparent decline in American responsiveness to their views. Above all, there was a genuine belief that the United States neither understood nor appreciated the complex nature and magnitude of the problems involved in evacuation from empire. Iain Macleod, the British Colonial Secretary at the time, was to be convinced that Williams never realised that there were white as well as black Africans! The Administration merely advocated the acceleration of the dismantling of empires, as one American columnist put it, 'without realising that the disintegration of the old empires at that speed was going to lead to a great deal of chaos and upheaval in the world which was not at all in our interest.'

Independence for many nations created almost as many problems as it solved (if not more). Between 1960 and 1966 military coups and mutinies took place in fourteen countries. Plots and counterplots were rife, political assassinations almost commonplace. Independence did not automatically bring the promised land. Rather did it bring disillusionment and, with austerity unpopular, the nationalist leaders settled for totally unrealistic development plans. They tried in vain to deal with problems which would have tested even mature political systems. The inevitable result was repression and denial of individual freedoms: the leaders became more preoccupied with their own survival than with anything else. If that were not enough, they had desperately to try to create a national consciousness where hitherto nationhood had been, at best a flimsy structure, at worst a divisive force. Probably in no country were the problems posed by independence more in evidence than in the Congo, a vast sprawling mass (mostly tropical jungle), covering over a million square miles.

The Congo gained its independence in the summer of 1960 with almost no preparation, and almost immediately disintegrated with its richest province, Katanga, promptly seceding. The power centres were leaderless, its leaders powerless. President Kasavubu dismissed Prime Minister Lumumba, Lumumba dismissed Kasavubu. He also attacked the provincial leader, Tshombe, for not recognising the authority of the Central Government but was in turn arrested by Colonel Mobutu for claiming that he was the Central Government! With such a power vacuum of obvious appeal to the Soviets, who had long sought a base in the heart of Africa, the Congo crisis was to be a major preoccupation of the Kennedy Administration throughout 1961. And, in so far as the only alternative to complete anarchy was a United Nations presence to re-establish order and authority, the crisis also brought the United States and Britain into unexpected and at times bitter, conflict.

President Kennedy's aim was the restoration of stability to a reunited and viable Congo and his chief instrument to achieve this was American diplomatic, economic and—to the extent of providing air transport—military support of the U.N. efforts to pacify the country and reconcile its factions. But, as in Laos, the situation in the Congo seemed to go only from bad to worse. Within a month of Kennedy taking office, Lumumba was brutally murdered. The Soviets and African nationalists, protesting vehemently at the assassination, quickly recognised Lumumba's old Vice-Premier, Antoine Gizenga, as the legitimate Congolese leader and promised him their support. Still backing the United Nations action, the Americans continued to recognise the government of Kasavubu. Yet in fact the danger of Soviet intervention was for Kennedy to prove a less difficult hurdle than the problem of Tshombe and Katanga. The President knew that, unless the Central Government could end the province's secession, Gizenga—indeed the forces of division throughout Africa— would have a field day.

Unfortunately for Kennedy, Tshombe appealed to many in the West as militantly anti-communist and Europeans, eager to safe-guard Katanga's copper, cobalt and other mineral assets, urged a policy of caution. As long as Tshombe talked co-operation, Britain and France held off the economic sanctions which the United States requested. But, with the U.N. having neither the funds nor the forces available to bring him down, Tshombe merely sat tight, thereby trying the patience of the Afro-Asians, who demanded that the U.N. take more positive steps to end the secession.

The United States agreed to supply more planes and equipment and even briefly considered sending in a squadron of American fighters to help end the secession more quickly. But this led to disagreement with Britain, which declined to support any U.N. attempts to impose a political solution. 'The United Nations forces are, of course, fully entitled to protect themselves when they are attacked,' Edward Heath told the Commons on 6 December 1961, 'but they have not got a permit from the resolutions to try to impose a political solution by force.' Suspecting that the U.N. action was only creating further anarchy in the Congo, the British Government initially refused to comply with a request to supply the Indian Air Force contingent of the U.N. force with bombs for their Canberras. Even when, after American pressure, Britain did tentatively agree to supply twenty-four bombs, she still stipulated their use for preventative action and withheld shipment until U.N. policy had been clarified. U Thant eventually withdrew the request for bombs because of British anxiety, but this did not lead to any relaxation in the British diplomatic offensive to end the war. Such efforts, however, only publicly revealed British and American differences on the handling of the crisis, with America on 13 December coming out in open opposition to the British proposal for an immediate ceasefire. 'It is becoming increasingly apparent', commented *The Times* (14 December), 'that Anglo-American differences in the conduct of Congo policy are as serious as any since the Suez crisis.' The differences were, however, basically over means rather than ends. Admittedly, Britain was prepared to accept a more loosely federated government than the Americans thought wise. But she still attached importance to bringing Tshombe into the Central Government. The British Government merely held that coercing Tshombe into accepting the more stringent federation would only make conciliation almost impossible and thus do more harm than good. Ultimately, the Katanga resistance was to be surprisingly swiftly ended by the U.N. force and the province re-integrated, though this was to do little to help solve the problem of creating a sense of nationhood.

The turmoil in the Congo was to be much of an eye-opener for the Kennedy Administration, highlighting the problems brought about by premature independence. With this experience acquired, the United States perceptibly moderated both its demands and remarks on colonialism. 'We agree with those who say that colonialism is a key issue in this Assembly,' Kennedy told the U.N. in September, 1961, 'but let the full facts of that issue be discussed in full . . . problems will be solved with patience, good-will and determination. Within the limits of our responsibility in such matters, my country intends to be a participant, and not merely an observer, in the peaceful, expeditious movement of nations from the status of colonies to the partnership of equals.' That the transition should, above all, be peaceful and orderly became the keystone of the Administration's policy. And it is perhaps ironic that, in the case of the transfer of power to British Guiana, it was America which was to urge the British Government to move more cautiously.

With a joint Indian and Negro population of about 600,000, British Guiana in 1961 already enjoyed a considerable measure of autonomy and was, by the standards then laid down by Britain, expected to gain full independence within a year or two. But an election in September, 1961, introduced an explosive element of uncertainty, when it brought to power the Indian Party, the People's Progressive Party, under the leadership of Dr Cheddi Jagan, widely considered anti-colonialist and quasi-Marxist. Deeply concerned to prevent any of the Americas following the Castro road, Kennedy feared that, if the colony received early independence under Jagan, Britain would only have dumped a communist 'time-bomb' at his back door. Not unsympathetic to American representations, Britain nevertheless held that only attractive offers of aid could help to prevent the colony from going communist. Even with aid, there was a fair chance of this happening: without it, communism was a certainty.

Initially prepared to give about $5 million in aid, Kennedy, after meeting Jagan in October, 1961, decided that, rather than make any concrete commitments, each project would have to be examined on its merits. Learning that this reversal of intention had upset Jagan, Britain expressed her concern that he should not return to his country disgruntled. Accordingly, a statement was issued in Washington which announced the establishment of a mission to determine what kind of aid could support British

Guiana's development, and which also committed Jagan 'to uphold the political freedoms and defend the parliamentary democracy which is his country's fundamental heritage.'

If Washington was inclined to suspect that the British wanted
only to get out of Guiana as quickly as possible, the Macmillan
Government could hardly be begrudged its sarcasm with Americans, who, having exerted self-righteous pressures to accelerate
the timetable of African independence, should now urge a postponement when the problems came nearer to home. Not wanting
to wallow in sarcasm, however, Britain came increasingly to share
the American apprehension, especially after race riots in George-
town in February, 1962, necessitated sending in British troops to
restore a semblance of order.

Washington, meanwhile, had become impressed with the Negro
leader, Forbes Burnham, whom Britain had earlier suspected of
being less responsible than Jagan. Burnham appeared not only
anti-communist but seemed also aware that there could be no
happy future for an independent Guiana as long as its leaders continued to incite racial animosities. London and Washington thus
concluded that an independent nation under Burnham would pose
considerably fewer problems for the West than one under Jagan.
And the way was open to bring Jagan down, for his parliamentary
strength had in fact been greater than his popular strength. He had
been elected Prime Minister on a minority vote. The obvious
solution, ingeniously devised by the British, was a system of
proportional representation, which was established in October,
1963, and which in 1964 was to achieve the desired end: namely,
the downfall of Jagan and his replacement by a coalition government under the more acceptable Burnham. Here then was a case,
not of the United States responding to British requests to
moderate its remarks, but of Britain responding to urgent pleas
from the United States to slow down the process of decolonisation!

If issues influencing the balance of power in Europe are to be
considered the occasion for alliance between Britain and America,
then observing the issues outside the European theatre, especially
towards the Third World, they have all too often been the occasion
of division between the two allies. In part such issues involved
conflicts of interests and priorities. But they have also involved to a
great extent conflicts of historical outlook. Britain has traditionally

espoused diplomatic principles oriented towards balance and compromise, tacitly assuming that one can rub along even with an adversary provided one does not permit moral enthusiasm for his defeat to get the better of political judgement. It is an outlook that has not always come easily to the United States, best exemplified by the different British and American approaches to the issue of the recognition of Peking. For twenty years, the two Governments had to agree to disagree, the United States, at least until 1971, vehemently refusing to promote any kind of *modus vivendi* between China and the rest of the world. In contrast, Britain not only recognised the People's Republic as an established political fact: to the chagrin of successive American Administrations, she even permitted limited trade contacts with China. The sale of six Viscount aircraft to communist China in 1961, for example, caused considerable resentment in Washington. But, if Britain refused to recognise the validity of American arguments, she equally refused to align herself with the highly intemperate speeches in the U.N. critical of the American position.

Neither Britain nor the United States have been able to stand aloof from the implications of the increasing involvement of the Afro-Asian bloc in world affairs. This involvement has produced attacks on both the United States and Britain, particularly in the context of colonialism. Anti-colonialism seems to have been a convenient outlet for the revolt of the rest of the world against Western domination. For Britain, the attacks were at their severest over the handling of perhaps her most difficult problem in Africa: the Central African Federation and the future of the white settlers in Southern Rhodesia. The very success of the independence movements elsewhere on the continent seemed only to increase the grievances about the dependencies which remained. Yet Britain felt she had enough problems in dealing with the hard, unswerving Prime Minister of the Federation, Sir Roy Welensky, without the U.N. interfering. Indeed she consistently refused to consider U.N. resolutions as in any way binding on the problem of Southern Rhodesia. The British position was one which fortunately the United States could in part support, and this underlined the basis of reciprocity between the two countries. For, where Britain declined to ally herself with the attacks on America, implicit in the resolutions on China, so the United States in turn sought to dampen down the attacks on British policy in Rhodesia. Adlai Stevenson best put the American position in June, 1962 when he told the General Assembly: 'the United Kingdom should have an opportunity to pursue further the steps that it has begun to take. . . . Surely Great Britain, on its record, is entitled to that courtesy and to that confidence.'

For his courage and steadfastness in pursuing the peaceful dismantling of the remaining parts of the British Empire, Macmillan earned both the confidence and the respect of his American colleagues. As it came increasingly to appreciate the problems involved, so the Kennedy Administration became more willing to defer to British wisdom and experience, particularly in solving the tricky problem of Rhodesia. Unfortunately for Macmillan, the attitudes of the whites in Rhodesia only hardened as they in turn became increasingly confident that Britain had 'lost the will to govern'. Refusing to permit the U.N. to interfere, Britain nevertheless took no steps herself. The course was thus set for U.D.I., the implications of which were to dominate British policy in Africa for years hence. U.D.I. was in some ways the price of Macmillan's avoidance of confrontation and his slow, but determined, retreat from previously established positions. For his policy, even if its forthrightness was to be warmly applauded by the Americans, nevertheless left in Africa a settler community which, not without reason, grew increasingly to believe that Britain was neither able nor willing to intervene in the running of their country.

1. Rupert Emerson, 'American Policy in Africa'. *Foreign Affairs*, Vol. 40, No. 2 (January 1962), pp.305-6.
2. John F. Kennedy, *The Strategy of Peace* (Harper & Row, 1960), Introduction.
3. *The New York Times* (25 March 1961).
4. At the Gridiron dinner in March, Kennedy remarked that he had just received a cable from Williams asking to prolong his stay in Africa. 'I felt I had better send this reply,' Kennedy told his audience: 'No, Soapy. Africa is for the Africans.'

15

It Never Rains—Kennedy and Macmillan's Departure

The slow but painful retreat from Empire was only one of many problems which faced Macmillan as he entered his last year in office. Another more pressing problem was the slump in the British economy in the winter of 1962/1963. The phrase 'never had it so good' was beginning to turn sour on him. It was in fact the worst winter since 1881 with stagnant production and mounting unemployment. By February, 1963, the total number of unemployed had reached 3.9 per cent of the working population, the highest figure since the fuel crisis of 1947. Full employment was in time to return but not before there had been renewed murmurings against Macmillan. Meanwhile, the Prime Minister had antagonised the Press with his handling of the Vassal case. An Admiralty clerk in the office of Thomas Galbraith, the Civil Lord, Vassal had in the autumn of 1962 been arrested for spying and duly convicted. Not satisfied to let the matter rest with Vassal's conviction, the Press had embarked on a vicious slur campaign against Galbraith and other Ministers: therefore, to clear his Administration of the charges of lack of probity, Macmillan felt compelled to establish a tribunal of inquiry. The Radcliffe Tribunal, as it was called, did clear Galbraith of the charges levelled against him, but it also resulted in the jailing of two journalists who had refused to divulge their sources of information. Fleet Street blamed Macmillan for the sentences and, having been made to look completely foolish over the affair, the Press was later to set upon the Prime Minister with vengeance.

Nor had Macmillan's foreign policy fared any better. The

Cuban crisis had shown the irrelevancy of Britain, the Skybolt affair had highlighted the consequences of reliance on American good faith. With the Common Market veto following so soon after, Macmillan was understandably depressed. For the collapse of his European policy, on which so many of his ambitions had been centred, marked, as Enoch Powell in 1970 put it, 'perhaps a final point in the story of Macmillan's Administration. And it probably appeared to him—as I know it appeared to other members of his Cabinet who were close to him—that perhaps that was the moment when he should have declared before history that his act was ended.' In short, by 1963 the Macmillan Government presented an unhappy spectacle of collapse and decay. Their ability and enthusiasm to undertake the proper responsibilities of government seemed almost overnight to have quite evaporated. The Prime Minister himself appeared only to lounge increasingly powerless in the heart of all this sorry drift and decay. Quite simply, he seemed exhausted.

With the Government ever more unpopular, the feeling grew, particularly after Harold Wilson's election as leader of the Labour Party at the comparatively youthful age of forty-seven, that the Conservatives needed a younger man to revive their fortunes. Macmillan was after all nearly seventy and a Gallup Poll in March, 1963, showed that three in five of a British sample felt that he should make way for a younger man. A blunt, if not exactly tactful, notice to quit had already been served by a prominent backbench M.P., Sir Harry Legge-Bourke. In a speech in February, 1962, which, though widely disowned, was nevertheless bold enough to state what privately many Tories were thinking, Legge-Bourke said that it was no disgrace for men like Macmillan, who had fought in the Great War, been active in politics between the Wars and borne a heavy responsibility in the Second World War, now to feel exhausted: 'It is no condemnation of those men if we should now say to them "Thank you for what you have done. Thank you for what you have tried to do. The time is coming for you now to hand over those responsibilities to men whose good fortune is not to have had to bear for so many grievous years the burdens you have borne." We must all put the country first and the country today needs unflagging vigour, undaunted hope, infallible faith and the forward look.'

The Tory Party, which had hailed Macmillan in 1957 as its salvation, was now, in its own inimitable way, preparing to dump him. In every way seemingly the epitome of what Britain required of its political leader in 1957, Macmillan by 1963 had become anathema to many segments of the British electorate. How then did he come to lose so much of his lustre so quickly? 'For so able a man to have come to seem so stuffy to the present generation,' wrote *The Economist*, 'for a man of such individual charm to seem so buttoned up . . . these are matters of psychology that a biographer, one day, will have to unravel.' If we are to put Macmillan's decline down to any single factor, it was probably that he never quite adjusted to the public mood of the early sixties, in its way so different from that of the late fifties. Britain in 1963 yearned for a leader, like Kennedy, who could give them hope and promise for the future, who could keep them excited. Instead, at least in the public mind, Macmillan had by this time come to be associated with an era and manner of politics that was simply outdated. He no longer excited the British electorate.

The climate of British politics in 1963 called for something more than Macmillan's political artistry. 'I am perfectly well aware', remarked Rab Butler in July, 1963, 'that people want us to give a fresh impression of vigour and direction before the next election.' 'We have not been successful', admitted Maudling at a fête in Cambridge, 'in obtaining the allegiance of the younger generation of voters, because we have not yet found a way of talking to them in language they understand or in terms of the ideals they cherish.' The idea of modernising with Macmillan carried a somewhat ridiculous ring about it!

Macmillan never did find a way of talking to the young in the language they understood, but what was his undoing was also to be Kennedy's greatest claim for posterity. In 1963, President Kennedy had seemingly become the hope, if not the hero, of liberals and even more of the young, the two groups in society which were to feel alienated most from Macmillan. Kennedy, in contrast to Macmillan, carried his message direct to the people themselves, over the heads of their governments. 'He spoke to us for the first time in the language of the present generation,' wrote Countess Maria Dönhoff for *Die Zeit*; 'a man who was able to project a vision of the future without moving an inch away from the reality of our times; a man whose many-faceted intellect grasped the essence of power; a man who knew every trick of the political game without having become a cynic in the process.' In Kennedy, the young and the liberals put great trust and confidence, as reflected in their demonstrations of enthusiasm during his triumphant trip to Europe in June, 1963.

Unwittingly, however, Kennedy's very ability to capture the public imagination only made things more difficult for Macmillan, increasing the sense of frustration felt in Britain towards his style of government. The dynamism of a young President drew ever more attention to the Prime Minister's age, placing in even sharper relief the irrelevancy of Macmillan in the modern era. It was an effect made more pronounced by the satirist's character assassination of the Prime Minister. Satire, at its heyday in 1963, served to give a platform for the protests of the younger generation against the aristocratic nature of Macmillan's Administration. Macmillan's tragedy was that, at this critical juncture in his premiership, he was utterly incapable of projecting any vision of the future. His patrician style, so acceptable in 1957, now turned out to be his greatest liability. And it is against this back-cloth of the rejection of old-fashioned snobbery that the Profumo scandal was to inflict such irreparable damage to his Administration.

The Profumo affair in retrospect proved to be only the climax of a chain of disasters for Macmillan, the confirmation that he no longer had a grip on affairs. A scandal can usually flourish only in the right soil, and the conditions of 1963 were perfect, with the growing suspicion that Macmillan's Government was steeped in corruption. The seeds had already been sown, the climate of public opinion was already in a state of high expectancy. In March, 1963, Charles Fletcher-Cooke, a junior Minister at the Home Office, had resigned. A public letter of his to Macmillan, revealing that he had lent his car to a former Borstal boy, was more than enough to signal his departure. Then came Vassal and the ridiculous attempts to imply homosexual tendencies of certain Ministers. And after that there was the Duchess of Argyll's divorce. On the surface it had nothing at all to do with politics but the climate of opinion in 1963 was such that it was almost enough to be a member of the Establishment to be associated in the public mind with Macmillan's Administration.

And then, in June, the Profumo scandal finally broke over Macmillan's head. Rumours of an affair between John Profumo, the Minister for War, and Christine Keeler, a 'model', had been ripe for at least six months before; but the Press, having been made a fool of over Vassal, maintained a stony silence. Profumo had been warned of the consequences of his relationship with Keeler, who was known to have associations with Ivanov, the Soviet Military Attaché, but he had consistently maintained that their relationship was on purely a social level. He had offered his resignation to Macmillan, but still conscious of the injustice suffered by Galbraith, Macmillan had persistently refused to accept it. After all, had not Profumo assured him and the House in March that there was nothing serious in his relationship with Keeler? 'His lie had been believed by his colleagues,' Lord Egremont was later to write, 'because his story was so incredible that it must be true. It was as simple as that. And anyone who scoffs at this explanation is not very wise in the ways of the world, because these things can and do happen.'[1]

Of course these things can and do happen and if anything, incredible as it may seem, the Profumo affair was, at least in American eyes, actually to enhance the reputation of British politicians. Long considered above such obvious human weaknesses, the picture of British politicians presented to Americans had been one of a dull and rather an uninteresting lot. Profumo had now changed all this and Washington merely chuckled at the observation that Christine Keeler had proved that mixed-manning after all did work! London, however, did not take the affair so lightly. The nation was outraged and the Macmillan Government assumed notoriety for its laxity and complicity. The British people may not always be shaken by the ways of the world, nor even scandalised by adultery, but they dislike intensely duplicity and, as he admitted in June, Profumo had actually lied to the House of Commons. A Gallup Poll after Profumo's confession showed that Labour's lead over the Conservatives was the highest for twenty-five years and Macmillan's rating was the lowest since Chamberlain. Fifty-four per cent of the sample expressed their dissatisfaction with his premiership. He was the one man who should have known the innermost truth of the scandals. 'It was the responsibility of the Prime Minister and his colleagues,' concluded the Denning Report in September, 'and of them only, to deal with the situation: and they did not succeed in doing so.'

Beyond the public indignation lurked more sinister implications, namely the laxity in British security. Sixty-seven per cent of the Gallup sample doubted if Macmillan had taken adequate security precautions and it was this, aside from the titillations, which was most to concern the American Administration. Following so soon in the wake of the Portland Spy Ring and the Vassal affair, the Profumo scandal brought to a head the mounting concern of Americans with British security arrangements. At the best of times extremely reluctant to impart information, American intelligence chiefs had long been interested in Ivanov, ever since his blustering threats at the height of the missile crisis to the question of who had tried to obtain intelligence from whom about plans to arm West Germany with nuclear warheads. Even if in retrospect the Profumo affair did not pose a major security risk, it was sufficient to lead to increasing demands that the United States restrict its information to Britain until she had tightened up her security arrangements. In July, however, MacGeorge Bundy declared that 'It is certainly not the view of the United States Government, at this stage at all, that there is a difficulty so grave in British security problems that we would have to re-examine co-operation in all kinds of fields, military, strategic, intelligence.' Kennedy had nevertheless raised the problem with Macmillan at their seventh, and as it turned out their last, meeting at Birch Grove in June, 1963.

The Profumo affair inflicted upon Macmillan, as he himself admitted, 'a deep, bitter and lasting wound', and Kennedy did not want to complicate matters for the Prime Minister. Indeed, genuinely fond of Macmillan, Kennedy had considerable sympathy for his friend's unenviable position in his last year in office. Told later, for example, that he had been soft on Macmillan at Nassau, the President had remarked, 'If you were in that kind of trouble, you would want a friend.'[2] But much as he wanted to help Macmillan, Kennedy was not prepared to get embroiled in British domestic politics. He was certainly not willing to be used in the way that he considered Macmillan had 'used' Eisenhower in the 1959 General Election. Political leaders in most countries had by 1963 begun to recognise that Kennedy's popularity could improve their own standing at home and Macmillan had at first hoped that the President's visit to London would give the British people an opportunity to forget the Profumo affair. Instead, the arrangements for the Birch Grove meeting, announced but a week before it took place, were, as one Macmillan aide confirmed, 'played very much to Kennedy's wishes.' The President preferred their talks to take place in the relative seclusion of Macmillan's country-house and was, accordingly, almost immediately upon his arrival in Britain whisked off by helicopter to Birch Grove.

While at Birch Grove, Kennedy was to get steamed up about an article that appeared in *The Sunday Telegraph* on that day (30 June), which had criticised the Press arrangements for the President's European tour. The article charged that they had been made to the advantage of the White House correspondents and to the disadvantage of European correspondents. The President was particularly annoyed with the accusation since, always conscious of the power of the Press, he had long sought, as far as humanly possible, to make friends of journalists, domestic and foreign. He may himself only have read two British papers, *The Sunday Times* and *The Economist*, but he went out of his way where possible to grant interviews to foreign correspondents. He had, for example, readily agreed to a television interview with European correspondents, which had in the end proved impossible only through France's refusal to have any part of it. Kennedy, not without reason, felt that its failure had been no fault of his own. Moreover, a visit such as the Birch Grove meeting inevitably tends to be considered by any President to an extent as an extension of domestic politics. But the same was equally true of a Prime Minister's visit to Washington, which traditionally involves a degree of special treatment accorded to British correspondents there. It was thus that, at Birch Grove, Kennedy called in his Press Secretary, Pierre Salinger, and the two men spent some time drafting a letter to the editor of *The Sunday Telegraph*, recording the full facts. Only after the letter had been drafted to the President's satisfaction did he go to his meeting with Macmillan.

The Kennedy–Macmillan meeting at Birch Grove went badly. Possibly following his Berlin trip, where he had been hailed almost as the second coming, and his Irish sojourn, the trip to Britain was for Kennedy inevitably an anti-climax. But it was more than this. Though they were able to decide policy issues, the President was to be greatly disillusioned with Macmillan. Previously such a stimulating source of information, Kennedy now found the Prime Minister so tired and so lacking in ideas. Macmillan could not convey any sense of excitement and optimism for the future because he did not feel any. The President was more surprised than upset that Macmillan had been unable to find the time to fit into the schedule a short meeting between Kennedy and Wilson, even though the Labour leader radiated none of the warmth which Kennedy had found in Gaitskell. Indeed the President had never quite been able to understand why Macmillan and Gaitskell, both of whom he liked enormously, had disliked each other so much. Gaitskell's tragic death in January, 1963, was to be regretted by Kennedy not just for the human loss but more for the vanished opportunity of the two men working together sometime in the future.

Kennedy's affection for Gaitskell did not, however, for a moment undermine his friendship with Macmillan, for whom he felt genuinely sorry. It was Kennedy's suggestion that his letter, praising Macmillan's efforts in the test-ban negotiations, be published. Unfortunately for Macmillan it did little to improve his standing at home. Macmillan's achievements were all too often inclined to go unnoticed. By the autumn of 1963 the British Press, having licked its wounds incurred over the Vassal affair, had all but crucified Macmillan. They had called him a megalomaniac, mad, senile, mangy and buck-toothed. He had been accused of lying, of complicity, even of treason. But the old boy had just soldiered on, and the end when it came was (almost providentially) due to chance. A prostate operation—which Macmillan was told would keep him out of action for weeks but which, to his intense annoyance, laid him up for days only—led to his resignation on 10 October 1963, followed by the most extraordinary internecine struggle for his successor.

Macmillan's departure was to be greatly grieved by President Kennedy. For three years the two leaders had worked together in the closest association. Every few months they had met and in between had exchanged frequent messages and telephone talks. They had got to know each other intimately. Theirs had been a relationship founded on mutual trust and friendship, the kind of relationship that permitted frankness and recognised honest differences. Their efforts in a whole host of co-operative ventures had greatly enhanced the intensity of the Anglo-American relationship. And now it seemed that, with Macmillan's exit, Kennedy would have to start all over again to build up such a meaningful rapport with the Prime Minister's successor. Tragically, the President was not to have time to do this, for it was only six weeks later that he was himself to be gunned down so brutally in Dallas.

1. Lord Egremont, *Wyndam and Children First* (Macmillan, 1968), p.188.
2. Quoted in Theodore Sorensen, *Kennedy* (Hodder & Stoughton, 1965), p.559.

16
Assassination and Martyrdom

Dr Johnson once remarked, 'It matters not how a man dies, but how he lives. The act of dying is not of importance, it lasts so short a time.' Yet surely few people do not remember where they were on Friday, 22 November 1963, when the world first heard of the assassination of John F. Kennedy. Who, indeed, will ever forget how the President's widow, having been witness on that day to the lowest level of human cruelty, maintained in the ensuing days the highest level of human nobility: how, throughout the burial rites, her slim, upright figure wavered not an inch in dignity, not an inch in grief? Few people do not recall the tensions and emotions intermingled as they laid President Kennedy to rest in Arlington National Cemetery: the lighting of the eternal flame by his brave widow; the young son saluting his father's memory; the silence of the grieving city broken only by the mournful tolling of a single bell and the monotonous roll of drums.

Literally millions of people were to be wholly involved in the death and burial of President Kennedy to an extent unthinkable before the age of electronic communications. Through television, the magnitude of the tragedy involved and overwhelmed us all in a way that would have been inconceivable but a few years before. Three previous American presidents had been assassinated but none, not even Lincoln's, had evoked such an immediate sense of grief and despair that the world felt with Kennedy's murder. 'I can recall no single blow in my lifetime,' Lord Boothby was to write, 'which has struck us all with such stunning force as the assassination of President Kennedy.'[1]

'Great Britain', Mr David Bruce remarked at the time, 'has never before mourned a foreigner as it has President Kennedy.' The traditionally undemonstrative British people unashamedly displayed their own grief and horror. We felt that we had lost not just a leader but a friend. 'We have lost our champion,' lamented the *Daily Mirror* (23 November 1963). We discovered that he had been more familiar to us than we had previously known or been prepared to admit. We had perhaps taken him too much for granted, for he had been the one Western politician of his era who had restored politics to its former position as a respectable and honourable profession. A television tribute given by the Prime Minister aptly summarised the grief experienced by the British people. 'There are times when the mind and heart stand still,' declared Sir Alec Douglas-Home; 'one such is now.'

In varying degrees, all of us felt such a standstill. 'To the whole of humanity struggling in the world of darkness,' remarked Macmillan, in a deeply moving personal tribute, 'it seemed a sudden and cruel extinction of a shining light.' Our anguish was universal, but it was also very individual. Millions of ordinary people suffered a personal loss. Countless thousands from all over the country were to file through the American Embassy in Grosvenor Square to sign the books of condolence. A requiem mass for the dead President filled Westminster Cathedral beyond capacity. The extremity of our dismay was perhaps the true measure of the grandeur of his achievement and our response to his murder will forever be a monument to the affection in which he was held in Britain. But why was it that, in common with the rest of the world, we felt such a desolation of spirit at the news of his death and such a sense of utter despair about the future which, for as long as he lived, had seemed so bright with promise? Was it not perhaps that we were simply being carried away by our emotions in the face of a stark human tragedy—the gunning down of a young President in the presence of his beautiful wife?

The personal tragedy was certainly the one that struck hardest. Here was a man only forty-six years of age, boyish in looks, young in heart, eager and vigorous in spirit. He had presented himself to the British public as an attractive, vital and friendly personality, the embodiment of youth, pulsating with fresh ideas and the political courage to espouse them. In British eyes, he had brought to international politics the excitement and the integrity of youth. He was of course no child: he was only fourteen months younger than Harold Wilson, and no one talked of Wilson's youthfulness! Yet Kennedy looked very young (to many, ridiculously young). He was tanned, handsome and rich, with a personal magnetism and a photogenic family. He united in one commanding person the idealism of some of the younger generation with the itch for success of the rest. The torch had been passed to a new generation of leaders and now it had been extinguished so cruelly soon, so unnatural seemed the deprivation. 'It is the realisation that the future held the promise of great accomplishments for Joe,' John F. Kennedy had written in an appreciation of his late brother, entitled *As We Remember Joe*, 'that made his death so particularly hard for those who knew him. His worldly success was so assured and inevitable that his death seems to cut into the natural order of things.' Millions of people felt the same sense of loss about John F. Kennedy's own passing. His worldly success had seemed so assured and inevitable that his death had tragically cut into the natural order of things. He had so much life and promise ahead of him until it was all so dastardly ended that day in Dallas.

Beyond the personal tragedy, the British nation shared the American anguish in a peculiarly special and poignant way. There was the great loss derived from the knowledge that, at least since 1940, Britain has increasingly been dependent upon American power and its exercise. 'The President of the United States,' wrote David Butler, 'is the President of Britain. However closely the British guard their independence, however scrupulously the President respects it, he still makes decisions that are more important to their fate than any made by the Prime Minister.' Everything a President does carries world-wide significance. 'When he creaks, they groan,' Sidney Hyman wrote, 'When he wobbles, they feel unhinged.' It was thus that, in the first shock reaction to Kennedy's assassination, we had a brief glimpse of the possibility that the scale in the international balance of power might be significantly, even dangerously, tipped. Understandably we were fearful of what the future might bring, our apprehension heightened by our lack of knowledge of the Vice-President, who seemingly had neither experience nor great interest in foreign affairs. Yet it was Lyndon Johnson who was to be the real hero during those traumatic days. He held the American nation together when they had yet to accept the death of Kennedy, let alone the succession.

Successful as Johnson was in taking over the reins of power, he was nevertheless unable to replace Kennedy in our affections. For Britain, the personal sentiments, biases and prejudices of a President often assume overriding importance, and, unlike his two immediate predecessors, Johnson had no close personal links with Britain. Thus did Nicholas Carroll write, 'For the British Government, the death of President Kennedy is an unqualified disaster.'[2] 'There has not been an American President for many years,' observed Michael Hilton, 'who had a more realistic, and at the same time sympathetic, appreciation of the value of the Anglo-American relationship.'[3]

It is perhaps remarkable how the British people felt that they could join in the activities of President Kennedy in a way that was simply not possible with a President of the United States thirty years before. Difficult as it is to explain, we felt Kennedy, like his predecessor, to be *our* President. We shared in the jokes and gossip about the White House. We took a fascinated interest in the vivacious First Lady who, in the hour of America's greatest need, gave them majesty. We delighted in the enchantingly informal pictures of the President at play with his children, attesting proof that every man, no matter how great and powerful, belongs to the one big family that is the human race. We shared not only the triumphs but also the misfortunes of the Kennedy family: their anguish was ours at the death in August, 1963, of their baby son, Patrick, born with a respiratory disorder which proved too much for his tiny heart. To an unprecedented extent, we immersed ourselves in the details, great and small, of the White House under President Kennedy. Whatever we thought of his politics, President Kennedy became part of our own national history.

But it is surely right to ask whether our instinctive judgement that here was a great man was not perhaps somewhat superficial? Only a very few people are in a position to gain their impressions of a man's character and worth at first-hand. Was it, therefore, not difficult—perhaps impossible—for the majority of the British people to distinguish between myth and reality? Did not the nature of Kennedy's death influence both our assessments

of his achievements and more, our expectations of future successes? Was not the halo fixed upon President Kennedy the day he
died? During those few agonising days, the Kennedy legend was
put before the television cameras and firmly established by them.
'His life, not his death, created his greatness,' argued Sorensen.
'In November, 1963, some saw it for the first time. Others
realised that they had too casually accepted it. Others mourned
that they had not previously admitted it to themselves. But the
greatness was there and it may well loom even larger as the passage
of years lends perspective.'[4]

To be true, he was a man on the verge of greatness, but how
could he establish his greatness in less than three years? Despite
his youth, he was given no chance to write the full history of his
times. Was it not, therefore, an ironic twist of fate that posterity
should relegate his greatness to legend, his martyrdom making a
myth of the mortal man? The legend was so absurdly built up in
the weeks following his death, the myth so absurdly portrayed,
that, as the passage of years has lent perspective, so history, not
cynically but inevitably, has come to challenge it. Hallowed in
1963, the Kennedy name no longer carries a mystique of majesty
about it. Indeed, with Jackie Kennedy's marriage to Aristotle
Onassis, with Edward Kennedy's involvement in the tragic
accident at Chappaquiddick in 1969, and more recently his
meddling in the Ulster Crisis, the Kennedy legend no longer goes
unquestioned in Britain. But this is not necessarily something to
be lamented. Only as the Kennedy name emerges from the slough
of public forgetfulness, which tends to follow the death of all
great men, will President Kennedy cease to be considered yesterday's hero (or villain for some) and instead become a properly
proportioned figure in history, who at least in Britain made a
lasting impact upon our politics.

1. Lord Boothby, *The News Of The World* (24 November 1963).
2. Nicholas Carroll, 'A Shift in East-West Relations', *The Sunday Times* (24 November 1963).
3. Michael Hilton, 'Effect on World Scene', *The Daily Telegraph* (23 November 1963).
4. Theodore Sorensen, *Kennedy* (Hodder & Stoughton, 1965), p.758.

17

To Move a Nation—Kennedy's Impact on British Politics

'Policies, it is true, are bigger than men,' commented *The Sunday Telegraph* (24 November 1963), 'but we must expect during the next year to be sharply, even shockingly, reminded of what the assassination means to the British as well as to the American people. We do more than offer sympathy: we share their mourning and their fears.' In so far as the intricacies of relations in the central power balance depend chiefly upon calculations of national interest, the historical process tends to produce its own cunning, for such objective determinations do not change much as a result of the advent of new decision-makers. But, however much the leadership given by Lyndon Johnson successfully allayed world-wide anxiety in the immediate wake of the assassination, we were indeed to be sharply reminded of what the Kennedy years had meant for Britain. The President's death marked, as subsequent events have confirmed, an end of an era in the history of the Anglo-American relationship. Since 1963, relations between Britain and America have become less intimate, less meaningful and generally of less importance. Instead of a working partnership, made effective by close personal ties, there is now a much more straightforward practical political relationship, with very little place for sentiment. In fact the Johnson–Wilson relationship was essentially one of mutual convenience between two extremely experienced, skilful political leaders, who both recognised, as a former Foreign Office official put it, that 'they had a good deal to offer to each other in different ways.' Even then, there were to be very difficult episodes in their relationship. However much Wilson may have assured the Commons on 21 December 1965 that 'We have reached a clearer understanding than probably at any other time since the Second World War', there was a period when President Johnson would not have turned a hand to help the Prime Minister. And Wilson in turn was to be so annoyed with the President's vetoing of his Vietnam peace initiative in February 1967 that he expressed the view 'that, in terms of influence on his master, the more I saw of certain of the White House advisers, the more I thought Rasputin was a much-maligned man.'[1]

Like Macmillan, Wilson attached great importance to the Anglo-American relationship, which (also like Macmillan) he believed could only be made effective through the establishment of a close rapport with the President of the United States. Unfortunately, he was never able to establish with Johnson anything resembling the intimate relationship between Kennedy and Macmillan. President Johnson's attitude to Britain was to be essentially patronising and parochial. ('It's an itsy-bitsy country, but it's the blood which counts,' he had once confided to a British correspondent in Washington, 'It's where I get my Herefords from!') Not once during the life of his Administration did LBJ visit Britain, not even for Churchill's funeral; and his foreign policy, by both necessity and design, came to be increasingly orientated towards South-East Asia, which, as Macmillan had warned in 1961, did direct American attention and interest away from Europe. Where Kennedy had been primarily concerned with events in the Atlantic alliance, Johnson was to be unable to see further than Vietnam. And over this crucial issue, of American involvement in the Vietnam War, the very foundations of the Anglo-American relationship were to be seriously, if not disastrously, undermined.

When Wilson became Prime Minister in October 1964, he found that the Johnson Administration was prepared to go to almost any lengths to bale Britain out of her economic crises, rather than see the £ devalued, a course of action which apparently was widely canvassed in the early days of the Labour Government. At their first meeting in Washington in December 1964, Johnson was disconcertingly brusque with the Prime Minister, urging him to construct a foreign policy which was in keeping with Britain's economic position; at the same time, however, he warmly welcomed assurances from Wilson both of support for the American action in Vietnam and also for a continuing British presence East of Suez. Even though he discreetly shelved his earlier promise to renegotiate the Nassau Agreement, Wilson nevertheless regarded that meeting as 'a foundation for the re-building of a "special relationship" in a constructive and radical form'.[2] And, on the surface, the talks had seemed to go well. But *The Sunday Times* Insight (7 May 1967) reported that Wilson had privately told an aide:' "Johnson's gone mad! We'll have to find a new ally." ' However true that may be, it was certainly not long after, when the Americans escalated the Vietnam War, that relations between the two Governments took a rapid turn for the worse.

Confident that the Anglo-American relationship was still the basis of British foreign policy, Wilson wanted to wield influence, and more, be seen to wield influence, within the alliance. But his first attempt to do so was almost a catastrophe. When the Americans announced their decision to bomb North Vietnam, as a reprisal against the sinking of an American ship in the Gulf of Tonkin, Wilson begged to arrange an 'eyeball-to-eyeball' confrontation with Johnson so that he, Wilson, could intervene to halt the bombing. LBJ was so furious with the suggestion that he abruptly cut off their telephone conversation: 'The decision to bomb North Vietnam has been taken by the President of the United States and had nothing to do with Harold Wilson.'[3]

There may be a much wider understanding in America today of why Britain did not enter the Vietnam War but in 1965, as one British columnist recalled, 'When they escalated the war, the Johnson Administration assumed that Britain would go in with them. They could never really forgive us.' Britain's refusal to give more than moral support put her, as a senior Johnson aide commented, 'almost in the position of France, of withdrawing to all practical purposes from the SEATO treaty.' Dean Rusk was particularly incensed by the British position. ' "All we needed was one regiment," ' he confided to Louis Heren one evening, ' "The Black Watch would have done. Just one regiment, but you wouldn't. Well, don't expect us to save you again!" '[4]

The American attitude to British policy in Vietnam was in fact not that different from Britain's attitude towards the American position over Suez. The United States has seen its vital interests threatened in Vietnam in much the same way that Britain in 1956 saw her vital interests threatened by Nasser. The fundamental issue in both instances was how far the community of interest in the Anglo-American alliance extended: for, in both cases, where the one ally refused to give active support, the other felt betrayed. But as long as the Prime Minister continued to emphasise a British presence East of Suez, Johnson managed to keep in check his suspicions of Wilson's Vietnam initiatives. He could thus hardly contain his fury when the British Government proposed that, as part of the devaluation package, British troops were to be withdrawn from their bases in the Far East and the Gulf. This was just the last straw for Johnson. Not altogether without reason, Britain was seen as opting out of her responsibilities. And with Wilson still insisting on making regular visits to Washington, even when there seemed to be no obvious advantage to be gained, LBJ became convinced that the Prime Minister was only playing electoral politics from the steps of the White House.

It was, therefore, no great surprise that when Edward Heath became Prime Minister in 1970 he should have found that the intimacy of Anglo-American relations, to which the Conservatives had been accustomed when last in office, had sharply diminished. By all accounts, in the past two years Mr Heath has managed to restore much of the cordiality in relations. He and President Nixon have certainly established a much more meaningful relationship. They are both conservatives of much the same stripe and their view of the world, and of the place of the Anglo-American relationship, appear to be very similar. 'They achieved an extraordinary closeness,' observed Henry Brandon of the Nixon–Heath summit at Camp David in December 1970, 'almost too close for the taste of some.'[5] Heath speaks not of a 'special relationship' but of a 'natural relationship'; and, at their Bermuda meeting in December 1971 (ten years to the day of the Kennedy–Macmillan meeting there), President Nixon declared that the Anglo-American alliance is now more important than it has ever been. The 'special relationship' has 'not broken up', remarked *The Daily Express* (22 December 1971), 'it has grown up!'

Such rhetoric is, of course, normal on these occasions, yet today it somehow fails to carry the desired conviction. For, whatever

Mr Nixon may say to flatter his principal ally, the Anglo-American relationship appears no longer to be as important to the United States as it was in the past. And it is no longer so important, as a senior Kennedy and Johnson official put it, 'because we have not had since 1963 the same kind of business to transact with Britain.' Britain no longer plays any decisive role in South-East Asia. There has been neither a Berlin crisis nor a Cuban missile crisis, which in the early sixties had drawn the two Governments together into a close working partnership. The Test-Ban Treaty has been signed, the 'Kennedy Round' has been completed. And, of course, hanging like a dark shadow over not only the relations between the two Governments, but also the relations between the two peoples, has been the Vietnam War. Undeniably it has been injurious to the image of Americans abroad, with Englishmen increasingly prepared to believe the very worst of American depravity.

America's involvement in the Vietnam War has been the most important single element in the tragic estrangement between the United States and its allies and, had he lived, President Kennedy might have handled it better than his successor. It is almost inconceivable that he would have made the miscalculations made by Johnson. But no one can ever be sure. 'It will indeed never be possible to measure the consequences of the loss,' commented *The Sunday Times* (24 November 1963). 'Great statesmen are rare at any time: great statesmen with the gift of hope are even rarer. . . . No one will ever know what opportunities might not have arisen if he had still been there to bring them to life.' In certain instances, however, what people believe might have happened can be as important in terms of public opinion on an issue as what actually happens. For the American nation, the Vietnam War is one such instance. To be true, it was in Vietnam that the communists were to call the bluff of a major promise of President Kennedy's given in his Inaugural Address: 'Let every nation know, whether it wishes us well or ill, that we shall pay any price, bear any burden, meet any hardship, support any friend, oppose any foe to assure the survival and the success of liberty.'

Vietnam was in fact the price paid for magnificent rhetoric but impossible policy. It was not a question of whether America was right to escalate the war but whether, physically and psychologically, she was able. And at a high price—the alienation from government of many segments of American society—we now know the answer: America simply cannot play St George to so many dragons. Nevertheless, for most people, in America, in Britain and around the world, the Vietnam War and its consequences are neither automatically nor obviously associated with President Kennedy. There were two thousand American troops in Vietnam when he took office and only sixteen thousand troops there by the time of his death. In the public's estimation, the Vietnam War is identified with Johnson and, to an increasing extent, with Nixon. Thus, looking back on those thousand days, which so many were to remember as a Golden Age, holding the promise of a bright and exciting future, they were to be less the beginning than possibly the end of an age. Certainly with Kennedy's death so also passed the age of American innocence. Men rejected their politics and turned to violence to achieve their ends; they questioned the usefulness of their institutions and challenged the very foundations of American society. The war created huge and bitter divisions in society which neither Johnson nor Nixon, both of whom, despite their efforts, remain basically 'unloved' and enigmatic characters, have been able to heal. Had he lived, President Kennedy perhaps could have led his country through their convulsions to a better and more stable order. Again, however much people fervently believe this, we cannot be sure. But of one thing we can be confident: there can have been few more cruel illustrations than the tragedy at Dallas of the great danger in relying on anything so fragile as human flesh. Yet even then, as the passage of years has lent perspective, so increasingly Americans have come to view the Kennedy Presidency with disappointment and disillusionment. He had promised them so much. He had pledged himself to get the country moving again. But by 1963 the United States, for many Americans, had moved neither very fast nor for that matter very far. It was in foreign affairs, more than in domestic affairs, that the Presidency of John F. Kennedy was to leave its mark: and, in certain respects, he was to be better remembered, held in higher regard, and make a more lasting impact in Britain than in his own country.

The British people have thought it fitting to erect monuments in London to only three American Presidents: Abraham Lincoln,

Franklin D. Roosevelt and John F. Kennedy. In Kennedy's case, they have also raised a memorial to him on the hallowed ground of Runnymede, opened by the Queen in May 1965, and established a scholarship scheme that will for ever bear his name. Remarkable as it was that Kennedy, in British eyes, should be placed in the same category as two of America's greatest ever Presidents: it was an honour made even more noteworthy by the fact that his Presidency lasted but a brief three years. How was it then that this young man, who held office for such a short period, should have so captured the imagination of the supposedly undemonstrative British people? What was it that this son of an unpopular American Ambassador to Britain did and stood for that made his achievements so paramount in our memories?

It was extraordinary how popular Kennedy proved to be in Britain where, as recently as 1969, by a significant margin, the British people (as reflected in a Gallup Poll) voted him The Man of The Decade.[6] 'Beyond doubt,' concluded *The Sunday Times* (24 November 1963), 'President Kennedy was the man the British people would have chosen if they had had the right to choose. Astonishing as it is to remember, President Kennedy won in 1960 by a tiny margin. [His victory over Nixon had in fact been the narrowest since 1888.] He would always have won here by a landslide against any opponent.' The British sense of judgement was attuned to his judgement. The slogans of the New Frontier did not have time to leave as deep an imprint in Britain as those of Roosevelt's New Deal. But they influenced men as widely different as Harold Wilson and Edward Heath. President Kennedy's desire to move forward in social and economic affairs all but mirrored our own almost obsessive needs. As Lord Boothby was to summarise his impact, 'Kennedy was the living embodiment of what we have all been longing for and have desperately missed . . . Youth, Energy, Courage and—above all—Hope.'[7]

Kennedy's personality roused impatience and hope of change and fresh aspirations in British politics. An unassuming manner and Edwardian elegance are no longer sufficient to meet the needs and aspirations of the British electorate. In place of the 'gifted amateur', who had for centuries assumed a patrician rule, we now demand total commitment and professionalism from our politicians. More than this, we look for a man who can offer the same kind of charismatic leadership as Kennedy did. Kennedy's style had been essentially a British style, in that his oratory was the kind to which the British people felt they could respond. But it made a lasting impact in Britain through the President's skilful combination of personal magnetism and 'telly-genetics'. Thus did the younger generation of British politician try hard (though without much success) to capture the same kind of image which Kennedy had, of somebody belonging very much to the modern world.

Kennedy's example was to herald a new era in the style and manner of politics in various Western countries. It greatly enhanced the fortunes of Willy Brandt, now Chancellor of West Germany, and paved the way for Pierre Trudeau, whose pitted skin and battered boyishness combined to make him touted as Canada's JFK. But of other Western political leaders, it was the British Labour Party policy-makers who were probably most visibly influenced in their attitude to America, and their approach to politics, by the personality of President Kennedy. And no single politician was more affected than Harold Wilson, who observed Kennedy with an admiration which developed rapidly into a form of hero-worship. A visit to the White House had long been considered by many a British politician as a must. Now the younger politicians went further: they imitated Kennedy's style, analysed his campaign techniques and permitted their publicists to portray them as 'another Kennedy'. Thus was Wilson's visit to the United States in the spring of 1963 put across by his public relations team as the visit of a Kennedy man, espousing Kennedy ideas, and discussing the future of the world, and especially the Anglo-American relationship, in modern, purposive terms.

President Kennedy fascinated Wilson as no politician had fascinated him since Stafford Cripps. The 'new broom'—energetic, vital, dynamic, technocratic—set for Wilson, and for many in Britain, in even sharper relief the kind of old-school tie incompetence, represented by Macmillan and Home, which he so despised. The new Administration of President Kennedy, Wilson, then Shadow Chancellor, told the Commons on 7 February 1961, 'are looking to new frontiers, while this tired, discredited, caste-ridden Government, boasting of nothing but a certain amount of Edwardian elegance, allows Britain to lag behind.'

A devoted student of Kennedy methods, Wilson was to model

his campaign in the 1964 British General Election very much on Kennedy's 1960 Campaign. As Kennedy had done with such effect so Wilson presented himself as the man to get his country moving again. He campaigned to free the country from the 'grouse moor conception' of leadership, continually emphasising the theme of purpose, 'social purpose, economic purpose, purpose in foreign affairs'. He may have been derided by Douglas-Home as a 'slick salesman of synthetic science', but who can deny that such a campaign reaped great dividends?

In government, Wilson was a faithful follower of Kennedy's style of decision-taking. He insisted on pulling an issue out of the bureaucratic rut in time and defended his own freedom of innovation and right of decision. Later he was to speak of the importance of getting in on emerging questions 'by holding meetings of all relevant Ministers at an early stage before the problem gets out of hand. That's one of the techniques the world owes to Kennedy.'[8] Like Kennedy, Wilson was to bring into the discussions only those Ministers whom he considered had a useful contribution to make, though in so doing he was on more than one occasion to upset some of his Cabinet colleagues.

Wilson further emulated Kennedy in attaching great importance to his dynamic First Hundred Days in office, which (as it had for Kennedy) was to produce unfortunate consequences. Neither Nixon, nor for that matter Heath, can be blamed for not having even attempted to match the youthful exhilaration of Kennedy and Wilson, for the examples of both men suggest that over-confidence can produce costly mistakes. For Kennedy, this was reflected in the considerable disenchantment in him produced by the Bay of Pigs fiasco. When he came to power, he had represented the finest idealism of American youth and his eloquent Inaugural Address had been all but a clarion-call to the youth in Britain and around the world. He had been represented in the three months between the Inauguration and the Cuban invasion as the last hope for the West, a brilliant and exciting hope, conveying the impression of a mature, responsible and, above all, intelligent American foreign policy. Now, through his own emphasis on the importance of his first hundred days, by this one failure, he seemed to reveal himself as but a continuation of past policy. Fortunately for Kennedy, (though the experience was not to be repeated in the case of Wilson), there remained enough reserve of good-will in Britain for him to overcome this temporary set-back. 'You really have got off very lightly,' Richard Crossman told Arthur Schlesinger of Britain's reaction to the Bay of Pigs. 'If this had taken place under Eisenhower, there would have been mass meetings in Trafalgar Square. Dulles would have been burned in effigy and the Labour Party would have damned you in the most unequivocal terms. But because enough faith still remains in Kennedy, there has been very little popular outcry, and the Labour Party resolutions have been the very minimum. But one more mistake like this and you will really be through.'[9] There were to be no further mistakes of that magnitude and, indeed, if Cuba was to be the occasion for Kennedy's greatest blunder, it also figured prominently in his greatest single triumph. His handling of the missile crisis, his calm determination and absence of display, was to be universally recognised in Britain as the most responsible management of a crisis in the thermonuclear age. 'To the world', reported *The Guardian* (23 November 1963), 'he will be remembered as the President who helped to bring the thaw in the cold war.'

President Kennedy's efforts to get a more meaningful East/ West détente were but to confirm the British judgement that he was a man to whom leadership came naturally. He had perhaps the ideal mental equipment for the nuclear age: an imaginative appreciation of power and a blend of caution, judgement and intuitive wisdom with which he wielded it. He was ruled by reason, common sense and by what was politically feasible. He possessed courage, moral and physical, extraordinary speed of thought and clarity of decision, high ideals and vision, a keen sense of history, and acute sensitivity to the problems of others, friend and foe alike. Above all, to operate these qualities, he possessed a personal dynamism and seemingly unquenchable energy. At this critical juncture in international politics, the world needed a leader with just such a synthesis of these qualities.

The Presidency is a unique institution. It places enormous and incredibly diverse responsibilities upon a single individual. It gives him inadequate authority as an outright gift but permits him to acquire whatever power he is capable of winning by leadership, combativeness, guile and sheer stubbornness from the people, the Congress, the states and a lumbering bureaucracy. In these times, the same qualities have to be extended to exercise Presidential leadership of the Western world, and this Kennedy perceived better than most. However difficult, on occasion, it proved to be, Kennedy tried always to work honestly with his allies. All the time, he treated them with respect and in turn he earned their respect.

Britain will, however, remember Kennedy not for what he did alone, but also for what he stood for and what he started. The energies which he released, the standards which he laid down, the goals which he established, the hopes which he raised and the purposes which he inspired are the same energies, standards, goals, hopes and purposes that will influence future British generations. He stood for excellence in an era of relative indifference, hope in an era of frustration and mortal danger, conciliation above confrontation. He gave men confidence in the future and in each other, lifting them beyond their capabilities. Last, but by no means least, he restored to the world pride and dignity in itself and gave a vision of the possibility of men living in peace and harmony with one another. Our loss was so great, said Macmillan, 'because he seemed, in his own person, to embody all the hopes and aspirations of this new world that is struggling to emerge—to rise, phoenix-like, from the ashes of the old.' Thus did the British people grieve as though they had lost a friend, even a brother.

Our dismay and despair was the greater for by November 1963 everything seemed to be moving in the right direction for Kennedy. Already, in under three years, he had presided over a new era in East/West relations, and a new era in alliance relations. His Presidency was just beginning to come into its own, and our loss, and the world's loss, was what might have been during his second term. For, at Amherst College, Massachusetts, in October 1963, he had offered to Britain, and to the world, his vision of the American promise: 'I look forward to a great future for America, a future in which our country will match its military strength with our moral restraint, its wealth with our wisdom, its power with our purpose . . . I look forward to an America which commands respect throughout the world not only for its strength but for its civilisation as well.'

America, under President Kennedy, was beginning to command

such respect for its civilisation. In his own person, he had represented what Britain liked best about America: he had restored decency to patriotism and had revived some of the romance about America. He had left us with a lasting impression of an America as it ought to be, as the Founding Fathers had conceived it—brave, energetic, gay, civilised, challenging, and, above all, young. His greatness was thus assured in Britain not by what he was alone but by what we wanted him to be: not by what he did alone but for what he promised to the young who have felt themselves, ever since, to be without a leader.

1. Harold Wilson, *The Labour Government*, 1964-1970. *A Personal Record* (Weidenfeld & Nicolson/Michael Joseph, 1971), p.365.
2. Paul Foot, *The Politics of Harold Wilson* (Penguin Books, 1968), p.212.
3. *Ibid.*, p.214.
4. Louis Heren, 'No Hail, No Farewell—The Presidency of Lyndon Baines Johnson', *The Times* (26 October 1970).
5. Henry Brandon, 'Almost a Love Affair', *The Sunday Times* (20 December 1970).
6. The actual figures of the Poll conducted at the end of 1969 were, from a sample of 1000: Kennedy, 146 votes; second was Churchill, with a vote of only 67; third, Dr Barnard with 48 votes.
7. Lord Boothby, *The News Of The World* (24 November 1963).
8. Quoted in Arthur Schlesinger Jr., *A Thousand Days* (André Deutsch, 1965), p.594.
9. Quoted *Ibid.*, pp.264-5.

Index